Hʏᴀᴛᴛ H. Wᴀɢɢᴏɴᴇʀ, professor of American literature at Brown University, is the author of *The Heel of Elohim: Science and Values in Modern American Poetry* (1950); *Hawthorne: A Critical Study*, which was selected in 1955 for the annual Explicator Prize; and numerous articles which show his concern with the most significant trends in American literature. A graduate of Middlebury College, he holds an M.A. degree from the University of Chicago and a Ph.D. degree from Ohio State University. Mr. Waggoner for fourteen years was a member of the English faculty at the University of Kansas City, before coming to Brown University in 1956.

William Faulkner

HYATT H. WAGGONER

William Faulkner

FROM JEFFERSON TO THE WORLD

UNIVERSITY OF KENTUCKY PRESS

Preface

ONE OF THE SIGNS of a writer's greatness is that continued study of his work does not exhaust its significance for us. This book has been written from the conviction that the large body of Faulkner criticism, much of it of very high quality, has not exhausted the meanings or fully defined the values of Faulkner's works. Critics have tended to concentrate their efforts on the novels that nearly everyone agrees are the greatest, to the neglect of others less great but deserving of careful study. This concentration on the high points of a career is natural enough, and proper enough too in a sense, but one of its results is that we have not yet fully perceived the outlines of Faulkner's career as a whole or the unity of the whole of his work.

I have attempted to get at this largest of the unities that may be discovered in a writer's work not by ignoring Faulkner's writings and concentrating on large philosophical questions, or by using his works merely to illustrate generalizations about Faulkner the man, the problem of the South, or contemporary social conditions, but by looking attentively at the writings themselves, noting signs of continuity and development, and relating these to Faulkner's many statements of intention. I would not argue that such a procedure is the only valid one, or even necessarily the best one, but only that it is capable of revealing some things that have remained dark.

The first ten chapters, accordingly, treat the fiction in the order of its publication, allotting to each novel a more or less extended discussion. Limitations of space made it impossible to treat the short stories in this way, but chapter nine, which interrupts the chronological presentation of the novels, attempts to relate the stories to the major themes that have emerged in the study of the novels and offers analyses of several stories taken to be representative. In the last two chapters I turn from specific works to consideration of problems common to the whole body of work, attempting first (in chapter eleven) to clarify the moral and religious implications of the fiction, concentrating on what I take to be central and determinative in Faulkner's writing, his uneasy relation to his Christian background; and finally (in chapter twelve) attempting to evaluate Faulkner's achievement thus far in his career.

Literary criticism is never definitive; criticism of a still living author, moreover, is exposed to special hazards of its own. The only justification for such a study as this lies in the hope that it may usefully supplement the explorations of others who have walked the same tortuous and rewarding trail.

ACKNOWLEDGMENTS

MY INDEBTEDNESS TO the Faulkner critics who have preceded me is I hope made sufficiently clear either in the text or in the notes of this book, but I should like to note here my largest debt to any earlier criticism. The many citations of William Van O'Connor's *The Tangled Fire of William Faulkner* will suggest how thoroughly I have used it but do not in themselves make clear what seems to me to be true, that despite its brevity and its pioneering, the book will long continue to be indispensable to Faulkner students.

I am deeply indebted to a number of friends who helped at various stages of the preparation of this book. Thanks go especially to Edwina Bender and Mary Jane Nelson, who typed the first draft of the manuscript, and to W. Stacy Johnson, Roma A. King, Barry Marks, and John Gardner, who read the manuscript and made many helpful suggestions.

For permission to reprint Chapter 11, a version of which appeared in *The Tragic Vision and Christian Faith*, edited by Nathan Scott, I am indebted to the Association Press.

Contents

CHAPTER 1

Explorations

SOLDIER'S PAY

MOSQUITOES

ONCE FAULKNER BEGAN to get his fiction published, in the mid-twenties, he attained his artistic maturity very quickly. Only three years elapsed between *Soldier's Pay* and *The Sound and the Fury*, but in the three novels he published in those years we may trace the growth of a major artist. *Soldier's Pay* is a wholly immature period piece containing a few passages of lasting power. In *Mosquitoes* the young artist finds his own voice and declares his independence. In the final third of *Sartoris* there is a prolonged demonstration of the sort of writing promised in *Mosquitoes*, a demonstration which the obvious unevenness of the novel does not obscure. *The Sound and the Fury* is a novel which demands comparison with the greatest in American, or any, fiction. By 1929 Faulkner was beginning his period of most rapid and successful production.

The opening chapter of *Soldier's Pay* makes us think of Hemingway, to Faulkner's disadvantage. The disillusioned returning soldiers, drinking to deaden their awareness of the great nothingness behind and before them, are like classroom examples of lost generation attitudes. If they are less revealing of the period than Jake

Barnes and Lady Brett it is because they are not so successfully created. They tell us they are in despair, and tell us why, and the voice of the narrator underscores their explanations. Julian Lowe sits "in a smoldering of disgusted sorrow," raising, now and then, "a sophisticated eye." Hemingway's Nick in *In Our Time* certainly feels both disgust and sorrow and he becomes what we might call "sophisticated," but no such words will be found in any description of him. The central fact in the awareness of the characters in *Soldier's Pay* is not very different from the fact that shapes the sensibilities of Jake Barnes and his group in *The Sun Also Rises*, the one expressed in the opening story of *In Our Time*, or the one that shapes the conclusion of *A Farewell to Arms*. But the expression of the central fact in *Soldier's Pay* is different:

> "Joe, do you know he's going blind?" she said abruptly.
> After a time her face became a human face and holding
> it in his vision he said:
> "I know more than that. He's going to die."
> "Die?"
> "Yes, ma'am. If I ever seen death in a man's face, it's
> in his. Goddam this world," he burst out suddenly.

What really emerges in this passage from *Soldier's Pay* is only a vivid impression of Gilligan's drunkenness: we feel the effort he has to make to attend to his questioner's words, to see her face, "holding it in his vision." We have not yet been made to feel the emotion behind his "Goddam this world." Faulkner has succeeded only intermittently in the creation of a world in the opening chapter of *Soldier's Pay*.

It is suggestive of the nature of Faulkner's creative gift that the second chapter, laid in the small Georgia town to which some of the victims of war we met in the first chapter are returning, is so much more interesting than the first. In a very real sense, this is the beginning of the part of the novel that still lives for us as successful fiction. It begins with a striking image prefiguring a theme as apparent in *The Sound and the Fury, As I Lay Dying, Requiem for a Nun,* and *A Fable* as here. Januarius Jones walks past the Episcopal church and sees the rector, his shining dome . . . friendly against an ivy-covered wall above which the consummate grace of a spire and a golden cross seemed to arc across motionless young clouds.

Januarius Jones, caught in the spire's illusion of slow ruin, murmured: "Watch it fall, sir."

Since the last chapter ends with Gilligan and the rector listening to a service in a Negro church, shabby "with its canting travesty of a spire," it is no exaggeration to call this image of a falling cross and spire the controlling image of the work. Between the two falling spires in *Soldier's Pay* lie all the parts of the book that remain interesting today, both in themselves and as foreshadowing the best in the later works. And implicit in the repeated image itself lies the dominant theme of most of Faulkner's major works, his tortured and ambiguous mixture of religious denial and affirmation.

Other good things in this book also reappear in more developed form in the great stories and novels. The paragraph describing Charlestown, for instance, foreshadows the section on the town and the courthouse in *Requiem for a Nun,* written nearly a quarter of a century later. Comparison of these illustrates the persistence of an interest as well as the development of a talent.

Charlestown, like numberless other towns throughout the south, had been built around a circle of tethered horses and mules. In the middle of the square was the courthouse—a simple utilitarian edifice of brick and sixteen beautiful Ionic columns stained with generations of casual tobacco. Elms surrounded the courthouse and beneath these trees, on scarred and carved wood benches and chairs the city fathers, progenitors of solid laws and solid citizens who believed in Tom Watson and feared only God and drouth, in black string ties or the faded brushed gray and bronze meaningless medals of the Confederate States of America, no longer having to make any pretense toward labor, slept or whittled away the long drowsy days while their juniors of all ages, not yet old enough to frankly slumber in public, played checkers or chewed tobacco and talked. A lawyer, a drug clerk and two nondescripts tossed iron discs back and forth between two holes in the ground. And above all brooded early April sweetly pregnant with noon.

There is perhaps no other evocation of a specific place, with its specific atmosphere, to equal this in any American writing of the period. Certainly there is none in the early work of Hemingway, who reached his artistic majority sooner but with whom Faulkner is not in competition in this passage, as he seemed to be in his first chapter. Only in the too consciously "poetic" last sentence is the picture blurred, the spell broken, as we become aware of the sensitive young man observing the scene. The two idioms, realistic and poetic, are not yet perfectly unified as they were soon to be in *The Sound and the Fury*.

But even before *The Sound and the Fury* Faulkner could at times achieve his special blend of realism and poetry, a feeling for fact and feeling for the human and imaginative meaning and emotional overtone of fact. He achieves it in the ending of *Soldier's Pay*, which is luminous with promise that a major writer is being born. Before the rector and Gilligan come in their walk to the Negro church with the tilting spire, the rector has been trying to comfort Gilligan:

> The divine put his heavy arm across Gilligan's shoulder. "You are suffering from disappointment. But this will pass away. The saddest thing about love, Joe, is that not only the love cannot last forever, but even the heartbreak is soon forgotten. How does it go? 'Men have died and worms have eaten them, but not for love.' No, no," as Gilligan would have interrupted, "I know that is an unbearable belief, but all truth is unbearable. Do we not both suffer at this moment from the facts of division and death?"

The rector, a sympathetic character throughout, seems to speak for the young Faulkner as well as for himself and to put the theme of the book into words. But the ending does not leave it there, in abstractions, even in abstractions dramatically conceived. For as they walked,

> The road dropped on again descending between reddish gashes, and across a level moonlit space, broken by a clump of saplings, came a pure quivering chord of music wordless and far away.

"They are holding services. Negroes," the rector explained.

They walked closer to the church and caught the words from
within. "Lead Thy Sheep, O Jesus." The soft light of the kerosene
lamps in the darkness, the words conveying to them "all the longing
of mankind for a Oneness with Something, somewhere," the sounds
of the voices blended in the hymn, all become entangled in their
thoughts and feelings, become the objective correlatives of the content of their awareness. The final sentences of the book, a little too
consciously, too poetically perhaps, catch up the theme and embody
it in a blend of perception and object:

> They stood together in the dust, the rector in his shapeless
> black, and Gilligan in his new hard serge, listening, seeing
> the shabby church become beautiful with mellow longing,
> passionate and sad. Then the singing died, fading away
> along the mooned land inevitable with to-morrow and
> sweat, with sex and death and damnation; and they turned
> townward under the moon, feeling the dust in their shoes.

"Feeling the dust in their shoes." In this first of Faulkner's novels,
after much intermittent reporting, philosophizing, and poeticizing,
we come at last to recognizably Southern dust in an image which
combines fact, meaning, and emotion. The image itself comes, one
suspects, from the Book of Common Prayer: "Remember, O man,
that thou art dust." The acute awareness of mortality it expresses
in context is the book's final reminder of how directly *Soldier's Pay*
grew out of Faulkner's reading, particularly out of his reading in the
later nineteenth century. But for once the literary echo is not a
blemish. The ending suffers only by comparison with the more
perfect embodiment of some of the same themes in the later novels.

Most of the work is of course not on this level at all. The reading
that the young author has been doing, for one thing, is too evident.
Jurgen and *A Shropshire Lad,* Oscar Wilde and Swinburne and the
experimental little magazines of the twenties, all are apparent, none
yet wholly assimilated. The young writer is still a little amazed at
the depth of his own disillusion. "Truly vice is a dull and decorous

thing," he tells us, in the accents of fin de siècle. *The Rubaiyat* supplies quotations to document a despair not very different, at times, from Housman's generalized sadness; where the method fails, it is sometimes because it does not clearly distinguish between genuine pathos and a self-directed irony which is never absent from the work for long. Here is Januarius Jones again, a faun-like character so disillusioned that only the pleasures of the chase are left him:

> Male and female created He them, young. Jones was young, too. 'Yet ah, that Spring should vanish with the Rose! That Youth's sweet scented Manuscript should close! The Nightingale that in the Branches sang, Ah, whence, and whither flown again, who knows! . . .' Wish I had a girl tonight, he sighed.

The effect here is chiefly ironic, and the quotation is dramatically functional in further characterizing the literate, decadent Jones; but similar quotations and allusions sometimes reach us in the voice of the author. The general effect of the literary references is wasteful. This is the most allusive of Faulkner's works. Only *A Fable* is so "literary."

The "poetic" passages are also wastefully used, as in this description of the end of a rainstorm in which the conceit is merely decorative, and that in a manner closer to Faulkner's nineteenth century reading than to his own experience:

> Before they were halfway through lunch the downpour had ceased, the ships of rain had surged onward, drawing before the wind, leaving only a whisper in the wet green waves of leaves, with an occasional gust running in long white lines like elves, holding hands across the grass. But Emmy did not appear with dessert.

When we compare this with the long simile describing the reporter's mother in *Pylon*, beginning "the fine big bosom like one of the walled impervious towns of the Middle Ages whose origin antedates writing, which have been taken and retaken in uncountable fierce assaults . . ." we see how much Faulkner was to develop his skill in the next several years. Humor is evident in both these figures in which a fecund imagination is given its head, but in the first we become aware of the humor only in the abrupt change of tone of the last sentence, after we have already decided that the elves are a little too much even in a "poetic" novel, whereas humor controls and informs the much more extended conceit in *Pylon* from beginning to end, without turning it into a mere joke.

Finally, the characters too are disappointing in *Soldier's Pay* if we read the book already knowing the characters of the later stories. Cecily Saunders, the empty and selfish flapper, foreshadows the Temple Drake of *Sanctuary* and others of Faulkner's young girls, but she is an even less believable creature of the author's satire than Januarius Jones. The unhappy, unbelieving Episcopal priest, Dr. Mahon, is the only character in the book whose suffering is likely to touch the reader. Mahon lives by a code the basis of which he has had to abandon; he has learned a definition of God not in the Prayer Book:

> "Circumstance moves us in marvelous ways, Joe."
> "I thought you'd a said God, reverend."
> "God is circumstance, Joe . . ."

Mahon's situation is not less moving because in his innocence he is unable to recognize the true character of Januarius Jones and Cecily Saunders. He is kind, but his traditionalism has become formalized and impotent by being cut off from its roots. He is the first in a long line of Faulkner characters in such a plight. Prefiguring the elder Sartorises, he is not unworthy to be compared with them.

Soldier's Pay, then, is as uneven as we generally expect a first novel to be. It lacks unity: it has not one center of interest but several, and its tone and style are erratic. As Faulkner himself has put it, he found out after writing *Soldier's Pay* that a book "had to have a design."[1] The book is also too "wise," too moralistic, and too full of the author's reading.

Yet we feel its defects far more acutely than we would if we did not have the later novels in mind when we read it. It still holds our interest even when it does not compel our belief. It suffers by comparison with the work of Hemingway of that time, and with Faulkner's own later work, but not conspicuously by comparison with most other novels of the period. It is, in fact, an immensely promising work: *that* is likely to be our final impression, along with a sense of its significance as a revelation of the interests and purposes which were to shape Faulkner's later career. Remembering its ruinous falling spires and trying to grasp their meaning for the greater works, we may recall a phrase from Joyce's *Portrait of the Artist*: ". . . how your mind is saturated with the religion in which you say you disbelieve." Early in 1925, about the time he was writing *Soldier's Pay*, Faulkner wrote in a newspaper sketch of "Jesus of Nazareth with two stars in His eyes, sucking His mother's breast, and a fairy tale that has conquered the whole Western earth."[2] *Soldier's Pay* first states the major themes and exhibits the major tensions of Faulkner's greatest work. The young author's intrusive comments are often as prophetic as his successful ending. Man seen as a creature driven, compelled, yet somehow free to choose, tradition seen as empty yet crying out for redefinition, the feeling of meaninglessness and the search for meaning—all are suggested in *Soldier's Pay*.

2

MOSQUITOES might be compared with *Portrait of the Artist*, though the comparison immediately suggests Joyce's greater self-absorption and his greater artistic maturity at this stage in his career. Each book is a survey of the artist's resources, a critique of the folk culture and of the literary environment, and a declaration of independence whose bravado could be justified only by later and greater works.[3]

The weaknesses of *Mosquitoes* are thoroughly un-Joycean however. Most readers have found that the fiction serves only as an excuse for an examination of art and life, especially art, in the mid-twenties. There is far more talk than action in the book, and the plot is, as the critics have been nearly unanimous in pointing out, negligible indeed. More important, only about half of the characters are successfully created, the others being either satirical stereotypes (the niece, Pat, for instance) or convenient mouthpieces for the play of ideas. The satire, though perceptive in places, is often unconvincing because lacking in complexity. The flappers of the period were not "sexless," as Faulkner suggests, merely because the clothes they wore concealed or de-emphasized their curves. The niece tells us more about Faulkner's distaste for the fashions of the day in clothes and manners than about the real young girls in the straight short shapeless dresses.

More serious is the lack of a clear controlling purpose capable of supplying unity to the work. The clearest evidence of this lack of artistic control is the contrast between the opening pages, with their satire in the manner of Aldous Huxley's "novel of ideas," and the closing pages, which amount to an exploratory exercise in the kind of writing that was soon to produce *The Sound and the Fury*. This contrast between beginning and ending is illustrated in the changing presentation of two of the chief characters, Mrs. Maurier and Talliaferro. Both in the opening were creatures of a bright, brittle, and superficial satire, wholly unsympathetic characters, butts of the young Faulkner's wit and disdain. But in the end Mrs. Maurier ceases to be a pasteboard figure and her "silliness" gets an "explanation" as Wiseman and Fairchild look at a likeness of her done by the sculptor Gordon:

> It was clay, yet damp, and from out its dull, dead grayness Mrs. Maurier looked at them, her chins, harshly, and her flaccid jaw muscles with savage verisimilitude. Her eyes were caverns thumbed with two motions into the dead familiar astonishment of her face; and yet, behind them, somewhere within those empty sockets, behind all her familiar surprise, there was something else—something that exposed her face for the mask it was, and still more, a mask unaware. "Well, I'm damned," Fairchild said slowly, staring at it. "I've known her for a year, and Gordon comes

along after four days . . . Well, I'll be damned," he said
again.

"I could have told you," the Semitic man said. . . . "I
don't see how anyone with your faith in your fellow man
could believe that anyone could be as silly as she, without
reason."

"An explanation for silliness?" Fairchild repeated. "Does
her sort of silliness require explanation?"

"It shouts it," the other answered.

Now Gordon's perception, expressed in clay, that Mrs. Maurier's
"silliness" springs from suffering, from despair, destroys the satirical
effect of the earlier portrayal of her: she ceases to be a target and
becomes a human being, taking her place in that crowd of tortured
and possessed human beings who people Faulkner's novels. The
effect of this transformation is to weaken the unity of the book,
which until its ending we have been invited to take as a satirical
novel of ideas. But it is also a momentary glimpse of the world of
the later novels, where compassion governs and understanding
grows from compassion.

Mr. Talliaferro, too, changes before our eyes from a ridiculous little creature who is seen from the outside with disdain to a pathetic
human being whose folly has a cause. As he pursues his last hopeless and absurd attempt to play the dangerous male, we are invited
to see him in a different light, a light in which comedy gives way
to pathos as we watch him struggle to achieve identity through
"love." Now, at last, we learn why Fairchild and the others have
tolerated him so long.

There are other examples of this, notably in the portrait of Mr.
Wiseman, but these will serve to illustrate the clear shift in purpose
and tone which something, perhaps impatience, has kept Faulkner's
critics from noticing. This transformation, from the feelings and
intentions which produced Januarius Jones in *Soldier's Pay* to those
which produced Benjy and Dilsey in *The Sound and the Fury*, is·
the real sign of the novel's immaturity. By too great and too sudden
a qualification it destroys the novel's satirical point, asking us to pity
those we have first been told to laugh at. To make such a qualifica-

tion effectively in the kind of novel this one started out to be might
be impossible even for a novelist of much greater skill than the
young Faulkner of *Mosquitoes*.

But the book is a promising performance by a young writer of
fiction still searching for his artistic identity, and it contains much,
despite its defects, that is of real interest.

The portrait of Sherwood Anderson as Dawson Fairchild, for
instance, is very perceptive. If the picture is somewhat unbalanced
because it does not pay tribute to Anderson's rare but genuine
achievements, it is something better than just: it is brilliantly
penetrating. The qualities of personality and outlook that made
Anderson fail in the bulk of his work, particularly in his novels, are
incisively laid bare here. Fairchild's "trustful baffled expression"
and his "tentative bewilderment" suggest essential qualities that
emerge not just in Anderson's failures but in the best things he did.
Even so fine a story as "Death in the Woods" betrays the *effort* to
find words adequate to the feeling, and to express ideas that remain
inchoate. Like Hemingway, Faulkner thought he detected in Anderson a crippling distrust of both intellect and art.[4]

The high point of the Anderson satire in *Mosquitoes* is Fairchild's
autobiographical story of love in the outhouse. He is trying, with
his usual humorless earnestness and honesty, to convey a memory
that is for him an epiphany of life's essence. The tale is a long one
of the youthful stirrings of love, of life's frustrations and its ironies.
The point is long in coming. Mark Frost, the poet, goes to sleep
before Fairchild comes to the climax. "Children are much more
psychic than adults," Fairchild ruminates, trying to explain to his
listeners why he followed the little girl to the privy with its side
for men and its side for women, trying to make clear his longing
and his curiosity and sense of a quite inexpressible meaning, trying
to make them understand why he did what he did when he got
inside, and why the golden haired little girl did what she did:

> "And I stood there, feeling this feeling and the heat,
> and hearing the drone of those big flies, holding my breath
> and listening for a sound from beyond the partition. But

there wasn't any sound from beyond it, so I put my head down through the seat."

Mark Frost snored. [Those who were still awake] sat . . . seeing two wide curious blue eyes into which an inverted surprise came clear as water, and long golden curls swinging downward above the ordure; and they sat in silence, remembering youth and love, and time and death.

The episode illustrates Faulkner's early mastery of the tall tale and suggests better than most of the writing in the first two novels the peculiarly Faulknerian blend of folk humor, a sense of the grotesque, and the interweaving of the absurd with the pathetic that was to distinguish much of his best later fiction. The parody is good parody, and it is good writing.

Seen in the context of all the talk about art in the book, the satire on Anderson reveals a good deal about Faulkner's developing conception of his role as artist. The talk takes two forms, negative criticisms of artistic fashions of the day, and positive statements of an artistic credo and program. The satire on Anderson is a part of the negative phase. Anderson was not simply a writer Faulkner had had the good fortune to know in New Orleans. He was the major American fiction writer of his generation, though few besides Faulkner, Hemingway, and perhaps Gertrude Stein recognized his importance at that time. Faulkner shared with him many traits, many attitudes, many aspects of sensibility. One of the reasons for the power of the tall tale of love in the outhouse is that Faulkner shared with Anderson almost everything but the humorlessness which he parodies in this grotesque epitome of "youth and love, and time and death." But the younger writer had to find his own way. The portrait of Anderson in *Mosquitoes* is a significant chapter in Faulkner's artistic self-discovery.

We may partially miss the point, today, of the criticism of Anderson's regionalism. Why did regionalism seem such a danger that the young writer had, for once, to be unfair to Anderson, exaggerating and misunderstanding his mid-western Americanism, attributing to him too emphatically the belief that "the function of creating art depends on geography"? The answer can be given very simply: to the young writer from Oxford, Mississippi, regionalism was the most obvious and alluring of temptations. The absorption in his local material, the love of his region, the feeling for family history that produced the Sartorises and made a provincial Mississippi county courthouse into the focal point of the perceptible universe could easily have produced a mere local colorist.

Another point should be remembered. In the mid-twenties regionalism seemed to promise a more luxuriant flowering in American literature than its later development actually produced. Not only Anderson with his *Winesburg, Ohio* but Masters with his *Spoon River Anthology*, Lindsay with his poems about mid-western figures written in mid-western accents, Cather with her novels of the Nebraska frontier and Frost with his New England poems all seemed to be following the regionalist's way. For a young writer who wanted his work to take a different course—partly because *that* course would be so easy and was so immensely attractive to him— what other way could be found?

The way is implicitly stated in *Mosquitoes*, chiefly by Mr. Wiseman, "the Semitic man," as he is usually called. A good many of the opinions that turn up later in Faulkner's writing as Faulkner's own and some basic to his later works are expressed by Mr. Wiseman. The creature of a double-edged, partly self-directed irony, he speaks both for the modern mind and for the critical part of Faulkner's mind. We shall miss much of the point of the book if we do not realize that he is portrayed with irony but not repudiation. He speaks for Faulkner, for instance, when he says that Fairchild's rebellion is too superficial to get him out of the shadow of Emerson and Lowell, that it betrays "a sort of puerile bravado in flouting while he fears," and, in the accents of Eliot, that what Fairchild lacks is "a standard of literature that is international."

Faulkner has never acknowledged a debt to Eliot, despite the frequency of Eliot echoes and allusions in Faulkner's later poems and in the fiction written up to the middle of the thirties.[5] Of Joyce he has said both that he read *Ulysses* in the middle twenties and that the artist "should approach . . . *Ulysses* as the illiterate Baptist preacher approaches the Old Testament: with faith."[6] A thorough study of Faulkner's early reading in relation to his changing theory and practice as an artist remains to be done; until it is, we cannot be certain what Faulkner had in mind as his standard. But there seems to me to be very little risk in hazarding the guess that the "international" standard was chiefly supplied by an expatriate American and an expatriate Irishman. In the work of both Faulkner found the "mythological" method which he was soon to begin to practice in his own way as he celebrated a dark Easter in *The Sound and the Fury* or took the Bundrens on their epic journey. In the work of both there was a sharpness and clarity of imagery that was never lost as the images expanded into symbols. From such reporting could come "epiphanies," if only the artist were sufficiently creative. I suspect that Fairchild has ceased to be an object of satire and is speaking for Faulkner when, toward the end, he says that "in art, a man can create without any assistance at all: what he does is his." Many years later Faulkner would insist to an interviewer that the allusions to the Passion in *The Sound and the Fury* were simply tools with which he worked to create the novel, as a carpenter works with the tools available.[7]

As the talk continues it becomes increasingly clear that Faulkner is using several of his characters to express his own views and that he himself hopes to write fiction which will transcend the reportorial and the regional to express "eternal and timeless" truth. Toward the end of the book, Gordon, Wiseman, and Fairchild drink and talk together as they wander through the streets. In this scene, a preparation for the experiments of *The Sound and the Fury* and *As I Lay Dying*, Wiseman defines the work of genius in the arts as the creation of "that Passion Week of the heart . . . in which the hackneyed accidents which make up this world—love and life and death and sex and sorrow—brought together by chance in perfect proportions, take on a splendid and timeless beauty."

Faulkner appears in his own person only briefly in *Mosquitoes*, and then as "a funny man. A little kind of black man . . . awful

sunburned and kind of shabby dressed. . . . He said he was a liar
by profession." The self-satire here is as pointed as it is in the
partial self-portrait in Mark Frost, "the ghostly young man, a poet
who produced an occasional cerebral and obscure poem in four or
seven lines reminding one somehow of the function of evacuation
excruciatingly and incompletely performed." Though Wiseman, not
Faulkner, is speaking in the passage defining the Passion Week of
the heart, a reader who has listened very long to Faulkner's voice
will recognize the accent, the sentiment, even the words. With such
a standard, with the genius to create such a Passion Week, Faulkner
hoped he might write something that, again in the words of Wiseman, would have "form solidity color."

It would be hard to find a phrase more suggestive of the writing
Faulkner was soon to do. Fiction which merited this description
would bring together once again ways of writing that had come to
seem poles apart. It would be aesthetically shaped, symbolic, not a
mere record or report ("form"). But it would also be real in the
only way fiction can be real ("solidity"). And it would owe something to the impressionists even while its solidity kept it from being
merely subjective ("color"). Joyce's fusion of disparate fictional
traditions comes to mind again, though *Mosquitoes* announces only
an aesthetic rebellion, not, like *Portrait of the Artist,* a religious and
cultural one too. Joyce's intention to "forge in the smithy of my soul
the uncreated conscience of my race," his intention to "discover the
mode of life or of art whereby [his] spirit could express itself in
unfettered freedom" finds no parallel in the Faulkner of this period.
The "fairy tale" has been lost, the spires are falling, but Faulkner is
not in rebellion. *Mosquitoes* might well have been entitled "portrait
of the young man as artist."

3

WHEN WE reread *Soldier's Pay* and *Mosquitoes* today we are
likely to be struck not so much by their immaturity, though

certainly they are immature, as by their surprisingly complete fore-shadowing of the great works which followed them. *Soldier's Pay*, it seems to me, is decidedly the less mature of the two novels. The way each of them expresses a theme common to both will serve to illustrate. In *Soldier's Pay* the author speaks in his own voice of one of the larger ideas underlying the novel: "Sex and death: the front door and the back door of the world. How indissolubly are they associated in us!" But in *Mosquitoes* Wiseman, at first the voice of modern reason and later in the book the voice of Faulkner himself, says

> "People in the old books died of heartbreak also, which was probably merely some ailment that any modern surgeon or veterinarian could cure out of hand. But people do not die of love. That's the reason love and death in conjunction have such an undying appeal in books: they are never very closely associated anywhere else."

What has happened between the two books in which these passages occur is a growth of critical, and self-critical, insight, with the resulting possibility of irony. One of the chief defects of *Soldier's Pay* is that its irony is intermittent. Irony does not inform the passage on sex and death, or the many other passages like it. We react to the author's wise statements with important reservations: yes, *but*. Our unspoken reservations, our sense of the missing quali-fication, our awareness that the "wise statement" is wise only if we adopt the attitudes from which it sprang and accept the frame of reference within which it has its meaning and its urgency—reserva-tions like these chiefly account for our feeling that *Soldier's Pay* is immature.

In *Mosquitoes* the voice of Faulkner is not heard except as we may discern its accents and sentiments in the words of Mr. Wise-man, the sculptor Gordon, and the poet Mark Frost. Faulkner has ceased to philosophize and begun to dramatize, ceased telling us about and begun to show us; just as important, he has stopped oversimplifying and begun to criticize his own insights. Without taking this step Faulkner could not have kept *The Sound and the*

Fury free of sentimentality: it would have became a simple elegy, a heart-felt lament. Without this step we could never have had the opening of *Absalom, Absalom!*, with its complex recreation of past-in-present, a past at once heroic, absurd, solid, false. Without it we could not have had the tragi-comedy of *As I Lay Dying*.

In *Mosquitoes* the Faulkner feelings and sentiments—the basic, pre-literary building blocks discernible in his greatest works—get the criticism they had to have if they were to become usable for the artist. If we think of *Soldier's Pay* as confessional and *Mosquitoes* as dramatic we shall be in a position to define the most significant difference between the two. Even if *Mosquitoes* were as bad a novel as the critics have generally thought, it would be very significant for Faulkner's later career that in it he distributes his ideas and feelings among Mark Frost, Gordon, and Mr. Wiseman. All the major characters except Jenny, Pat, and Mrs. Maurier are given lines which the author himself might have spoken in *Soldier's Pay*. But since all of them are seen with amusement, the result is a sanity and a truth not present in *Soldier's Pay*. The self-satire in the portrait of Mark Frost is one measure of that sanity, that capacity for self-criticism. The assignment of most of the wise sayings to "the Semitic man" with the descriptive name, the author's anti-type who speaks for all the wisdom unknown in Jefferson and explains away so deftly the romance of the Sartorises, is another. Out of the double, or multiple, vision here implied were to come all of Faulkner's finest works; and also, when the ambiguity became unresolvable, the tension too much to bear, his most typical failures.

That is why, quite apart from its own intrinsic merit, which I think is considerable, we shall be repaid for a close reading of *Mosquitoes*. Again and again we find in it, not only in the larger aspects of its structure but in its details, the clues we need for an understanding of the later development. The "baroque plunging stasis" of Andrew Jackson's statue as perceived by Gordon gives us the clue to the mature Faulkner's recurrent feeling about human life: motion and stillness, life and death, so irreconcilably opposed and intermixed that only an oxymoron can express them.[8] Fairchild's realization that, in contrast to fiction as known in the past, "In life, anything might happen; in actual life people will do anything" prepares us for *As I Lay Dying* and for Miss Burden and Joe Christmas in *Light in August:* prepares us, in fact, for the whole world not only of Yoknapatawpha but of *Pylon* and *The Wild Palms* and all the rest. The narrator's impatience with "Talk, talk, talk; the utter and heart-breaking stupidity of words" foreshadows a central theme of *As I Lay Dying.* It also gives evidence that the artist is achieving, painfully, the necessary sophistication about the tools of his own craft: the realization that he must make the words serve his fictional purpose by disappearing to make way for the images, the characters, the actions that can exist only through his words but that must never seem to consist of, or be perceptibly dependent upon, words.

The trouble with *Soldier's Pay,* again, is that the words do not become transparent vehicles for the fictional realities they are supposed to create. The rhetoric, some of it quite moving, constantly calls attention to itself; it refuses to die as rhetoric that it may live in character and action. It is a commonplace of criticism to say that Faulkner is a sort of Southern orator, a rhetorician, a speaker in love with, and therefore very willing to trust, words. But his willingness to trust and to explore as fully as possible the resources of words is a potential weakness as well as a source of his greatest strength. Without the distrust of words announced for the first time in *Mosquitoes* he might have produced later only the sort of achievement we get in the speeches of Gavin Stevens—a rhetorical rather than a fictional achievement.

In short, the self-criticism of *Mosquitoes* is the act of judgment without which Faulkner could not have produced his best work. When he inserts, between scenes, "Voices without; alarums and excursions, etc." his use of Shakespeare is on a very different level from the use of his reading in *Soldier's Pay.* It means that the young writer is not taking his own novel too seriously and that he is not taking himself—and the Sartorises—too seriously. If he manages to create a career for himself at all, it will not be as an elegist. If

Mosquitoes rejects the little sophisticated Bohemia it pictures, it rejects also, in no less emphatic terms, the most obvious alternative. Life, the Semitic man says, "everywhere is the same." This is the fact overlooked by the regionalists he criticizes. "But man's old compulsions, duty and inclination: the axis and circumference of his squirrel cage, they do not change. . . . And he who has stood the surprise of birth can stand anything."

CHAPTER 2

Apprenticeship

SARTORIS

NOT UNTIL *The Sound and the Fury* would Faulkner fully show what he could do when writing by the standard he had discovered and announced in *Mosquitoes,* but *Sartoris* achieves the ideal with intermittent brilliance. It is rich with scenes and characters only a major novelist could have created. Though most of the faults that marred *Soldier's Pay* and *Mosquitoes* may be discovered here too, they have become mere interruptions, lapses. *Sartoris* is not, as a whole, a mature novel, but while he was writing it Faulkner attained his maturity.

Young Bayard Sartoris is our chief stumbling block, as Donald Mahon was in *Soldier's Pay.* Like Mahon, he is inadequate as tragic hero. Intended meaning and achieved content come apart in him, as in Mahon. The portrayal of Bayard, unlike that of his prototype, emerges finally as a fine solid portrait of a neurotic young man, but like Mahon, Bayard is inadequate as the carrier of the theme. Only in the last third of the novel can we believe that his actions spring from the causes assigned to them. In Quentin Compson of *The Sound and the Fury* Faulkner achieved at least a more credible if not, for some readers, a wholly convincing solution to the problem of presenting the sensitive young man of the lost generation faced with the emptiness of life. In the creation of Quentin the psychological and philosophical perspectives seem to complement each other and not to be alternative and contradictory explanations of the despair. In the creation of Bayard, Faulkner failed.

He failed, that is, if we assume that Bayard is intended as a sympathetic character. If, instead, we take him as many young readers today seem to prefer to do, as a satirical portrait, we of course come out with a very different judgment of him. Richard C. Carpenter, for instance, has developed an interesting interpretation, based on parallels between the McCallum episode and *The Inferno*, of Bayard as a betrayer punished, like Dante's Ugolino, by being imprisoned in ice, and of *Sartoris* as "in part an exploration of the Christian myth of sin, guilt, and redemption."[1] But though Bayard may very well be interpreted in the McCallum episode as guilt-ridden and suitably damned, it seems to me doubtful that this conception of him effectively controls the portrait in the novel as a whole. This is not to say that the parallels with *The Inferno* stressed by Mr. Carpenter are not genuine but that the novel finally lacks unity of conception.

The immediate reason for Bayard's despair in the first two-thirds of the book seems to be grief for his brother John, killed in an aerial dogfight which Bayard witnessed and tried but was unable to prevent. But Bayard sees John's death as a particular manifestation of the general doom. He grieves not just for John but for the Sartorises and for man. His violence is his way of forcing out of consciousness what he cannot allow himself to think about. Like Nick in Hemingway's "Big Two-Hearted River" he contrives ways to keep from thinking; when the contrivance fails, his thoughts are more than he can bear.

> Then sowing time was over and it was summer, and he found himself with nothing to do. It was like coming dazed out of sleep, out of the warm sunny valleys where people lived into a region where cold peaks of savage despair stood bleakly above the lost valleys, among black and savage stars.

The image of the cold peaks close to the savage stars points as clearly to a kind of waste land as the sandy deserts do in Eliot's poem; though it is significant that the context of the novelist's image does not attribute the lifelessness to loss of faith, as does the poem, but to a discovery of unalterable truth. Sterility may be brought about, or remedied, by man; the waste land reflects a failure of man's values. But dying stars suggest a cosmic drive toward death that man is not responsible for and cannot remedy.

The image points, that is, not toward Eliot but toward Dreiser,[2] one of whose self-portraits pictures him sitting at his window handkerchief in hand wiping away the tears of pity for mankind lost in a world of nothing but matter in motion. The year *Sartoris* was published the British astrophysicist Sir James Jeans in his best-selling book *The Mysterious Universe* was explaining to the public the significance of *dark* stars: they gave evidence of a world *running down* to final darkness and death, in accordance with the second law of thermodynamics. The "black and savage stars" are Bayard's special and master symbol. The image occurs later in the book without verbal change. But though it bears the stamp of 1929, it is, in another sense, traditional: Hawthorne understood this blackness, and Melville's Ahab accused the gods of this savagery.

Bayard's recognition of the truth about the world shapes his character and his reactions—or so at least I think we are intended to believe. As Narcissa looks at him lying on the bed in his cast after his accident, she realizes that

> He was so utterly without affection for anything at all, so—
> so . . . hard . . . No, that's not the word. But "cold" eluded
> her; she could comprehend hardness, but not coldness. . . .

She cannot comprehend his coldness because she does not fully understand the depth of his loss: she can understand his grief for John but she does not know the meaning Bayard sees in John's doom. She is shut out of the region he inhabits by her unreflective faith in life. "He watched her with wide intent eyes in which terror lurked, and mad, cold fury, and despair." Though the immediate occasion of the terror and despair here is a literal nightmare from which he has just awakened, in a sense all Bayard's life, waking or sleeping, is a continuous nightmare. He is cold with the fore-knowledge of the coldness of death. Like the sympathetic char-acters Hemingway was creating at the same time, as he voyages "alone in the bleak and barren regions of his despair," he cuts with his own hand ties that he knows would otherwise be cut despite him, proving himself one of the initiated by the deliberate sacrifice of a part of his humanity.

> She took his face between her palms and drew it down, but his lips were cold and upon them she tasted fatality and doom. . . . And they would lie so, holding to one an-other in the darkness and the temporary abeyance of his despair and the isolation of that doom he could not escape.

For brief intervals he finds forgetfulness with Narcissa—"Far above him now the peak among the black and savage stars, and about him the valleys of tranquillity and of peace"—but he can never forget for long what Narcissa knows only momentarily, after he has gone from her, as she looks with Miss Jenny at the miniature of John—then "she realized as she never had before the blind tragedy of human events." Bayard seems meant as a character whose personal tragedy springs from his overwhelming conscious-ness of the human tragedy.

The content of Bayard's awareness is like that which shapes the sensibility of the old waiter in Hemingway's "A Clean, Well-Lighted Place," though the two respond to their vision of nothingness differently at last. After his terrible first night at the McCallum farmhouse, alone beside the sleeping Buddy in the darkness and the cold that penetrated and embraced him (in "the season of dissolution and of death"), he knows how to value the next morn-ing: ". . . now he could rise and go where they were gathered about a crackling fire, where light was, and warmth." The McCallum episode draws much of its power from the extended and elaborate symbolism of light, warmth, and order in contrast with darkness,

cold, and disorder. In this episode Bayard is acceptable as an
initiated or "aware" character: we feel that he is facing the truth,
as less perceptive characters are not.

But the reader has difficulty taking him this way, both before
this and later. His reaction seems too extreme, his vision too
obsessive and unqualified. He seems too sick a man to be a tragic
hero. We are likely to think of him as a case of war nerves. We
find his rationalization for getting drunk with Rafe McCallum unconvincing:

> "I've been good too goddam long," Bayard repeated
> harshly, watching McCallum fill the two glasses. "That's
> the only thing Johnny was ever good for. Kept me from
> getting in a rut. Bloody rut, with a couple of old women
> nagging at me and nothing to do except scare niggers."

During the first two-thirds of the book Bayard seems properly
motivated only when he is very drunk. Then we can accept his
emotions, accept even the inflated language of his thoughts:

> His head was clear and cold; the whiskey he had drunk
> was completely dead. Or rather, it was as though his head
> were one Bayard who lay on a strange bed and whose
> alcohol-dulled nerves radiated like threads of ice through
> that body which he must drag forever about a bleak and
> barren world with him. . . . Nothing to be seen, and the
> long, long span of a man's natural life.

The whole initial presentation of Bayard is lacking in the clarity
and definition necessary to make him a solidly created character.
Faulkner seems to have been of two minds about him. On the one
hand we have Miss Jenny's judgment, that he is a fool who is as
well off dead as alive and whose destruction was the result of his
pride and self-pity. On the other hand, we seem to be asked to
accept him as glamorous, right, justified, an aware man among those
only partially aware. The judgment, the objectivity, the irony in
the portrait of him is intermittent. There is an ambivalence in the
creation here which never rises to the level of intentional ambiguity.
Young Bayard dates *Sartoris* as no other character does.

A good deal is made of the fact that young Bayard's traits are not simply his own, that he is the last of a long line of such men, proud, rash, violent, doomed. But this broadening of his case to include all the male Sartorises is another embarrassment. The Sartorises are as closely identified with the writer as young Bayard is; and, as portrayed, they are unworthy of the writer's sympathy and the reader is unable to share the identification. That the Sartorises are, in the essential features of the legend, the Faulkners, may help to explain the author's lack of objectivity. But explaining the cause of a creative failure is not the same as analyzing its nature or effects. The fictional problem presented by the Sartorises in the book centers on the fact that the reader cannot feel for them what he is invited to feel, cannot see them as the creatures of inexpressible glamour and romance that they are supposed to be. Nothing that he has learned about them in the course of the novel has adequately prepared him to accept the final apostrophe to the name and the idea of the Sartorises:

> The music went on in the dusk softly; the dusk was peopled with ghosts of glamorous and old disastrous things. And if they were just glamorous enough, there was sure to be a Sartoris in them, and then they were sure to be disastrous. Pawns. But the Player, and the game He plays ... He must have a name for his pawns, though. But perhaps Sartoris is the game itself—a game outmoded and played with pawns shaped too late and to an old dead pattern, and of which the Player Himself is a little wearied. For there is death in the sound of it, and a glamorous fatality, like silver pennons downrushing at sunset, or a dying fall of horns along the road to Roncevaux.

Whenever the Sartoris idea is directly approached we get a tortured rhetoric that fails to communicate because of the very urgency of its effort. When the family doom is in the foreground, we sometimes seem to be reading not *Sartoris* but *Soldier's Pay*.

The trouble is not that there are no critics of the Sartoris legend in the novel. The Jeb Stuart story early in the book burlesques the legend. Aunt Jenny deflates the Sartoris men frequently and effectively, and now and then the narrator, in passages not attributed to or meant to characterize any character, agrees with her judgment of them. But Miss Jenny's sharpness gets its edge from the love behind it, and the non-dramatic negative judgments of the narrator are outnumbered and outweighed in emotional content by passages like the final one about the Player and the Pawns. When we hear about "the bitter struggling of [young Bayard's] false and stubborn pride" we do not know what to make of it: false and stubborn pride are not in themselves glamorous or romantic, and false pride and a neurotic suicidal impulse are not the traditional connotations of the sound of the horns on the road to Roncevaux.

2

TO SAY so much may seem to grant the validity of the harshest negative judgments and I have said that I think these are mistaken. Theme and vehicle do fall apart in the book, and the finally achieved content is not much more than a sense of doom. Yet *Sartoris* has many elements of greatness for all that. Defying easy analysis or neat schematization, it retains its hold on our imaginations even while we grant its failure as a work of art.

Sartoris is memorable in just those elements which are fiction's traditional province. Most of its people and most of its situations live. We sense its vitality immediately in the opening scene, and in the best parts of the novel we are already beyond the apprenticeship. Faulkner has been quoted as saying that in the midst of the composition of *Sartoris* he "discovered that writing is a mighty fine thing; it enabled you to make men stand on their hind legs and cast a long shadow."[3]

All of the characters in *Sartoris* except young Bayard cast a long shadow, especially the old men and women. Old Bayard and Miss Jenny are certainly the most memorable of the main characters. But it reveals the extent of Faulkner's growth since *Soldier's Pay* and *Mosquitoes* that even the people we meet only briefly, like Dr.

Peabody and Old Man Falls, are solidly created. Horace Benbow and Narcissa are unforgettable in their vitality and their poignance. Even in the section devoted to Bayard's visit with the McCallums, where the emphasis is not so much on individuals as on the family and on a way of life, the people come through: Henry with his soft hands, Buddy with his medal. Snopes is perfect in a different way: seen from the outside, in terms only of his actions, he is a behavioristic portrait. His fictional greatness we are not likely to estimate accurately unless we recall how "villainous" he is, and how difficult, if not impossible, we find it today to believe in any "villain" in fiction—yet how convincing this one is.

From the opening sentences, when Old Man Falls comes for his regular visit with old Bayard, these people are alive. Even young Bayard is unable to spoil the episodes in which he appears. His getting drunk in town with Rafe McCallum is less impressive than his later adventures that afternoon and night with Suratt and Hub and later with Hub and Mitch. But this is because early in the day, when he is less drunk, he talks and thinks more of his doom, and the Sartoris glamour comes between us and the action. The Thanksgiving dinner is memorable Faulkner, and of course the visit to the McCallum place has been recognized as great by all the critics. Christmas in the Negro cabin is a scene not greatly excelled anywhere in Faulkner's work.

One thing that distinguishes some of the best scenes of *Sartoris* from its weaker ones, and from the earlier works, is the presence of irony. We sense an aesthetic distance in the picture of old Bayard that we do not feel in the picture of his grandson, except in the last quarter of the novel. Sympathy, and even love, are apparent in the portraits of old Bayard and Miss Jenny, but not complete identification. The distinction to be made here is difficult to get at but real. In the portrait of Old Man Falls, for example, we note admiration and even a kind of idealization, as in the figure of old McCallum: these are "the old people," the embodiment of a way of life for which there is an unexpressed but clearly felt nostalgia. But there is no trace of sentimentalizing in the portraits.

But of course the characters cannot be separated, even in our attempts to analyze them, from the scenes to which they give life and from which they get their own life. If we are to uncover the secret of their vitality we shall have to look directly at their actions. The writing in the best scenes of Sartoris seems to me distinguished by a special blend of solidity and luminosity. It is full of precise details accurately and fully reported without comment. Hub and Suratt squatted easily on their heels, but Bayard sat with his legs outstretched. Old Man Falls was not simply slow, deliberate in his actions: he picked laboriously and interminably at the knotted string around his parcel. This is the sort of "reporting" for which Hemingway was already becoming famous and which Flaubert had practiced long before.

And the details are functional, revealing, luminous with meaning. Old Man Falls's tedious deliberation is related not only to his advanced age but to his attitude toward life. It does not simply reveal his character: in a sense it *is* his character. He strengthens the point when he tells why he refuses a ride to town: he has too little time left to hurry his pleasures. Or again, the deafness of Old Man Falls and old Bayard: they sat without hearing the noises of the bank, periodically shouting at each other, "two old men cemented by a common deafness to a dead period." These details become symbolic. Functional parts of a total vision, they both express the vision and direct our emotional response to it. This aspect of the writing reminds us of what Fitzgerald had done in *The Great Gatsby* and what Anderson had done, without being able often to repeat, in a few of his finest stories. Only the best fiction has ever been marked by this degree of luminosity.

3

ONE WAY to define the special quality of *Sartoris* is to call it a very conventional novel that finally abandons every convention it

draws upon. In breaking through the stereotypes of Southern
romance and lost generation attitudes it achieves fragmentary
greatness.

The central situation, for example, of the disillusioned soldier
returning home from the First World War to fight the inner battles
of the "lost generation" was a commonplace of the period. The
convention was so strong that it dictated the style even of passages
in which young Bayard is not on stage: "Early in December the
rains set in and the year turned gray beneath the season of dissolution and of death." The trouble with this is not that we wish to
object to the meaning attached to the seasonal change but that the
statement is too little prepared for, too explicit, and too obviously
related to the loss suffered by the lost generation.

Or again, when young Bayard balances his sense of guilt against
his sense of doom, alternately accusing himself and accusing a God
in whom he cannot believe, the writing takes a too-familiar direction:

> *You . . . are afraid to face the consequences of your own
> acts.* Then again something bitter and deep and sleepless
> in him blazed out in vindication and justification and
> accusation; what, he knew not, blazing out at what, Whom,
> he did not know: *You did it! You caused it all; you killed
> Johnny.*

This fits in too neatly with "the black and savage stars," parallels
too closely the rebellious atheistic humanism of the twenties and
of the nineteenth century. Byron, Swinburne, Melville, and Mark
Twain had similarly accused God. The conversation at the end of
the book between Dr. Peabody and his son in which the older man
remarks that the soul cannot be found by dissection was conventional in 1929, when Joseph Wood Krutch published his popular,
accurate, and symptomatic book *The Modern Temper,* with its
chapter on the disillusion of the laboratory.

But there is nothing conventional about Bayard's visit with the
McCallums. With minor exceptions there is nothing conventional

about any of Part Four. Young Bayard in this section ceases to be a literary stereotype and becomes a sick young man with whom we can at last sympathize.

There are other conventions illustrated in the earlier parts of the book just as decisively broken in Part Four. The portrayal of the Negroes is one of them. The convention demanded that the Negro be portrayed, as Quentin puts it in *The Sound and the Fury,* not as a person but as a "form of behavior." There is no reason that I know of for considering the actions of Simon or Isom or of the Negro church deputation as necessarily exaggerated or untrue or even, perhaps, atypical; but the Negroes in question are presented not primarily as people but as forms of behavior, and somewhat stereotyped behavior at that. The whole attitude is epitomized on an early page in a narrator's comment: "'Chris'mus!' Joby exclaimed, with the grave and simple pleasure of his race. . . ." We miss the humanity we always expect in Faulkner, the comprehensive sympathy, in the episode of the church committee come to collect the money Simon has spent: the scene has humor at the expense of compassion. The conventional attitude being uncritically adopted here shuts out compassion, except in certain permitted circumstances under definite conditions, channels it and renders it harmless to the convention. The Negro is childlike and amusing. The only use of the word *nigger* (except where it is fictionally significant for characterization) that I recall in all the works of Faulkner occurs in *Sartoris,* in the author's own voice, in the middle of the magnificent little essay on the mule.

But when Bayard moves out to the McCallums', he leaves behind him the Sartoris convention of the Negro. He seems to feel it perfectly natural when the McCallum Negro cook offers to shake hands with him in greeting, and he treats the Negro men on the place without condescension. "Forms of behavior" have become persons, certainly for the reader, perhaps for Bayard. There is not the slightest trace of the convention left by the time we get to Bayard's Christmas day in the Negro cabin. The two Christmases,

Joby's and that of these people, are in the sharpest contrast. The change is from a convention uncritically followed to a convention broken by fresh vision and real creativity.

The same thing may be said of the evocation of the Sartoris way of life as contrasted with the McCallum episode. The former follows to a considerable extent the tradition of romantic local color, with nostalgia and idealization about equally blended. In view of old Bayard's actual end and of what we have learned of the South in other Faulkner works we wonder about the adjectives *peaceful* and *kind* in the following passage, describing old Bayard and his favorite dog:

> Then together they spent the afternoon going quietly and unhurriedly about the meadows and fields and woods in their seasonal mutations; the man on his horse and the ticked setter gravely beside him, while the descending evening of their lives drew toward its peaceful close upon the kind land that had bred them both.

Beginning with "while the descending evening," the writing here becomes not only lifeless but positively bad. But with this we may compare the evocation of the McCallum way of life. The McCallum episode is a kind of idyll, but there is no trace of the conventional in it.

The same point may be illustrated by contrasting the descriptions of nature in the early and the later parts of the book. Faulkner in most of his work continues a long and valuable tradition of nature writing in American fiction, but in a number of passages early in *Sartoris* he writes in the borrowed romantic language of an un-criticized convention:

> From her silver casement the moon looked down upon the valley dissolving in opaline tranquillity into the serene mysterious infinitude of the hills, and young Bayard's voice went on and on, recounting violence and speed and death.

An impression of the serenity of nature as a backdrop for human anguish is often an effect achieved by the nature descriptions in

Faulkner's later works, but it is not achieved in this kind of language, dictated by this convention. It is achieved in *Sartoris,* too, but not until Bayard approaches the McCallum farm. Then we have one of the most powerful and effective nature descriptions to be found anywhere in Faulkner; and in it, significantly, Bayard comes alive without our being told anything of his agony or his doom:

> Up the last hill the tireless pony bore him and in the low December sun their shadow fell long across the ridge and into the valley beyond, from which the high shrill yapping of the dogs came on the frosty, windless air. Young dogs, Bayard told himself, and he sat his horse in the faint scar of the road, listening as the high-pitched hysteria of them swept echoing across his aural field. Motionless, he could feel frost in the air. Above him the pines, though there was no wind in them, made a continuous dry, wild sound, as though the frost in the air had found voice; above them, against the high evening blue, a shallow V of geese slid. "There'll be ice tonight," he thought, watching them and thinking of black backwaters where they would come to rest, of rank bayonets of dead grass about which water would shrink soon in fixed glossy ripples in the brittle darkness. Behind him the earth rolled away ridge on ridge blue as woodsmoke, on into a sky like thin congealed blood. He turned in his saddle and stared unwinking into the sun that spread like a crimson egg broken on the ultimate hills. That meant weather: he snuffed the still, tingling air, hoping he smelled snow.

It is possible to find literary antecedents—in Eliot, chiefly—for the sunset imaged as congealed blood and a crimson egg, but if these images suggest that another convention has replaced the one echoed in the "silver casement" of the moon, at least it is a convention liberating in its effect here, suited to the needs of the fictional situation and of Faulkner's deeper sensibility.[4] Perhaps a writer can only break with one convention by adopting another, more adequate one. At any rate, the conventions that seem early in the book to be accepted uncritically are cast aside one by one before the end, and in that process the book comes to life and rises toward greatness.

4

IF SARTORIS fails in its aim at tragedy and convinces us finally only of sickness, the reason for its failure has something to do with the extreme difficulty of our believing in a tragic hero. Young Bayard could have been more skillfully presented, but no doubt we should have had trouble taking him even so. We tend today instinctively, without even being aware of the extent to which we are doing it, to psychologize, to explain away man's choices of good and evil, his actions, his "character," to use a word already beginning to sound archaic, by seeing them as mere results of hidden causes. The heroes of fiction in our culture are usually psychological victims.

It is not surprising then that young Bayard seems only partly tragic hero. He affects us chiefly as a neurotic whose "case" we feel might be easily explained and cured. Even if he were more consistently presented as tragic hero, would it be possible for us to believe in him? The image of man changes and believable pictures come to seem lifeless and false conventions. The image presented by classic tragedy and by high religion is not that which our culture presents to us.

The problem here, implicit in *Sartoris* only as a kind of ambivalence in the portrait of young Bayard, is explicit in *The Sound and the Fury* in Quentin Compson's effort to believe in man by believing in the possibility of sin. In *Sartoris* two perspectives, one traditional, one contemporary, are at odds; each destroys the other, destroying therefore the possibility of any final meaning. In *The Sound and the Fury* several possible perspectives are presented and explored, including the traditional one that Bayard so unconvincingly embodies and that Quentin tries to believe in.

CHAPTER 3

"Form, Solidity, Color"

THE SOUND AND THE FURY

IN THE YEAR IN WHICH *The Sound and the Fury* was published Faulkner made a point, for a while, of carrying a cane and wearing spats, serving notice on Oxfordians of the role he had chosen for himself. The young artist had not yet been acknowledged as artist. There would be time later for him to adopt the role of Mississippi farmer.

But the mask of the artist was not merely a gesture of defiance of local mores. The gesture indicated attachment as well as separation, and the attachment was that which had been suggested clearly enough in *Mosquitoes*. That novel's rejection was a rejection, as we have seen, of the whole local and immediate context of the artist in America, a rejection of Anderson's tradition of regionalism and naturalism as much as of the folkways. The combination of the usual interpretation of *Mosquitoes* with the usual undervaluing of *Sartoris* makes it harder to understand Faulkner's development: it makes a "mystery" of *The Sound and the Fury*. The spats and the cane were the young artist's substitute for the beret he had worn briefly in Paris. *The Sound and the Fury* was created in the context in which Joyce, Pound, Eliot, Gertrude Stein, Conrad, the later James, and Ford Madox Ford were finding ways of expressing a new sensibility.

In the fifteen years before *The Sound and the Fury* was published, poetry had moved from Georgian sententiousness through imagism to symbolism, and fiction was taking a similar course. Ford had described the ideal novelist in Jamesian terms as an "impressionist" and located his superiority in the fact that he "renders the world as he sees it, uttering no comments." But Joyce, rendering the world as he saw it and uttering no comments, had found a way of making the necessary comments seem to utter themselves. Eliot had termed Joyce's method of writing "the mythological method."

The shock which the opening section of *The Sound and the Fury* gave its readers was the shock of pure experience rendered without the kind of interpretation Faulkner had provided so liberally in *Soldier's Pay.* A part of what Faulkner had learned as he came to artistic maturity was what he was later to express with characteristic overemphasis: "I am not responsible for the statements of my characters. . . . I am not responsible for anything lost or found in any pages of my books."[1] *The Sound and the Fury* is the first book in which Faulkner was able consistently to practice his art as he had come to conceive it. The artist is now a creator, the "liar" of *Mosquitoes.* But he creates in order to render life in all its "form solidity color." The form, the solidity, and the color are all here: *The Sound and the Fury* is a work of art, not a "slice of life," it "renders" the specific without comment, it heightens the emotional and imaginative color of experience concretely recaptured and evoked. The result is a "passion week of the heart" that makes clear how sensitive and creative was Faulkner's response to the new symbolic techniques of such writers as Joyce and Eliot. *The Sound and the Fury* is very much a product of the twenties, by which of course I do not mean that it is "dated" in a bad sense.

By 1946, when Malcolm Cowley remarked on the oddity of the fact that all of Faulkner's books were out of print, *The Sound and the Fury* had still received very little serious and responsible criticism. Significant criticism of Faulkner's work as a whole hardly exists before George Marion O'Donnell's *Kenyon* piece in 1939. Several years before Lawrence Bowling wrote his early analysis of the technique of *The Sound and the Fury,* in 1948, Malcolm Cowley had confessed himself puzzled by it. Three years after Bowling's essay the authors of the first book-length critical analysis of Faulkner emphasized what seemed the opacity of the work in their remark that "the novel *The Sound and the Fury* presents peculiarities of style and meaning which make it practically meaningless unless read with the aid of insights proffered by Freudian theory of dream-work."[2] Mr. Howe felt it necessary several years ago to begin his perceptive chapter on *The Sound and the Fury* by defending the arrangement of the sections of the novel against the common charge that the order is arbitrary, irrational, or needlessly difficult. How a whole generation missed the point of what had happened in American literature when *The Sound and the Fury* was published is at least as great a mystery as how the apprentice novelist of *Soldier's Pay* and *Mosquitoes* came to write it.

We are likely today to profit by the reminder that the novel is in some ways more traditional than it once seemed. Some of Faulkner's best critics, particularly George Marion O'Donnell and Robert Penn Warren, have made clear, perhaps with some strategic exaggeration, the traditional elements in Faulkner's themes; but critics of *The Sound and the Fury* have been unanimous in their emphasis on the "experimental" form of this novel. But a quarter of a century is a long time in the conditions of modern life and literature, long enough at least to render the experimental familiar if not conventional, long enough to enable us to see properly what was new and what was old in the experiment. Now in mid-century, Joyce and Eliot are "old masters," initiators of a tradition long since not only accepted but assimilated and currently being modified or even rejected by a second or third post-Joyce-Eliot literary generation. *The Sound and the Fury* no longer needs to be either defended or attacked for its departure from an earlier tradition. Its own tradition is already mature in the work of writers of early middle age.

In one sense *The Sound and the Fury* continues in modified form the tradition of nineteenth-century fiction. It tells the story of a family over a period of about thirty years, following a generation from early childhood through the chief remembered events of their lives to maturity or death. Faulkner has recently characterized it as "a tragedy of two lost women: Caddy and her daughter."[3] Though the manner of telling is untraditional ("I wrote it five separate times trying to tell the story. . . ."), the story told is more like the story told in *David Copperfield* or *Henry Esmond* than like that told in *Ulysses*. Here it is not the shifting of a cake of soap from one pocket to another that reminds us of the outer, objective world but death, marriage, and death again. In *Ulysses* the events of Bloom's day, as they are in themselves, are mostly trivial. The significance lies chiefly in what they are made to recall by being placed in a framework of echo and allusion. In *The Sound and the Fury* the events themselves are significant: recast in a different telling, they would serve for a traditional, pre-Joycean novel. That they are *not* told in that manner is of course of the essence; but we should not lose sight of what is told in our concentration on the manner of telling.

This is the story of the Compson family, from some time in the early 1890's until April 8, 1928, when Benjy is thirty-three. The cast of characters is large, as it was in the typical Victorian biographical novel, and characters present in the early years drop out of the story later, except as they are retained in memory. The Compson children are born in the 1890's. The earliest childhood memory seems to be of the way the buzzards "undressed" Nancy, presumably a cow—that is, tore away the flesh and left the bones. The death of the children's grandmother, "Damuddy," is a crucial event in the growth of their awareness, as is the renaming of Benjy, at first named Maury after the mother's brother. Caddy's getting her drawers wet in the branch, the events of the day before her wedding, the wedding itself, the day of Quentin's suicide in Cambridge, Benjy's castration, the burial of their father, and the girl Quentin's elopement and flight with Jason's money are other events which might be subclimaxes in a novel more traditionally told. When the story ends the only Compsons left are Benjy, an imbecile; the mother, a moral and emotional invalid; and Jason, who has rejected the ways of the Compsons. Father and Quentin have died, years ago, and Caddy and her child Quentin have disappeared. The story tells of the disintegration and disappearance of a family.

What may trouble the reader is the difficulty of dating some of these events, or of filling in the events between them. But for the most part the precise dates and the exact chronological order of the events do not matter. When they do matter they are clearly given.[4] But to reconstruct the chronology roughly will be necessary before we can analyze the effect of the novel's departure from a straight chronological method of narration.

Quentin is the oldest child; Candace, called Caddy, next; Jason next; Maury, renamed Benjamin and called Benjy or Ben, the youngest. Significantly, it is chiefly by what we know of and through him that we are able to order our chronology. Since Quentin finished his first year at Harvard and died in 1910, the children were probably all born between 1890 and 1895. By 1928 Caddy's daughter, called Quentin after her uncle, is seventeen.

One of the principal means of placing the events in the first two sections, where the shifts between past and present are so frequent, is to note which little colored boy is taking care of Benjy. Versh, who looks after Benjy in the events of the earliest memories, is I suppose Dilsey's child, perhaps her oldest. We may imagine him as a little older than the first Quentin. T.P., who takes his place in later events, is probably about Quentin's age. He is apparently another, younger child of Dilsey. Luster, who is caring for Benjy in 1928, is presumably one of Dilsey's grandchildren. Versh, T.P., and Luster establish the order of these memories, as definitely as they need to be established.

The reader needs no dates more exact than this for the fullest aesthetic experience of this novel, any more than he needs to recall the exact date of the month and day of the week when his own grandmother died for the memory to be vivid and detailed and the event important in the shaping of his life. All that we need to know here we either gather as we read or we can reconstruct after reading, as one might first recall in detail the moments or hours of any past event in his own life and then search his memory for clues to the precise date when the event took place. Thus the night Damuddy died must have been some time between 1896 and, say, 1899; that is close enough, at any rate. Quentin's suicide is established, almost to the hour, 1910; Caddy's marriage is the same year. Roskus, husband of Dilsey and father of Versh and T.P., died not very long after Caddy's marriage and departure, probably between 1910 and 1915. Father died when Caddy's daughter Quentin was still a baby, perhaps in 1911 or 1912.

All the events of early childhood, before the complications of puberty set in, are first presented in Section I. They make up the bulk of Benjy's section, and we depend almost entirely on him for our knowledge of them. These are innocent memories in several senses—events innocently remembered, without special bias and without apparent interpretation. If these events foreshadow the future (Jason with his hands in his pockets, Caddy with the stain on her bottom) Benjy cannot tell us what they prefigure. His is the innocent mind.

For the events occurring between, say, 1906 and 1910, when the children were in their adolescence and earliest maturity, we depend about equally on Benjy and Quentin. Some of the events of these years are recounted twice, once from Benjy's point of view, once from Quentin's; but of course the experience of an event as recalled by Benjy is not the same as Quentin's experience of the same event. Insofar as may be, Benjy's memories still give us the events in themselves, as they really were, whereas Quentin's memories of this period are still more colored by his obsessive interpretations than were his memories of the earlier period. To the extent that we depend on Quentin rather than on Benjy for memories of this period, we find it more difficult here than in the memories of the earlier period to know what "really" happened—between Caddy and Quentin, for instance, in the scene at night in the brook, which we know only through Quentin: how much has he invented, imagined, dreamed, wished? By contrast, both earlier and later events recalled or experienced by Benjy are clear, external, objective—the burning of his hand, for instance, of which we know little, but can trust what we know. The innocence is in process of being lost in this period and by the end of it has been lost by all the Compsons except Benjy. Benjy's innocence is inviolably prelapsarian.

For the events during the last, and longest, period of the story told in the book, we depend almost entirely on Jason, who remembers as subjectively as Quentin, though with a quite different bias. There are only a few memories of this period, after Caddy's departure, left to Benjy; we cannot depend any longer on his memory to establish the norm. If we try, for instance, to judge Caddy's conduct after her marriage when she brought her baby home to be cared for by its grandparents, we are left only with whatever conjectures we may form as we attempt to allow for the distortion introduced by Jason. If we could turn to a passage in Benjy's section for his memory of this event we should still be in doubt, perhaps, but in doubt of a different kind. We could make our own interpretation of the event with some confidence, as we can of the time when Mother scolds about Benjy's not having his mittens on. We know exactly what she says on that occasion, and we can penetrate to the motive behind her words of seeming motherly devotion as even she cannot; we end by knowing her better than she knows herself. But Jason seldom remembers precise words or events, so that before we can interpret the events that are recalled only in his section we must first interpret *him,* as he is revealed in the total context of the work, and then try to decide what really occurred. Jason's corruption interposes a whole series of screens between the reader and reality, as it does between Jason and reality.

Finally, for the events of Good Friday, Saturday, and Easter Day,

1928, the story's present, we have three sources, Jason, Benjy, and the omniscient author: Jason for Friday, Benjy for Saturday, omniscient author for Easter. Since the separate events of these three days are closely connected, what we have in effect is a continuation of the multiple perspectives which have come to seem a necessary condition of our appropriation of the past. The interaction of these perspectives has prepared us to accept the interpretation implicit in the impersonal reporting of the last section.

If we relate the chronology of the events in the story, in other words, to the four-part structure of the book, we find that, with one important exception, the "scrambling" of time, the chronological disorder which has been so often attacked and defended, is less extreme than we may have been led to expect. The events of 1896 to 1906 occur first and we encounter them first, in Section I. Later, in Section II, we reencounter some of them. The events of the next period, 1906 to 1910, we get chiefly in Section II, though some of them we have already encountered in the first section. Though we have had a few glimpses of the events of the third period, 1910 to 1928, in the first section, we get our fullest account, and of most of them our only account, in Section III. The events of the last three days in Easter Week we get in Sections I, III and IV. Here is the only conspicuous exception to the predominance of chronological order.

From this juxtaposition of chronological order and aesthetic order, or from a simple adequate reading, emerges a story of three generations of the Compsons, not a perversely obscure puzzle or exercise in literary "experimentalism." Chronoligical order and order of presentation finally come together: this is one of the reasons for emphasizing today what it may still seem perverse to some to emphasize, that this is a more traditional novel than we have realized.

Perverse? Strategic and useful, rather, I hope. It is true that if we center our attention not on the larger aspects of structure, on the arrangement of the sections and the relation of this arrangement to the story being told, but on the smaller units of structure, on the order of events within any one of the first three sections, we may get the impression of disorder. But this "disorder" is of a kind to which we are thoroughly accustomed by now, the shuffling back and forth in memory between past and present; and there is a significant, a very immediate and human point of view from which it seems not "disorder" at all but *our* kind of order, the order of human experience, human reality, before "inward" and "outward" are abstracted from the whole, separated. If this mixing up of events from past and present puts a barrier in the way of the inexperienced or inattentive reader, it contributes to the illusion of reality felt by the prepared reader.

Thus Benjy's section, where past and present are most thoroughly mixed, has been found by most of the critics to be the most immediate in the book. Benjy lives in the present in terms supplied by the past and recalls the past through the stimulus of the present. Both past and present are rendered sharply in Benjy's section, though the past gets most of his attention. Quentin, too, moves back and forth between past and present, though his changes of focus are not quite so abrupt or frequent, so that his section seems to have occasioned fewer complaints about its "difficulty": and it too is immensely vivid. The events of Quentin's last day that are related to his past or to his present purposes, and the events he relives from the past, are as immediate, as concretely present to the reader, as any events in modern fiction.

But Jason's section is not immediate in the same way. Though he is the only "practical" and "sane" narrator so far, concerned with action, with public events, with "reality," yet in his section the quality of the actual present is rendered hardly at all. His mind moves back and forth between a colored version of the past and a wishful projection of the future, both calculated to help him "get even." Thus though his section is the easiest to read so far in the book, it is the least vivid and immediate: in fact, we could not understand it at all if we had not been prepared for it by Benjy and Quentin. We have only to compare, even on a quite literal level, the clarity of the events of Quentin's last day with the murkiness of those of April 6, 1928, narrated by Jason, to see the difference. The blending of past and present in the novel may make some passages difficult at first reading, but the final effect is to focus and clarify both past and present.

2

BUT OF COURSE no service would be done by insisting too much on the "traditional" aspects of *The Sound and the Fury*. Once we have recognized that this novel which seems to break so sharply with the story-telling tradition of the novel tells a story of the objective world peopled with solid, memorable characters engaged in and suffering significant experience, we may move another step in our effort to define the special quality of the work. To do so is necessarily to consider the significance of its departures from tradition. That we may most easily and effectively understand the function of the form through a consideration of the characters is another reminder that this experiment ends not by destroying but by strengthening novelistic tradition.

Benjy is one of the great idiots of literature. The tale he tells, like his frequent bellowing, is full of "sound and fury" but whether or not we should say that it signifies nothing depends on the context in which we ask the question. For the Compsons the story ends in Father's bitter cynicism and alcoholic death, Quentin's despair and suicide, Jason's unhappy corruption; for the Compsons the story ends in loss and perversion and death. But for the reader this tale first told by an idiot signifies much indeed. And its significance is very largely dependent on the fact that we experience it first through Benjy and judge the experience finally by means of the standard offered by Benjy.

If Benjy is prelapsarian, Adam before the Fall, he is also, and

in the end I think more significantly, a Christ image. Not that he
is in any sense an allegorical symbol of Christ. He simply reminds
us of Christ, and of the values associated with Christ.[5] Like
Dostoyevsky's Prince, he is a kind of modern Christ, impotent to
save us but supplying a standard by which we are judged, and,
perhaps, may know ourselves lost. He is thirty-three, the story he
first tells culminates on Easter—an Easter without a Resurrection—
and the jimson weed he sometimes plays with has another local
name, angel's trumpet. There is even, early in his section, a kind of
Epiphany when he and the other children come out of the darkness
to find father on the steps, in a beam of light, and then "He stopped
and took me up, and the light came tumbling down the steps on me
too. . . ." Clearly Benjy is an impotent, helpless Christ, however
unorthodox we may think the Christology implicit in the portrait—
and I suspect that it is not much more unorthodox than Dostoyevsky's in *The Idiot* or Melville's in *Billy Budd*. As St. Paul writes in
I Corinthians, 1.19,27: "For it is written, I will destroy the wisdom
of the wise, and will bring to nothing the understanding of the
prudent. . . . God hath chosen the foolish things of the world to
confound the wise; and God hath chosen the weak things of the
world to confound the things that are mighty."[6]

To call Benjy a Christ image is not, of course, to prejudge the
ultimate meaning of the book. In what sense, if any, the theme can
be called "Christian" is a question which it would be wholly
premature to take up at this point. Faulkner himself has recently
stated the necessary *caveat*. The artist, he has reminded us, uses
whatever myth is available to him as artist: which is to say, he
need not be personally committed, committed in his role as a
citizen, to the myths he uses as artist.[7] As we should not conclude
—at least without much more and different evidence—that Faulkner
personally holds all the views he attributes to Gavin Stevens, so it
would be very poor critical procedure to conclude that Faulkner
when he wrote *The Sound and the Fury* thought of himself, or
ought to be thought of, as a Christian.

Nevertheless, we must recognize Benjy as a Christ image. If his values prevailed, the family might be saved. But he is castrated and eventually sent to Jackson, where he will not embarrass Jason, the prudent Compson who can see no purpose served by continuing to care for this idiot brother with his bawling for the lost Caddy and the broken angel's trumpet. This Christ is not crucified: he is rendered impotent and removed from the scene. All the other characters in the book are finally judged in terms of their relationship with Benjy. The Mother would be an unsympathetic character anyway, with her neurotic, self-pitying illness, but the negative reaction we have to her is focused most sharply in those scenes and reported actions when she most clearly reveals the embarrassment and distaste behind the conventional sentiments of mother love she utters. Caddy would be a neutral character, dimly seen and perhaps unsympathetic, if we knew her only through Quentin. Her genuine love for Benjy is the crucial fact that determines our attitude. Judged within the frame of values decisively determined by Benjy's function in the story, she emerges a creature of pathos. We assent to the judgment involved in Benjy's perception that she smelled like trees; and we note that this is the most difficult act of intelligence in his section, where almost everything is simple discrete perception without connections except with similar perceptions in the past, which is not even recognized as past. And it is Jason's attitude toward and treatment of Benjy that most decisively determines our judgment of Jason, making us see him as self-condemned to existence in a Hell of his own making. Quentin's inadequacy is given sharper definition by the fact that though he feels pity for Benjy, or perhaps more accurately feels the pathos of the situation of which Benjy is an expression, he never is able to carry his generous feelings into effective action. "Faith without deeds is dead." Quentin is not a doer of the word; one of the "wise," he is confounded equally with the prudent.

After Caddy's departure only Dilsey is left to love Benjy and express her love in action. She continues patiently to serve him, protect him, honor him. When she takes him to church for the Easter service, she has to defend her action (who else would take care of him while she was gone?) even to her daughter Frony:

> "I wish you wouldn't keep on bringin him to church, mammy," Frony said. "Folks talkin."
> "What folks?" Dilsey said.
> "I hears em," Frony said.
> "And I knows whut kind of folks," Dilsey said, "Trash white folks. Dat's who it is. Thinks he aint good enough fer white church, but nigger church aint good enough fer him."
> "Dey talks, jes de same," Frony said.
> "Den you send um to me," Dilsey said. "Tell um de good Lawd dont keer whether he smart er not. Dont nobody but white trash keer dat."

Only Dilsey remembers his birthday and sees that he has a cake, as she alone of those on the Compson place properly celebrates Easter, thus officiating at two rites not unconnected. (Mother, in contrast, dreads Christmas, which has become for her, like the family honor she "protects," like Benjy himself, only a burden.) After Caddy is gone only Dilsey has compassion for Benjy—not only compassion but even a kind of respect. Only to her is he not a "thing" but a "person," even in his repulsive helplessness. Her position in the novel is determined by her relation with him more than by anything else. It may not be utterly fanciful to see her as becoming, finally, a kind of foster-moster of Christ, the enabling agent of a revelation at once spiritual and aesthetic.[8]

Benjy responds to love and truth, and establishes for us the norm of love and truth. He is not taken in by his mother's false displays of affection: he is aware of them only as the meaningless words and gestures that they are, responding not to them but to the tone and situation that express the truth behind the words. Only in his section of the first three in the book can we be perfectly sure that what the mind perceives actually occurred. Quentin did not commit incest but only wanted to; much of his revery is fantasy. Jason interprets the world subjectively; his revery is largely wishful thinking, almost as much fantasy as Quentin's. Benjy's perceptions give us the facts prior to interpretation. His reactions, and the reactions of others to him, enable us, by an act of the moral and aesthetic imagination for which we alone are finally accountable, to make the interpretations which he cannot make for us.

Quentin has seemed to many readers the least impressive of the major characters. As Mr. Howe, for example, has said, "Where Benjy recalls a world, Quentin nurses an obsession."⁹ Finding Quentin a Hamlet-figure, Mr. Howe also finds him "too weak, too passive, too bewildered for the role of sensitive hero." His problem is credible but "it cannot carry the weight in the novel that Faulkner intends." Now I am not going to argue that Mr. Howe is wrong in his feeling that Quentin is less effectively conceived and presented in the novel than the other major characters. Mr. Howe may be right. The aesthetic burden that Quentin carries is as large as the burden of guilt that he feels; it may indeed be too much for him. But I do not believe that we have yet adequately identified his "problem." If we can do so, we shall be readier to decide how well he fills his role.

Quentin's problem is centered in his relation with his sister Caddy, but even for him this is not the end of the matter. His obsession with her chastity, her "honor," and with her "guilt" after her affair with Dalton Ames, is in part at least a result of his effort to localize, to pin down and define, a larger problem. His desire to commit incest with her—unfulfilled only because of himself, as she says "I'll do anything you want"—is a wish to *sin*. But "sin" is not a word one uses in a naturalistic frame of reference; when the word is seriously used it is defined as willful disobedience of God's commandments. The word defines a world. If God is gone and there are no commandments, then perhaps only the calculations of expedience and the distinctions of social and anti-social behavior remain. In such a world there is no "sin," but only effective or ineffective behavior in relation to immediate goals, goals as much created and destroyed by time as the actions they dictate.

Quentin's father had made all this clear to Quentin:

> He said it was men invented virginity not women.
> Father said it's like death: only a state in which the others
> are left and I said, But to believe it doesn't matter and he
> said That's what's so sad about anything not only virginity.
> . . . If we could just have done something so dreadful and
> Father said That's sad too, people cannot do anything that
> dreadful they cannot do anything very dreadful at all they
> cannot even remember tomorrow what seemed dreadful
> today and I said You can shirk all things and he said, Ah
> can you. . . .

It is not surprising that Quentin's memory of this talk with his
father leads him into the picture of death by water that immediately
follows:

> And I will look down and see my murmuring bones and
> the deep water like wind, like a roof of wind, and after a
> long time they cannot distinguish even bones upon the
> lonely and inviolate sand. Until on the Day when He says
> Rise only the flatiron would come floating up. It's not
> when you realize that nothing can help you—religion, pride,
> anything—it's when you realize that you dont need any aid.
> . . . Jesus walking on Galilee and Washington not telling
> lies. . . .

Quentin cannot rest in his father's cynical unbelief nor achieve
Dilsey's faith; but he cannot endure a world in which he can do
neither. His brooding on Caddy's loss of "honor" is a result not
only of an incestuous wish but of an unbearable nostalgia for a
world in which "honor" was conceivable. He cannot find the will
to live in a world from which not only honor but the very possibility
of dishonor has evaporated. He longs for the possibility of significant action. He longs for what the radically pragmatic will call
"absolutes." The world he finds himself in is the world pictured in
Eliot's "Sweeney Among the Nightingales," in which the shock of
the last phrase, picturing the "stiff, dishonored shroud" of Aga-
memnon, depends upon our feeling of the utter incongruity of
"dishonor" in the context of the scene pictured in the poem.
Quentin's desire to sin, to do something "dreadful," is a perverse
reflection of his desire to test the possibility of holiness.

This aspect of Quentin's problem was defined long ago by Eliot in his essay on Baudelaire. Eliot wrote: "So far as we are human, what we do must be either evil or good . . . and it is better, in a paradoxical way, to do evil than to do nothing: at least, we exist. It is true to say that the glory of man is his capacity for salvation; it is also true to say that his glory is his capacity for damnation."[10] Quentin found that he had no capacity either for salvation or for damnation. Caught in a world of inaction, he is unable to achieve any human identity in terms whose validity he recognizes. If he can't be St. Francis, of universal charity, he would like at least to be Conrad's Kurtz, that "lost, violent soul"; but in fact he is neither. The conception of Quentin owes something—indirectly, probably— to Dante, and more, directly, to Eliot. In him there is something of Prufrock, something of Gerontion, and something of Eliot's analysis of Baudelaire.

But there is more to his problem than this, complex though it already is. He is also so obsessed with time that several critics have contended there is too much time symbolism in his section, and that this is an intrusion of the author's sentiments which results in a distortion of character. This opinion would seem inevitable if Quentin's concern with time were not consistent with what we know of his character and his situation. But it is, I think, consistent, connected with Quentin's concern for honor, and an expression finally of the deepest themes of the whole work. The emphasis on clocks and watches in this section is made wholly functional by the depth and complexity of these connections.

It is not simply, as has been suggested, that the clocks in the store window, each telling a different time, imply that the "times" are wrong, the world out of joint, and Quentin inadequate to the job of setting it right. All the main characters in the book, not only Quentin, live in a world in which time is the most significant dimension. When Quentin's father gives him his watch he gives it to him as "the mausoleum of all hope and desire":

> I give it to you not that you may remember time, but that you might forget it now and then for a moment and not spend all your breath trying to conquer it. Because no

battle is ever won he said. They are not even fought. The field only reveals to man his own folly and despair, and victory is an illusion of philosophers and fools.

Father has prepared Quentin for his reflections on his last day:

> Like Father said down the long and lonely lightrays you might see Jesus walking, like. And the good Saint Francis that said Little Sister Death, that never had a sister. . . . Father said that. That Christ was not crucified: he was worn away by a minute clicking of little wheels.

Benjy is not capable of Quentin's and Father's concern with time; he is even, in a sense, unaware of time, making no distinction between past and present. But he grieves continually for what time has taken from him; the present is alive for him chiefly as it recalls the past. Mother cannot accept the realities of the present at all. Thanks chiefly to Dilsey she is able to continue her evasion and live in a world of make-believe fashioned out of a colored version of the past, in which she was a lady and brother Maury a gentleman. Jason races against time. He spends his life doing just what Father hopes Quentin may not do, futilely trying to catch up with what has already fled. The magnificent scene in the last section in which Jason tries to overtake the escaping girl Quentin epitomizes his way of dealing with time but is only the climax of a series of revelations. If Quentin is obsessed with time, all the Compsons are defeated by it.

But Dilsey is not. She knows the right time, whatever the clocks may say. The ruined kitchen clock presents no enigma to her:

> On the wall above a cupboard, invisible save at night, by lamp light and even then evincing an enigmatic profundity because it had but one hand, a cabinet clock ticked, then with a preliminary sound as if it had cleared its throat, struck five times.
>
> "Eight oclock," Dilsey said.

Knowing a "time not our time," she is able to *use* time practically and humanely, without haste and with the only constructive results achieved by anyone on the Compson place. She has time to take the unneeded hot water bottle slowly, painfully up the stairs and time to make a birthday cake for Benjy. She is the only major character not obsessed, frustrated, defeated by time. She acts as though she had "all the time in the world." And of course in a sense she has, if her religious beliefs are justified. She lives in two worlds, one in and one out of time. For her, Christ was crucified, not worn down by the minute clicking of little wheels. She has time to celebrate His resurrection and to take Benjy with her. She does not need to hurry. She is not anxious.

Quentin's problem, then, is the problem of all his family. As the most reflective, self-conscious member he brings it to the conscious level and his section is full of watches, with and without hands. But his problem is also his own in a special way, connected with his concern for Caddy's "honor" and his desire to commit incest. The contrast between his reaction and Jason's to Caddy's promiscuity and marriage will suggest a part of the point. Jason is concerned in this instance, as always, only with "results." The most tangible result is Caddy's child, the girl Quentin, and Jason's section centers on his reactions to her and his attempts to use and control her. Quentin is concerned with nothing tangible at all, only with "honor," which he associates with a bygone world that held to the "timeless" virtues.

Quentin's rare actions and his fantasies are then the results of his effort at definition. His incest wish is the reverse of his desire to protect Caddy's "honor." If he cannot force Caddy to acknowledge the importance of his standard, he will prove its significance by violating it "dreadfully." And the standard itself is connected in his mind with a definition of man, a definition quite different from his father's. "Man the sum of his climactic experiences Father said. Man the sum of what have you. A problem in impure properties carried tediously to an unvarying nil: stalemate of dust and desire." For Quentin, "honor" recalls a situation in which man defined himself as a free and responsible moral agent in a world with an eternal dimension. The human animal of his father's definition only behaves, and behavior has only a temporal significance. To be able to sin would be to prove the existence of a "time not our time," to touch the edge of the eternal.

If he is concerned with the shadow rather than the substance of virtue despite the reality and urgency of his moral and spiritual quest, it is because the shadow is all that is left him. In him the old order has been reduced to empty formalism, the shadow without the substance, but it is not because he has not tried to recapture, or recreate, the substance. He did not really commit incest with Caddy but he really *wished* to do so. Quentin is ultimately concerned with honor and dishonor just *because* he recognizes these concepts as archaic, destroyed by time. His tragedy is that he cannot himself believe what he tries to get Caddy to believe, cannot attain the only belief which for him would make life meaningful. He locates his values in the past, in the Old South, because it once conceived the world as only Dilsey can conceive it now. His obsession with honor and sin springs not only from his childhood experiences but from his mature concern with the possibility of a world in which honor and dishonor are not made by time but by human choice and are not destroyed by time but preserved unto everlasting. If he could only sin he might be saved.

But he can do no morally significant act, either good or bad. His world and his life are woven of the stuff of fantasy. If Dilsey is the only morally effective character in the book, Quentin is the only one completely incapable of significant action. Just as he was mysteriously frustrated in his wish to do "wrong" at home—to commit incest with Caddy—though he had, seemingly, not only the desire but the opportunity and her acquiescence, so in his last day he is frustrated in his desire to do "right," to help the little girl who is lost and who reminds him of Caddy. He cannot find her home, cannot communicate with her, cannot even make others understand or believe what it is he wishes to do. Quentin can only exist, for a while, in time, and then cease to exist. His only alternative to time is nothing.

So the clocks and watches in Quentin's section are not function-less, pointless and heavy-handed intrusions by the author to get us to pay attention to—what? They are connected, in all directions, with everything in the work. And the emphasis on them may be seen as right in another way, too: it is motivated, "in character," as we know Quentin in his situation. This after all is his last day alive: he knows it, he has already determined it, and he is naturally more concerned than ever with time, with the hours and the very minutes. Much of what he recalls of the past, as in the opening pages of his section, is connected with time because this dimension of experience, as he faces death in a matter of hours, naturally forces itself more than ever on his attention. Everything, he has discovered, is "a matter of hours," so that he is truly the representative modern man. His awareness is decisive in a book whose story begins not in birth but in death—the memory of the buzzards undressing Nancy—and ends on Easter Day with a frustrated attempt to drive to the cemetery. Quentin is a Prufrock figure more than he is a Hamlet figure.[11]

Jason can be understood more easily. He is much less complex than Quentin, though Faulkner's treatment of him seems to me in no way oversimplified. Since he is so unsympathetic a character, so near an approach to what it was once customary to call a villain, the wonder is that Faulkner was so successful with him. Perhaps a part of the secret of it is that though he is utterly corrupt morally, we are invited to pity rather than to hate him. He is as much a victim of time as Quentin, though he takes and makes his fate differently. Every member of his family, every situation fails him. It seems to him a personal affront that his father dies penniless, that his brother commits suicide after a year at college, thus having "wasted" the money got from the sale of the pasture that might have sent *him* to college, that his mother is an invalid, his sister a "whore," his younger brother an idiot. He must eat a cold dinner because his mother has let the "nigger" go to church—"Blame you? Blame you for what? You never resurrected Jesus." The sound of the bells ringing for the Easter service in "Nigger Hollow" as he prepares to try to catch Quentin and the man from the traveling show—with too little time—is an irritation that multiplies his anguish.

Dilsey judges him well, as she does all the affairs and people of her household: "You's a cold man, Jason, if man you is." Jason can only calculate because he has no love; and the only absolutely practical standard he knows is his own material self-interest. Benjy remembers Jason's walking with his hands in his pockets, as though "holding his money," and remembers too his reply when Quentin tried to get him not to tell what had happened at the brook. Quentin reminds him of a favor once done—" 'You remember that bow and arrow I made you, Jason.' "—" 'It's broke now,' Jason said." Even as a child he seems to have acted by the standard which he later verbalized as that of being interested only in results: a broken bow promised no results and so could enter into no calculation that he cared to make. For him, that is true which gets results; that is binding which promises results. He is bound by no "absolutes."

He is not, as are all the others in some way, even the mother in her vicious and pitiable delusions, taken in by intangibles. He knows the value of a dollar, and of a minute. Thinking of a man who gives money to the church, he laughs to himself. "I often think how mad he'll be if he was to die and find out that there's not any heaven, when he thinks about that five thousand a year." Mr. Howe has properly remarked that Jason is characterized in part by the fact that he shares the most widespread and virulent American prejudices: he hates both Jews and Negroes.[12] But his hatred goes further and deeper: Negroes and Jews are only convenient targets of a more generalized hatred that governs his whole life. He hates everyone who does not directly minister to his needs, and he hates even those who do if they claim any independent existence apart from him, any recognition of their status as persons and not simply conveniences or objects in his world. He never even approaches the relationship which Buber calls the "I-Thou" relation.

That is why he has to get rid of Dilsey even though she will work for nothing. That is why he "likes" Lorraine: each of them uses the other, in an arrangement mutually profitable. Whatever our ethical beliefs, in the context of this novel we are made to see that Jason and his kind poison all human relationships as he would poison the pigeons on the square if only the Methodist minister, "talking all about peace on earth good will toward all and not a sparrow can fall to earth," did not stand in the way. His proposed solution to the pigeon problem epitomizes his whole approach to life: it would be cheap and practical and in no way inexpedient, if his basic convictions about life are justified. Jason is Quentin's anti-type, a Compson who has self-protectively become a Snopes. He does not regret the loss of value because he does not grant any reality to superpersonal or transpersonal value. He has, in his own eyes, no illusions: he is a thoroughgoing naturalist. It is Jason's world that Quentin cannot bear.

Dilsey is for most of us the only completely sympathetic character of the book, I should imagine, despite Faulkner's stated intention that the work be considered Caddy's and her daughter's story. (Benjy we sympathize with but cannot perfectly identify ourselves with. Removed from the ordinary human sphere by his idiocy, he is not quite "one of us" as Dilsey is.) Patient, loyal, loving, strong, she preserves the best values of the past and retards the family's race toward destruction. She is one of the great sympathetic characters of all fiction, completely unforgettable once one has encountered her and wholly admirable without the slightest trace of idealizing or sentimentalizing in the portrait. From the moment she appears at the door of the cabin in her best dress of purple silk she holds our interest and compels our admiration.

And not only because of what she does and says in the last section, which is effectively hers even though told from the narrative point of view of omniscient author. Her entrance that dismal Easter morning has been thoroughly prepared for: we are ready to appreciate her before she ever appears at the center of the stage.

The glimpses we have had of her, especially in Benjy's and Jason's sections, have prepared us for what we are now to witness. One of the reasons why the novel could not start with this last section, as some have suggested it should in order to lessen the difficulties of Benjy's section, is here illustrated. If we were to read this section first we should find it not easy, except on the most superficial level, but obscure, and not utterly convincing but forced and perhaps even melodramatic. We should either not get the effect of Dilsey at all, or we should obscurely sense it without being prepared to accept it. We have had to learn to depend on her to deflate Mother's insincere rhetoric with truth ("'I'm afraid to,' Mother said. 'With the Baby.'—Dilsey went up the steps. 'You calling that thing a baby,' she said."), control the irresponsible caretakers of Benjy, protect the others from Jason. We have found her the one stable and dependable element in the situation. We have been prepared to accept her as chorus and judge, and to feel the full impact of her reaction at the end of the visiting preacher's sermon:

> In the midst of the voices and the hands Ben sat, rapt in his sweet blue gaze. Dilsey sat bolt upright beside, crying rigidly and quietly in the annealment and the blood of the remembered Lamb.

We share her emotion because we have seen with her what the preacher sees, "de darkness en de death everlastin upon de generations." We know her words are not idle ones when she says "I've seed de first en de last." We have so learned to trust her wisdom that we are compelled to assent in some sense to her judgment of Benjy and herself: "'You's de Lawd's chile, anyway. En I be His'n too, fo long, praise Jesus.'"

3

A JUDGMENT of such far-reaching consequences, resting on and carrying with it so many other judgments, could be aesthetically compelling only if its context had been fully prepared. It will seem the right verdict only to a reader who has shared the experiences that make up its context, who has been led to an assent which he would not have given initially. That is why, finally, we cannot imagine this novel arranged otherwise than as it is.

The novel may be said to move from the concrete to the abstract, in several senses. It moves from Benjy, immersed in time and able to hold its treasures only because he is unable to think in abstractions; to Quentin, who meditates on time and longs for assurance that values are timeless, but who can escape from time only into death; to Jason, who is concerned with the concrete moment only insofar as it can be translated into his "practical realities," money and power, which are finally as abstract as Quentin's "honor"; to Dilsey, whose faith in timeless intangibles enables her to live in time and deal with concrete experience without frustration and without despair.

Benjy's section is concrete because he is bound, limited, subjected to the immediacy of the given-in-experience. Paradoxically, there is a kind of escape from the tyranny of time in Benjy's complete subjection to time: for Benjy the moment *is* eternal, always present, forever recallable. This relationship of his to time is one of the reasons why we see him as not only the potential savior but man before the fall, not yet having destroyed (only because he *cannot*, perhaps) his right relation to the eternal, a relation of trust and love. In Benjy we get the concretely realized flow of experience. The first section establishes the quality that the ending states for us in the last sentence:

> The broken flower drooped over Ben's fist and his eyes were empty and blue and serene again as cornice and facade flowed smoothly once more from left to right; post and tree, window and doorway, and signboard, each in its ordered place.

Benjy does not fight time. The order he experiences is not of his making. Quentin fights it with "ideals," attempting by sheer will to escape its dominion. Jason is a rationalist: he tries to conquer it by careful planning. Dilsey submits herself to it because her faith gives her hope that the sound and the fury are not final. Like Benjy, she preserves the values of the past and responds to the values of the present.

In still another sense the novel moves from the concrete to the abstract: it moves, in the successive sections, from the sensory to the interpretive, from Benjy through Quentin and Jason to Dilsey. The arrangement is essentially one we might call "inductive" if the word did not suggest logic rather than art. The structure of the novel, in short, invites us to participate in the process by which the judgments implicit in the last section are arrived at, invites us by first immersing us in the facts and then arranging for us a series of perspectives. Quentin's and Jason's perspectives are opposite in character and quality but alike in subjecting the raw data of Benjy's perception to Procrustean interpretations, "idealistic" or "realistic." The last section moves beyond realism and idealism, affirming at once the qualitative richness of Benjy's experience and the human values which he was partially able to respond to but unable to define or protect, implicitly acknowledging the values Quentin was unable effectively to believe in and Jason cynically denied.

The "objectivity" of the last section is, then, only formal: the reporting seems objective because we have known Benjy, Quentin, and Jason. We have been immersed in experience, and in two versions of experience-as-interpreted: when we stand off and look at what we have known, it looks the way we see it in the last section. The objectivity here is a technical achievement made possible by the total form of the work; its implicit perspective is based on judgments which we ourselves have been brought to the point of making. If the last section is in one sense the simplest, in another it is the most complex.

Structurally, then, and at the deepest level of meaning, there are movements in two directions going on here. Benjy's experience is at once more subjective and more trustworthy than Jason's.

Quentin's view of life, and the resultant shape of his experience, are at once more "realistic"—because not dependent on an act of faith—and more subjective than Dilsey's. Paradox is at the center of the vision. The order achieved in the last section has been achieved through difficulty, formally and thematically. The easy-reading, formalized, traditional order of the last section would be, aesthetically, too easy if the three sections that precede it had not prepared us for the narrator's way of ordering, just as, religiously, Dilsey's affirmation of a supersensible order would be too easy if she had never suffered the sound and the fury. Insofar as we can achieve an unbiased reading of the novel, our faith in Dilsey is a response both to the order which we have seen her bring to the lives she touches and to the order which her section brings to the book. Theme and structure are one thing in *The Sound and the Fury*. Both assert the possibility of achieving a difficult order out of the chaotic flux of time.

The possibility; a difficult order. There is little joy in this Easter day. Dilsey wears purple, a liturgical color that suggests the sadness of penitential seasons—the color for Advent and Lent. It is not without its meaning that the saving positive values, the ordering beliefs, are embodied here in an idiot and in a representative of an ignorant and despised people. As the words that might save us come to us fragmented and in an unknown tongue at the end of *The Waste Land,* so the Word here is revealed only in the senseless bawling of an idiot and proclaimed only by the bells ringing down in "Nigger Hollow." The novel allows us to make of this what we will, and we shall make somewhat different interpretations of it depending on our fundamental beliefs. But there are perhaps a few aspects of the theme on which we may all agree.

Our first reaction as we try to hold the whole work in mind and think of its meaning for us may well be a sense of the impossibility of thus wrenching apart "form" and "content," even temporarily and after preparation. The reaction may well be a sound one, and at any rate constitutes an implicit tribute to the richness, solidity, the full aesthetic achievement of this work. But we can and do, sometimes usefully, generalize about the meanings embodied in works of art; it is not impossible to do so here. First, then, we note that by the end of the novel there has been a reversal of the meaning first suggested by the title, or at least a significant qualification of it. The idiot has turned out to be the carrier of the values we accept: the tale he tells signifies much, and if one of its meanings is that life is at last "a stalemate of dust and desire," it is only one, and not the one that the idiot himself suggests to us. Nor Dilsey. In her innocent ignorance she continues to live by what was once, according to St. Paul, "foolishness to the Greeks" and is still foolishness to Jason.

But the sound and the fury will not be dismissed as unreal, or the private fate and preoccupation of the Compsons. If the saving values are no longer held except by an idiot and an ignorant old woman—and, in a sense, putatively, by a maladjusted neurotic heading for suicide—then they are effectively lost to us. Quentin cannot simply *decide* to believe in the reality of sin, and so in the reality of a timeless order. In this fictional counterpart of *The Waste Land* a situation is presented and diagnosed: no remedy is proposed. The flower Benjy clutches as the shapes flow by in the final scene has a broken stem, and Jason has effectively prevented him from reaching the cemetery. When they turn to the left around the square Benjy can only bawl his grief, not re-establish the right direction. The fact that he bawls is the final reminder to us of his role as a Christ image: in folklore, the *left* has often been associated with the *sinister,* as the etymology of *sinister* itself reminds us. But the fact that he can do nothing more than bawl is also a final reminder that this Christ is powerless; the Word swaddled in darkness, "unable to speak a word."

Only when we import into our consideration of this novel ideas we have gained from other, later Faulkner stories are we likely to feel that we can confidently resolve this ambiguity. If we think of the role played by the Negro in the later fiction, in which he sometimes achieves an explicitly redemptive status by endurance and acceptance of suffering, we may be tempted to resolve completely the irony of Dilsey's Easter; too completely, I think, as though we were to read all the meaning of the *Four Quartets* back into *The Waste Land* because we have discovered its potentiality there.

Yet we may say that from the apparent meaninglessness of Compson history, something has emerged, some meaning, some value, some real if not publicly recognized order. If instead we say that out of the obscure and fragmentary expressions of inward experience that form the first three sections, Dilsey and Ben and Mother and Jason emerge as characters in the final, objective section and a story emerges there whole and clear and ready for our judgment, we shall be saying very much the same thing. Every aspect of the form is functional here—but to say even that is to imply a dichotomy that does not exist. As the plot is "hidden," so the theme is hidden. As characters finally emerge, full-bodied and wholly memorable, from a texture and structure that may seem until we have completed our reading too lyric and fragmented to produce character, so a dramatic impact unexcelled in the modern novel remains as a final impression of a novel in no obvious or traditional sense dramatic.

One way of putting the greatness of *The Sound and the Fury* is to say that we begin by seeing it as a marvelously precise and solid evocation of a specific time and place and family and end by realizing that it is more than this, that the concrete has become universal: an anatomy of a world, a world recreated, analyzed, and judged as it can be in only the greatest fiction.

CHAPTER 4

Vision

AS I LAY DYING

THE THEME ANNOUNCED by the falling spire of *Soldier's Pay*, continued as a subsidiary and peripheral interest in the talk of Mr. Wiseman in *Mosquitoes*, suggested by the image of the "black and savage stars" of *Sartoris*, and implicit everywhere in *The Sound and the Fury*, is squarely at the center of Faulkner's fifth novel, from the title to Anse's last words, "Meet Mrs. Bundren" —the new Mrs. Bundren.

The structural metaphor in *As I Lay Dying* is a journey through life to death and through death to life. Literally, the journey is undertaken to bury the dead and get some new teeth. Another and unexpected result is a new Mrs. Bundren. Behind a story at once grotesque and elementally traditional lies a search for a lost center of value, a direct probing of ultimate questions, a continuation of Quentin's futile search for *human* meaning. In *The Sound and the Fury* a recalled way of life led to the question of what effect our attitude toward time—Dilsey's, Father's, Jason's—has on our way of life. Here time stops, for Addie in one way, for the family in another, for the reader in still another; then begins again when Pa comes up to the wagon "kind of hangdog and proud too, with his teeth and all" and what is left of and added to the family goes back to take up the ordinary daily routine of the Bundrens, back to ordinary time. Addie Bundren is safely buried in Jefferson at last and Darl is on his way to Jackson, where his visions will result in no more barn-burnings. The Bundrens take up where they left off. As Faulkner has recently said of them,[1] they cope with their fate pretty well.

Since Darl is the member of the family who "sees" the most, and sees most objectively, it is fitting that we get our introduction not only to the Bundrens but to the symbolic reverberations of their journey first through him. What Darl sees is true, and what he thinks always reveals more than his own idiosyncrasies. (What Cora Tull sees, on the other hand, sometimes *didn't* happen, or didn't happen that way; and what she thinks may or may not be revealing of objective reality.) Vernon Tull gives us a clue to Darl's function in the story when he says of him, "I always say it aint never been what he done so much or said or anything so much as how he looks at you. It's like he got into the inside of you, someway."

Darl tells us in the first chapter that Cash is a good carpenter, and before long we have ample evidence that Darl is right. "Addie Bundren could not want a better one, a better box to lie in." Darl's opening chapter is factual, imagistic, objective. We learn immediately to trust him, whether he is noting the figure of Jewel striding just five feet in front of him or pondering the facts of birth and death: "It takes two people to make you, and one people to die. That's how the world is going to end." His meditation on emptying yourself for sleep is one of the earliest pointers toward the central theme. Is there anything left after you have been divested of the items of consciousness that have made up your day?

> In a strange room you must empty yourself for sleep. And before you are emptied for sleep, what are you. And when you are emptied for sleep, you are not. And when you are filled with sleep, you never were. I don't know what I am. I don't know if I am or not. Jewel knows he is, because he does not know that he does not know whether he is or not.

After they have crossed the river and while Jewel and Vernon
are in the water trying to retrieve Cash's tools, Darl watches the
ludicrous, fantastic, and pitiful scene and formulates the judgment
which his factual reporting of the situation has led the reader to
accept:

> From here they do not appear to violate the surface at all.
> . . . It looks peaceful, like machinery does after you have
> watched it and listened to it for a long time. As though
> the clotting which is you had dissolved into the myriad
> original motion, and seeing and hearing in themselves blind
> and deaf; fury in itself quiet with stagnation. Squatting,
> Dewey Dell's wet dress shapes for the dead eyes of three
> blind men those mammalian ludicrosities which are the
> horizons and the valleys of the earth.

Darl is concerned to establish the line between being and not-
being. When his mother died was there simply a dissolution of the
clotting into the "myriad original motion," or was there something
else, something that could be described in Cora Tull's religious
language? Darl does not ask himself these questions formally
because there is no need to: he ponders them so constantly that
he is of little use to his family in their ordeal. If the scene beside
the river suggests to him first the answer his mother would have
given to his questions, it suggests also a very different answer, a
Biblical answer. And his reply to Vardaman when asked "Why
does she want to hide her away from the sight of man, Darl?"
suggests, too, with its Scriptural echo, that he has weighed Cora
Tull's faith: "'So she can lay down her life,' Darl says." Darl
presents us with both the facts and the issues that spring from
them. He arrives at no solution and is sent to Jackson.

Dewey Dell also leads us into the central theme, though unlike
Darl she is only very dimly conscious, when she is conscious at all,
of the implications of her own words and thoughts. Dewey Dell
wants an abortion. Since she cannot get one at New Hope, she
has her own reason for holding Anse to his promise to her mother
that he would bury her in Jefferson. As they begin their journey
and her new hope of freedom from the life growing within her is

put to a severe trial by the slowness of their progress, she does not ponder the irony Darl knows: that only her mother's death, making necessary a trip to Jefferson, could have given her this new hope. But what she experiences has more meaning for the reader than for Dewey Dell.

Anse's people buried their dead at New Hope, only three miles away. If Anse had buried Addie there, there would have been no need to risk the perils of flood and fire. New Hope is the obvious place for Anse to bury his dead, as all the conventional, normal people believe, and several of them, notably Tull and Samson, tell him. But they pass the fork in the road with the sign first brought to our attention by Darl and later concentrated on obsessively by Dewey Dell: "a white signboard with faded lettering: New Hope Church. 3 mi." The whole chapter assigned to Dewey Dell in the first day of the journey centers on this signboard and its implications. It begins with "The signboard comes in sight" and ends with Dewey Dell's agonized prayer, "I believe in God, God. God, I believe in God." In between we have her thoughts as she ponders the sign ("it can wait") and her own terrible need to hurry ("I wish I had time"). The sign saying New Hope seems to her "empty with waiting." It seems to take forever to get to it but finally they are beyond it and the copula changes to past tense. For her there is no irony in her observations and thoughts:

> It blows cool out of the pines, a sad steady sound. New Hope. Was 3 mi. Was 3 mi. I believe in God I believe in God.

In Vardaman's chapters the religious theme is at once most precisely defined and most hidden from casual reading. Vardaman is first seen carrying a fish, immediately after Anse has said "The Lord giveth" and Tull has agreed with the implied interpretation of the significance of Addie's death: "It's true. Never a truer breath was ever breathed. 'The Lord giveth,' I say." Vardaman's first words in the book tell us the fish "was full of blood and guts as a hog."

If this seems an unusual description of a fish, it is fitting for a fish so unusually large, both physically and metaphorically. The fish was a symbol of Christ to the early church, the church that centered its teaching in the new hope offered in the gospel, or good news, of Christ's resurrection. Symbolically it is appropriate then that Vardaman in the first chapter assigned to him should be wholly preoccupied with the great fish he has caught. He can *feel* where it was in the dust. Jewel's horse, both "an *is* different from *my* is" and somehow an illusion, seems to disappear in the darkness: "It is as though the dark were resolving him out of his integrity, into an unrelated scattering of components"; but the image of the fish is strong and clear to Vardaman, no illusion. "I am not afraid." Vardaman has a childlike faith in the efficacy of his fish. The chapter ends with "Cooked and et. Cooked and et." When Cora Tull tries to question Vardaman about his mother's state, she "can't get nothing outen him except about a fish."

Not to labor the point: the fish which Vardaman pictures "all chopped up . . . laying in the kitchen in the bleeding pan, waiting to be cooked and et" parallels Christ killed and ritualistically eaten and drunk to prevent the death of the believer. Vardaman does not accept his mother's "change" as final; or does not mean the same by "dead" as the others do. She has somehow *become* the fish: when the fish is eaten she will live on hidden away "from the sight of man." The thing they put in the box was not his mother: "I know. I was there. I saw it when it did not be her. I saw. They think it is and Cash is going to nail it up." When the fish is eaten "she will be him and Pa and Cash and Dewey Dell and there won't be anything in the box and so she can breathe." The Prayer of Humble Access in the Communion Service according to the Book of Common Prayer ends with the petition that we may "dwell in him, and he in us." Vardaman's chopping up of the fish is ritual magic to prevent his mother's death. Believing it to have been effective, he opens the window by her bed and bores holes in the top of the coffin "so she can breathe." We have been prepared for his next chapter, which consists simply of "My mother is a

fish." Vardaman is the true believer. He hovers in the shadows
and watches Cash "going up and down . . . at the bleeding plank."
Worshipper, priest, altar, and the Last Supper are all suggested by
Vardaman's early chapters.

It is natural then that as they walk over the flooded river on the
sunken bridge, in "a scene of immense yet circumscribed desolation
filled with the voice of the waste and mournful water" it seems to
Tull, who is more frightened than he has ever been, that without
Vardaman he would never have done so foolhardy, so apparently
impossible a thing:

> It was that boy, I said "Here; you better take a holt of
> my hand," and he waited and held to me. I be durn if it
> wasn't like he come back and got me; like he was saying
> They won't nothing hurt you. Like he was saying about a
> fine place he knowed where Christmas come twice with
> Thanksgiving and lasts through the winter and the spring
> and summer, and if I just stayed with him I'd be all right
> too.

Tull does not recall for us the Biblical parallel of this scene, in
which, as St. John tells the story, "they see Jesus walking on the
sea . . . and they were afraid. But he saith unto them, It is I; be not
afraid." But Darl is conscious of the parallel, and of the irony it
contains, when he sees the wagon upset by the log ("'Log, fiddle-
sticks,' Cora said. 'It was the hand of God.'"):

> It surged up out of the water and stood for an instant up-
> right upon that surging and heaving desolation like Christ.

Vardaman, like Dilsey, has what has sometimes been called "the
perfect faith of the little child." It enables him in this instance not
to move mountains but to walk confidently where more circumspect
adults like Vernon are afraid. Vardaman's obsession with his fish
is something more than a childish fantasy.

By the time we encounter, through Darl, the log "like Christ"
we are prepared to realize the significance of earlier portents.
Without being conscious of the echoes in his words, Tull has already

reinforced Vardaman's identification of his mother as a fish. Addie, he tells us, "laid there three days in that box" before the journey even began. "On the third day"—unless Vardaman's fantasy may be trusted—"they got back and they loaded her into the wagon and started and it already too late"—too late to cross the river by the bridge and too late for proper burial: the corpse had already begun to smell in the summer heat. (But Vardaman: "My mother is not in the box. My mother does not smell like that. My mother is a fish.") What we learn of Addie through the others reinforces the theme we have first seen through Darl.

When we come to Addie's own chapter toward the end of the book we find another dimension added to the theme. Addie's whole life, as she sees it, has been one long attempt to escape her aloneness by breaking through mere words to the reality of things. The result of our learning to know her from her own point of view, then, is to bring us to see the people around her in a new light. We see that they can be divided into those who, like Anse and Cora, live by, are taken in by, empty words, and those who, like Darl and Cash in their different ways, penetrate to the reality of things. With this distinction of Addie's in mind, we are able to see another level of meaning in the Tulls' sense of outrage at Anse's refusal to break his promise and bury Addie at New Hope: the Tulls, led by Cora, have been taken in by words, the words of the "fairy tale" of traditional Christian faith.

But Addie had foreseen the reaction of those more conventional than she, with their faith in words. She would not be buried there, for she remembered all her life how her father "used to say that the reason for living was to get ready to stay dead a long time." Unlike Cora, who confidently sings "I'm bounding toward my God and my reward," Addie has no faith. Cora is probably right for once, at least from her own point of view, when she says that "the eternal and the everlasting salvation and grace is not upon her": Addie is lonely, hard, loving only Jewel, embittered by having Anse for husband and Whitfield for lover, both of them men of words. Neither is any cure for her aloneness. In her despair she "learned that words are no good." Anse had a word for what happened at night: "Love, he called it." "And when Darl was born I asked Anse to take me back to Jefferson when I died, because I knew that father had been right."

> And so when Cora Tull would tell me I was not a true mother, I would think how words go straight up in a thin line, quick and harmless, and how terribly doing goes along the earth, clinging to it, so that after a while the two lines are too far apart for the same person to straddle from one to the other; and that sin and love and fear are just sounds that people who never sinned nor loved nor feared have for what they never had and cannot have until they forget the words. Like Cora, who could never even cook.

The theme by this time could be suggested in a question: is Cora's piety mere cant? Are we to believe, with Addie, that her father had said the final word on living? Addie's father had taught her as Quentin's father had taught him: that living has no final meaning or direction, that people are the mere momentary clottings of arrested motion that Darl sometimes saw them as being. What is man, and what is his destiny? These are the questions which form the central theme of *As I Lay Dying*.

If we read attentively we are never allowed to forget that these are the questions we want answered. Cora Tull's piety, sincere but self-righteous, is a constant reminder whenever she is on the scene. As she falls into clichés that distort the reality (saying, for instance, of Darl, "His heart too full for words") she prepares us to feel the full force of Addie's distinction between words and things. Even when her words do not distort, they seem the result of a formula not very intelligently applied. "Riches is nothing in the face of the Lord, for He can see into the heart": this is not wholly inappropriate, but it serves to remind us that Cora cannot "see into the heart" at all, as Darl can, cannot truly discern the motive behind the deed. Her judgments are the conventional judgments of her time and place and faith: at their best they contain the kind of truth that inheres in her convention. All she discerns in Vardaman's obsession

with the fish is that "He's outen his head with grief and worry"—
which is true enough on one level, but insufficient. "It's my
Christian duty," she says frequently, giving us each time both
greater knowledge of her as a type of dogged and joyless and not
very perceptive Christian and greater understanding of the theme.

Anse too supplies many casual running reminders of what is
going on here below the surface. "The Lord giveth" is a kind of
refrain on his lips, and his musing on his luck sometimes breaks
into explicitly religious terms: "I am not religious, I reckon. But
peace is [in] my heart." Like Jewel ("because if there is a God
what the hell is He for"), Anse thinks of God only when he pities
himself, but that is often enough to keep us reminded how his
misfortunes parallel and depart from those of the Vicar of Wake-
field and Job, two other "misfortunate" men, who also had comforters
like Cora Tull who did not comfort.

Tull's characterization of Cora—perhaps she's a little *too* religious,
but still it's better to be on the safe side—and Dr. Peabody's meditations on death both serve the same purpose. Halfway through the
novel the religious theme is fully established. Thereafter the number of explicit religious references diminishes as we go with the
Bundrens on their archetypal journey.

2

THE THEME established by the religious symbols and echoes is
strengthened and deepened by the pure imagery, by images that
are not in themselves symbolic but take on depth and complexity
of suggestiveness from their association with the more clearly
symbolic images that make up their context. One image pattern in
particular, in a work enormously rich in imagery, seems prominent
and continuous enough to deserve to be called the stylistic key to
the vision that shapes the novel.

In Darl's second chapter, the third in the book, he watches

Jewel and Jewel's horse in a scene which impresses him as uniting somehow great violence with perfect stillness. As Jewel subdues his horse by cutting off his wind, the horse and Jewel suddenly, momentarily, become quiet:

> Then they are rigid, motionless, terrific, the horse back-thrust on stiffened, quivering legs, with lowered head; Jewel with dug heels, shutting off the horse's wind with one hand, with the other patting the horse's neck in short strokes myriad and caressing, cursing the horse with obscene ferocity.

The violence of horse and man has been momentarily arrested and now Darl watches them as "they stand in rigid terrific hiatus." The image is one of confused and contradictory movement arrested and defined.

"Rigid, motionless, terrific . . . rigid terrific hiatus." The words are Darl's, recording an observation seemingly free of interpretive bias; but they are also favorite words of Faulkner's, idiosyncrasies of his style. And here they are functional keys to the whole book. *As I Lay Dying* stops time, creates a stillness full of arrested and incomplete motion, allows us to inspect the "myriad original motion" and try to discern its pattern. If this is what any work of art in some sense does, it is also the peculiar effect, the controlling metaphor, of this work.

It is not without significance that we get this image through Darl. Darl takes no sides on the issues he sees embodied in the events he records so accurately. He is detached, able to record objectively, very different from Jewel, Cash, and Vardaman. He can observe accurately because he is beyond caring. A less sympathetic character than Cash, he is, throughout most of the novel, more perceptive. He is pure mind, without will and without love or hate. (It is significant that he does not have the last word in the novel. That is given to Cash, who knows less but cares more.) Darl stands above the division of people suggested by Addie's thoughts, into those who are taken in by words and those who are not. He listens to what Cora says as carefully and remembers her words as faithfully as he does those of Jewel and Dewey Dell. He is untouched by Dewey Dell's emotional response to New Hope. He neither hopes nor fears: he observes, speculates, wonders.

Darl and Cash divide between them Faulkner's conception of the artist in his multiple roles of seer, maker, and man. Darl is the seer, a Tiresias who foresuffers all. Cash is the artist as craftsman, maker, and as the committed man. Together Darl and Cash remind us once again how similar Faulkner's initial idea of the artist is to Eliot's. Cash comes closer, probably, to representing Faulkner's conception of his own complex role, but Darl points to an aspect of Faulkner's self-image never completely dropped even when he came, later, to emphasize more the moral function of art. Gavin Stevens surely speaks for an aspect of Faulkner when he pictures himself in *The Town* looking down at Jefferson "unanguished and immune." When Darl sees Jewel and his horse in a "rigid terrific hiatus" he announces the dominant image pattern of the book.

The image is difficult to analyze. Out of context its union of opposites may seem merely confused or idiosyncratic. "Rigid" suggests that arresting of motion in time, that grasping of the event before it passes into oblivion, which was a part of Quentin's effort in *The Sound and the Fury*. Quentin "succeeded" only in death, and "rigid" takes us back to the title and central situation here. In death the violence of motion and emotion is arrested and man may be studied, grasped, dissected. As Darl sees Jewel and the horse with perfect distinctness only by stopping time, so Addie's meaning for the family becomes clear only at her death. When Addie dies the Bundrens experience, each according to his capacity and in his own way, a sudden halting of the flow of normal time as they have known it. Her death is an interruption, a stoppage, a cause and an opportunity for reflection, if only for Anse's "The Lord giveth."

But the motion begins again even before it has ceased, so that "rigid" alone, without the implications of motion in "terrific," would be quite untrue to what really happens. The rigidity is "terrific" because of the violence which has preceded and will follow it. There is nothing of what we ordinarily mean by "quiet," "peaceful" or "still" in the scene of Jewel's subduing his horse which prompts Darl's words, or in the story that unfolds before us in the novel. "Terrific" is one of Faulkner's distinctive adjectives, revealing his sense of the "outrage" which is life. We find it frequently in all his stories: it is one of the threads of continuity uniting such different works as the Yoknapatawpha tales and *Pylon*. But no story ever more fully justified the sense of outrage than *As I Lay Dying*. For here the reassuring limitations, the comforting restrictions and blind spots of unimaginative "sanity," of the polite, the conventional, the well-ordered "normal" world are wholly broken down, swept away by the flooding in of a larger, more ultimate perspective, by a direct confrontation with what we normally contrive to ignore. In Thomas Mann's story "Railway Accident" it took only the slight jar of a minor accident to reveal to the narrator some realities he had been quite unaware of while he was comfortable and apparently secure. Here we endure with the Bundrens fire and flood and the stench of a rotting corpse. Darl's word "terrific" for Jewel and his horse characterizes the larger action of the novel as well as the smaller one to which it directly applies. What Darl sees in the pasture is an epiphany of all that is about to occur.

Rigid and terrific at once: but not for long. Only for the timeless moment of the artist's vision. Motion arrested is resumed: a "hiatus," a pause, a gap, an interruption. Addie's death makes a gap in the Bundren routine. Things do not go on quite normally between her death and the acquisition of her successor. The action of this interval is apocalyptic, for Darl and for the reader; it is shaped by the demands of the myth-making impulse. Normal action is interrupted by Addie's death and is resumed (for the rest of her survivors though not for Darl) with the introduction of the new Mrs. Bundren. In the "hiatus" Darl sees that the log that kills the mules and breaks Cash's leg is "like Christ."

The implications of Darl's image of Jewel and the horse are

abundantly reinforced. Here is Darl observing the sunset the day his mother died:

> The sun, an hour above the horizon, is poised like a bloody egg upon a crest of thunderheads: the light has turned copper: in the eye portentous, in the nose sulphurous, smelling of lightning.

"Like a bloody egg": aesthetically this novel takes up where the last section of *Sartoris* left off. The suggestions conveyed by this image are the same as those of the passage in which young Bayard approaches the MacCallum place in a sunset like "thin congealed blood" and "a crimson egg broken on the ultimate hills," though the writing now is more economical. The single image here conveys what the two images together convey in *Sartoris*, and conveys it without the need of the comment offered by "ultimate." "Bloody" suggests death, life cut off: a *bloody* egg is one that was fertile, that gave promise of life, that would have hatched: the chicken within was living, developing. "Bloody" in Darl's image compresses the meaning in the "thin congealed blood" image of *Sartoris*: congealed, dead. And a "bloody egg" is "crimson," but in Darl's image the color has taken on an added dimension.

Behind the images in both novels lie Eliot's "Prufrock" with his picture of a sunset "like a patient etherized upon a table" and another poem of Eliot's, "A Cooking Egg." Darl's vision, again, is the artist's vision. The "bloody egg" superimposes life and death, wrenches them from their normal separation in time, stands them up together against the light to see what common pattern will fit them. The image reinforces that of the "rigid terrific hiatus," points to a moment when time stands still, unites a beginning and an end. It precedes the Vardaman chapter in which Vardaman's thoughts form an unconscious comment on the service of Holy Communion, which celebrates and re-enacts an end and a beginning. Much later in the novel we begin to realize that it makes a difference how we think of the implications of this image: beginning and end, or end and beginning. Both are contained in a bloody egg.

Darl's thoughts supply many more reinforcements of his perception of the rigid terrific hiatus. Toward the end, when he no
longer needs to be established as a "real" character and the language
he uses can be even freer of the limitations of realism than it has
been from the beginning, he thinks that "in sunset we fall into
furious attitudes, dead gestures of dolls." The implications of
"rigid" are here expressed in "sunset," "dead," "dolls"; those of
"terrific" in "furious"; those of "hiatus" in the undivided image. Or
again, on the conditions of the journey: "we go on, with a motion
so soporific, so dreamlike as to be uninferant of progress, as though
time and not space were decreasing between us and it." On Jewel
in the doorway of the burning barn: "like a flat figure cut cleanly
from tin against an abrupt and soundless explosion." On approaching Jefferson: "we can see the smoke low and flat, seemingly unmoving in the unwinded afternoon," in which the prefixes deny and
negate the roots so sharply in "unmoving" and "unwinded" that
"still" and "quiet" could not be substituted as synonyms because
they would convey only half the meaning.

The central effect of these images of Darl's is to arrest motion:
not to replace it with quiet or peace or stillness, but to see the
motion and the stillness as somehow, in a way that cannot be translated into other, plainer language, one. Darl communicates this
more adequately than the others; his mind is more sensitive, his
language more expressive. But the others perceive in some degree
what Darl perceives. Peabody, the most thoughtful "normal" character, comes closest to echoing Darl when, after his meditation on
death, he characterizes the land: "opaque, slow, violent; shaping
and creating the life of man in its implacable and brooding image."
The opposition between "slow" and "violent" and between "implacable" and "brooding" is noteworthy chiefly because it reinforces the
tension in Darl's "rigid terrific hiatus."

Dewey Dell's whole experience of the approach to and the
passing of the sign saying New Hope has the same effect. This is
also the dominant impression we get from the fording of the river,

at least as we see that action through Darl. The wagon seems to take forever to tip over, seems to rest motionless and interminable half tipped over, with the log against it. The journey as a whole has this quality of arrested motion, as of "fury in itself quiet with stagnation," somnambulist, dreamlike, yet still "terrific" in its rigidity; the quality of "terrific arrested plunge" and "baroque plunging stasis" assigned in *Mosquitoes* to the statue of Andrew Jackson and so, by implication, to the whole function and effect of art; the quality named in *Sartoris* as "a dynamic fixation" and "doomed immortality and immortal doom." Darl sees well when he sees Jewel and the horse in "rigid terrific hiatus."

3

ANALYSIS OF a work of art is always in danger of distorting the object it takes apart, destroying the uniqueness and self-existence of what it tries to understand. I have gone directly to what seems to me the center of *As I Lay Dying* because I believe that the act of critical understanding must in some sense grasp the whole before it can grasp the parts. But we are not likely to respond to the work in this way, in this order, when we first read it.

What strikes us first, so forcibly as to impress us immediately with the greatness of the novel, is a unitary experience of people in context. None of Faulkner's novels, and perhaps no novel in modern literature, contains more vividly and fully created characters, wholly alive and distinct and unforgettable, engaged in actions that seem so inevitable that we accept (but do not forget) their grotesqueness, actions to which the characters give and from which they get their reality. Whatever else it may be, *As I Lay Dying* is a great novel in the Dickens genre.

Darl has the opening chapter, but we become aware in his early sections not so much of him as of the objects of his perception. In somewhat the same sense as Benjy's, his mind is a transparent glass through which we approach the reality he passively watches. Darl is walking with Jewel, and the picture he gives us is distinct, exact, and moving in its suggestion of violence, but in it we see Jewel more as an object in the landscape than as a person. In the second chapter Cora leads us further into the situation and reveals, in the process, a good deal about herself, but still no person emerges full and complete from her rambling remarks. Anse is, I think, the first person in the book to emerge clearly, distinct and "understood," and this despite the fact that the third chapter, Darl's second, concentrates more on Jewel and his horse than on Pa. The portrait begins with the opening sentences of the chapter, "Pa and Vernon are sitting on the back porch. Pa is tilting snuff from the lid of his snuff-box into his lower lip . . ." and continues after an interruption, "Pa's feet are badly splayed. . . ." We begin to see Pa, to feel that we know him, as we do not yet know—because we do not understand—Jewel.

Anse Bundren is one of the most perfectly realized characters in all fiction. He is at once ludicrous and pitiable, but we are never for a moment invited to exercise our sense of superiority toward him, to see him as outside the human context, our context, as simply an exhibit of the shiftless and wretched "poor white." The difference between our apprehension of Pa and our apprehension of characters from the same class and section in the works of Erskine Caldwell written in the same period is distinct, and of the greatest importance. Caldwell's people are dehumanized. The reaction they invite is either a mixed amused superiority and condescending pity or else political fury, a determination to "change the system" that produced them. They are the products of a predominantly political and abstract understanding, true caricatures, partial creatures, dependent on the author and his views, with their humanity left out despite the generalized pity that surrounds them.

Pa is highly grotesque but in no sense a caricature. He is utterly pitiable but we dare not condescend to him. He is the product at once of the clearest and sharpest awareness and of a love so complete that his absurdity is absorbed in his humanity. He is a person. He is one of us. He is both a type and an individual, as we all are. Shiftless, lazy, weak, well-meaning, self-pitying, stubborn, not very intelligent, he "can't seem to get no heart" into anything he does except burying Ma and getting his store teeth.

Pa's ludicrousness would be too much for us to credit if it were revealed by author's comments instead of by his own actions and in his own words:

> With that family burying-ground in Jefferson and them of her blood waiting for her there, she'll be impatient. I promised my word me and the boys would get her there quick as mules could walk it, so she could rest quiet.

Since Addie is not yet dead, only gravely ill, Jewel's reply seems appropriate: "'If everybody wasn't burning hell to get her there,' Jewel says in that harsh, savage voice." The situation has in it an elemental absurdity and an elemental naturalness, and both the absurdity and the naturalness unite in Pa. Only the greatest art could make us accept him. His emotional reaction to Ma's death, for instance, his sincere if inadequate love for her, would seem to be in the sharpest contrast to his frequently expressed sense that her death is an opportunity—an opportunity to get new teeth. If the artistry were less perfect we should succumb to the temptation to interpret him as *either* genuinely bereaved *or* hypocritical in his clumsy expressions of sorrow and really glad of her death because of the chance to get to Jefferson it affords. But no: Pa is both sad and pleased, regretful and hopeful: he is human. Darl sees and presents the full humanity. Ma is dead:

> Pa stands over the bed, dangle-armed, humped, motionless. He raises his hand to his head, scouring his hair, listening to the saw. He comes nearer and rubs his hand, palm and back, on his thigh and lays it on her face and then on the hump of quilt where her hands are. He touches the quilt as he saw Dewey Dell do, trying to smooth it up to the chin, but disarranging it instead. He tries to smooth it again, clumsily, his hand awkward as a claw, smoothing at the wrinkles which he made and which continue to

emerge beneath his hand with perverse ubiquity, so that
at last he desists, his hand falling to his side and stroking
itself again, palm and back, on his thigh. The sound of
the saw snores steadily into the room. Pa breathes with a
quiet, rasping sound, mouthing the snuff against his gums.
"God's will be done," he says. "Now I can get them teeth."

The beauty, the power, the passion of the whole book is implicit
in this one paragraph. The perfection of it can be seen as either
moral or aesthetic, or, perhaps better, as both at once. Here is a
compassion so complete that it does not sentimentalize and thus
does not blur the sharpness with which Anse is seen, a compassion
consistent with full awareness, a compassion which never asks us to
deny what we know, to suppress our sense of the absurd, but which
compels us to accept Anse as he is, and as we are. There is no
suspension of irony here and no withholding of compassion for the
sake of a "funny scene": there is perfect vision, holding in suspension the contradictory reactions of humor and pity, irony and love,
a sense of the absurd and a sense of the tragic.

Such passages prepare us to accept without any discounting
Tull's less sensitive, less shaded apprehension of Pa greeting the
mourners as they come to the house:

Anse meets us at the door. He has shaved, but not good.
There is a long cut on his jaw, and he is wearing his Sunday
pants and a white shirt with the neckband buttoned. It is
drawn smooth over his hump, making it look bigger than
ever, like a white shirt will, and his face is different too.
He looks folks in the eye now, dignified, his face tragic
and composed, shaking us by the hand as we walk up on to
the porch and scrape our shoes. . . .

We are ready to accept now the dignity, the composure, the awareness and expression of tragedy. Those who have interpreted *As I
Lay Dying* as comedy are right, but only half right: it is also high
tragedy. We accept Vernon's perception of Pa without denying or
discounting or even qualifying the Pa Darl has seen, the night
before, as the rain began:

> Pa lifts his face, slack-mouthed, the wet black rim of snuff
> plastered close along the base of his gums; from behind his
> slack-faced astonishment he muses as though from beyond
> time, upon the ultimate outrage.

Since Pa is at the center of the book, the novel could be wholly successful only if he were fully acceptable as a tragicomic figure at the center of a tragicomic action. The greatness of *As I Lay Dying* is revealed, not exhausted but revealed, in Anse Bundren.

Our interpretation of the central theme of the work is more dependent on what we think of Addie. She is a problem. There is an unresolved ambiguity in the portrait of her which would have to be counted a defect in the novel if it were not functionally related to the theme. Addie is the only character whom we do not see directly, except in fragmentary, undecisive glimpses as she lies dying. What her life has really been like, what *she* really is, we can know only as we apprehend it through a series of screens. Knowing her requires a more complicated and indirect act of judgment than knowing any of the others. She dominates the action at all times, living and dead, but we are never in a position to judge her directly, face to face, without intermediary, by her actions and her appearance and her words.

This is no less true in her own chapter than in the others. Her thoughts are obviously a rationalization, revealing a particular and peculiar perspective, natural, right, in character, and often shrewdly perceptive of objective facts. But these thoughts are as biased by personality as are all the other inward visions except that of Darl, who is beyond normal hope and fear and self-interest. Addie's thoughts are marvelously revealing, of her and of the others, but she is not, I think, as she has sometimes been taken to be, an author's spokesman, a convenient mouthpiece for the theme. Yet her central concerns, her search for a "violation" of her aloneness and her effort to know words from things, are connected with the central theme of the work, and we must make a decision about them before we can feel ready to say what that theme finally says to us. But if Vardaman is right in connecting her in his mind with a fish, we should not expect the most patient study of all that is revealed of her, by herself and by others, to resolve the ambiguity. The interpretation of Addie involves a doubtful and difficult act of decision.

Some critics have interpreted Addie as a wholly sympathetic character, the "heroine" of the work even in death; others emphasize her sadism, her misanthropy, and her bitter rejection of a life too hard for her to bear. The "traditionalist" interpretation points up an important aspect of the portrait when it emphasizes her effort to achieve a relation of love with others, to break through the barriers of separation. She is a redemptive character—Vardaman's fish—because she recognizes both the difficulty and the necessity of love. But this reading of her neglects another aspect of her personality, an aspect very sharply at odds with this interpretation.

Cora Tull sees her as the victim of a pride that would never humble itself, her bitterness as the result of frustrated self-concern. We can say flatly that Cora is simply wrong only if for reasons of our own we have accepted Addie's estimate of Cora and Addie's own schematization of words and things. We know from Darl and in other ways that she has really loved only Jewel: Cora cannot be entirely wrong then in her statement that she has never been a "true mother" to the others. We know from Addie herself what her feelings were toward the children she taught in school before she married Anse: after school she would go "where I could be quiet and hate them. . . . I would look forward to the times when they faulted, so I could whip them." She rejected not only the children she taught and all but one of the children she bore, she rejected life itself: "I would hate my father for ever having planted me." This side of her nature makes it difficult to interpret her as a wholly redemptive character.

Is Cora then right about Addie? It seems clear that Faulkner would not have us think so, yet the question cannot be wholly dismissed. Cora may be self-righteous and unintelligent, but there is too much evidence not of her own invention to support her judgment of Addie for it to be thought of as wholly beside the point. Even Addie's effort to get beyond her aloneness can be interpreted as not Christian love so much as an attempt at self-assertion: "with each blow of the switch: Now you are aware of me!" The very expression of her search for community is ambiguous: "my aloneness had to be violated over and over." Violated? If she is right, that "sin and love and fear are just sounds" so that the words of faith so continually on the lips of her antithesis, Cora Tull, are perfectly empty and meaningless sounds, then perhaps "violated" is the right word for what she sought. But if the outlook of historic Christianity, of which Cora's inadequate pieties are a simple-minded fundamentalist expression, is taken as the standard, then Addie comes to seem a descendant of Ahab of *Moby Dick*. She responds to the presence of pain and suffering in the world not in resignation and humility and a desire to make of suffering accepted a precondition of grace, a necessary part of a desired "imitation of Christ," but with bitter and violent rebellion and rejection not only of the world but of others and of love. Ahab's rejection of the request of the captain of the *Rachel* and Addie's rejection of her children come to seem parallel actions. Or, to turn back to a book equally relevant to *Moby Dick* and *As I Lay Dying*, Addie reminds us, as we think of her in the Biblical perspective, of a Job to whom the Lord never did speak, a Job left with only his sense of outrage and his false comforters.

Addie is presented with as much compassion and more sympathy than Anse. Where he is tragi-comic, she is tragic. If this were not so, the ambiguity in her portrait would be destroyed. Her sadism, her bitterness and coldness, are presented almost entirely in her own chapter, through her own words, as she reviews and justifies her life. To Vardaman she becomes a fish because to him her death is inconceivable. To herself she is a lonely and frustrated woman whose whole life has been a waiting for this death. To Jewel she is the only person he ever loved; to Jewel she is, Darl says, a horse.[2] To Anse she is the faithful wife whose efficiency and dutifulness have compensated for his own complete ineffectualness. To Cora Tull she is a sinner. To us she is, and I think will remain, an enigma.

Just because of this, she tempts us to a kind of speculation more appropriate to allegory than to the kind of novel *As I Lay Dying* is. Is she the result of a breaking up of the role of Christ and a distribution of the disunited functions among several characters? Is she, in other words, whether willingly or not, while alive the sacrificial savior and when dead the body sacrificed? If we take her this way we get a certain insight into not only her role but the way in which the others are defined by their relation to her. Cash, the carpenter, loyal, patient, long-suffering, and forbearing, acts the human role of Christ; Jewel, who saves the body in the trials of fire and water, the role of "divine" champion; Vardaman, to whom she is "transubstantiated," the role of devout believer.

But if this is the way we should take her as allegorical symbol, we are not, I think, forced by the nature of the work to reach any final decision on such matters as we read. *As I Lay Dying* is not an allegory, and any final decision we make about Addie will be in some sense beyond the book, on grounds that cannot be weighed in solely aesthetic terms, and this despite the fact that all the chief characters in the book may be seen as defined by their relation to her and to her demand for reality.[3] The art by which Addie is created declares itself insufficient to define her character, and in that declaration lies its final perfection. Addie is, in a peculiar sense, the only character in the book who is not wholly self-sufficient and self-existing: she is the product of the imaginative apprehension of the others in her life, of the understanding contained in her own self-image, and of the imagination of the reader. She is the only character watched and remembered by Darl, the artist, whom he does not, in Tull's words, take us "inside of." She remains shadowy in all his reflections, ubiquitous and defining but undefined.

We are never for a moment asked to believe that Vardaman is literally correct in his idea that this mother has physically, or even in some transempirical sense, become a fish. It should be equally clear that we are not asked to accept either Cora's judgment of

Addie or Addie's judgment of herself. All we know of Addie is insufficient to enable us to make positive final judgment, confident that we have overlooked none of the evidence and have properly assessed the significance of all of it.

It is not Addie but Cash who has the last word in the book, as Dilsey does in *The Sound and the Fury*. Unlike Darl and like Dilsey, he is an "engaged," a "committed" character in the Existentialist sense; and he is also, for most readers I suspect, the most sympathetic character in the book. The role assigned him foreshadows Faulkner's Nobel Prize speech, with its conception of art's moral and therapeutic justification. It is he who utters the words that come closest to stating the theme:

> But I ain't so sho that ere a man has the right to say what is crazy and what ain't. It's like there was a fellow in every man that's done a-past the sanity or the insanity, that watches the sane and the insane doings of that man with the same horror and the same astonishment.

Cash is an artist in his carpentry, respecting his materials, working the wood according to the grain and turning out a good job not for any "practical" motive but simply because he cares about good workmanship. Cash is the artist seeing, caring, and taking pains, the artist as man and maker. "A fellow can't get away from a shoddy job." As a carpenter he foreshadows Isaac McCaslin, the redemptive character of "The Bear" and other later stories. If we take him as normative in the work and base our interpretation on him—on what he *is* and *does* as well as, or perhaps more than, what he says—we shall I think not go far astray. Like the Bundren family, we may *depend* upon Cash. What his approach to life would seem to imply is a sacramental view of nature—all nature—without a specific historical Incarnation: a religious view of life but not one that, in the historic sense of the word, can be called Christian. Divinity in Cash's world is immanent but not transcendent. If this is a correct interpretation, it makes the novel, once again, foreshadow the later work, especially the nature mysticism of some of the stories in *Go*

Down Moses. To say that *As I Lay Dying* asserts the emotional and imaginative, but not the logical, validity of Biblical and Christian symbolism is perhaps another way of saying much the same thing.

4

IN SOLDIER'S PAY and *Mosquitoes* Faulkner had found the words for his feelings and his vision, the words to suggest the quality of the world he experienced. He had written in *Mosquitoes* of "the equivocal derisive darkness of the world," a world in which as the sculptor Gordon had said, "Only an idiot has no grief." And in that novel of definition he had had Mr. Wiseman define the mark of the true artist as the capacity to know "that Passion Week of the heart . . . in which the hackneyed accidents which make up this world—love and life and death and sex and sorrow—brought together by chance in perfect proportions, take on a kind of splendid and timeless beauty." In *Soldier's Pay* he had apostrophized "Sex and death: the front door and the back door of the world" and had foreshadowed Anse's precipitous remarriage with "The saddest thing about love, Joe, is that not only the love cannot last forever, but even the heartbreak is soon forgotten."

But these are rhetorical statements of abstract "truths," summaries of the experience of the young artist. In *Soldier's Pay* and *Mosquitoes* he had not, except fragmentarily and imperfectly, found the images which would convey the quality of the experience itself. The words tell us about experience, but as we read we are aware of the gap between the thing in itself and the word for it. We know that we are being given an interpretation, plausible perhaps, appealing perhaps, but not inevitable. The words, as Addie said, go straight up, do not cling to earth with the doing.

Partially in *Sartoris*, especially in the last section, magnificently in *The Sound and the Fury* and *As I Lay Dying*, Faulkner learned how to make words cling to earth, to make them, in the *seeming* of art, disappear in the presence of the doing, become not simply translucent but transparent vehicles of the hackneyed accidents of sex and death in the equivocal derisive darkness of the world. In *As I Lay Dying*, as in *The Sound and the Fury*, he found the images that made the wise sayings of the young artist unnecessary.

"Equivocal": two voices, the voice of Addie and the voice of Cora, speaking equivocally of the meaning of life and death. Addie's death, Dewey Dell's pregnancy and hope of abortion, the stench of the corpse and Anse's new duck-shaped Mrs. Bundren—these are the substance of "sex and death." The plot of the novel could be summarized as a journey that begins at the "back door" and moves to the "front door" of the world, progressing en route through a "Passion Week of the heart."

The perfect craftsmanship of the novel may be seen in many ways. A purely structural analysis centering on the arrangement of the sections, with their contrapuntal balancing of perspectives, would highlight it. As in *The Sound and the Fury*, we begin with the facts themselves, seen in their purity by Benjy in the earlier novel and here by Darl, the uncommitted man. We end with the judgment of Cash, the committed man, as we did with Dilsey's, after viewing the action from the varying perspectives of a series of other characters. The characters through whom we have our constantly shifting view of the events in *As I Lay Dying* exhibit several kinds of faith and unfaith and several degrees of closeness to the action. Their reactions range from the obsessive attachment of Jewel to the distant speculation of Dr. Peabody. Anticipating the more radical irony of *Absalom, Absalom!*, *As I Lay Dying* lets us overhear the voices of those variously involved without ever resolving the conflict in the impersonal tones of the author.

The beauty of the work is felt most immediately in the unforgettable solidity of the characters and the vividness of the incidents in which they reveal themselves: Darl drinking water out of a wooden bucket, Cash planing the boards for the coffin, Dewey Dell picking down the row with Lafe toward the secret woods—incidents clear, sharp, perfectly realized in all their qualitative richness, so that they become a part of our own memories along with those few incidents we really remember out of the many we forget.

But it seems to me that we may approach an understanding of the greatness of As I Lay Dying best at this point if we think of its vividness, its sheer immediacy, and at the same time try to hold in mind the lines of suggestion, of meaning, that radiate from it. In it we have a perfection of "realism" in the basic and non-historical sense of the word—not an effort at documentation, not a cataloguing of the details of surface perception on the assumption that only "physical facts" are real, but an illusion of experience acted and suffered. But in the seeming paradox of art's achievement of the "concrete universal," we also find symbolic meanings that are quite literally inexhaustible. Its forms are no less solid, its colors no less pure, because they are given added dimensions in their association with the basic Western myth. The novel not only re-enacts the Eucharist, it is incarnational in its very form. In it the word becomes flesh, meaning is embodied, idea takes on substance and substance gets form and so meaning. In its perfection of embodiment lies the "splendid and timeless beauty" of the novel.

CHAPTER 5

Outrage and Compassion

SANCTUARY

LIGHT IN AUGUST

THE MOOD AND THE ATTITUDES present in much of
Faulkner's work of the early thirties, particularly in *Sanctuary*, are
expressed in simple, almost outline form in a seventeen-page short
story which he published in 1931 as a separate booklet, *Idyll in the
Desert*. The sense of outrage and the feeling of pity given such
powerful and beautiful embodiment in the novels here finds expression in a fable.

A man suffering from tuberculosis comes to the Southwest for a
cure. His paramour leaves her husband and children to be with
him and care for him. He recovers from the disease and she con-
tracts it. He deserts her and marries a younger woman, leaving her
alone to die. When, shortly before her death, she sees him with
his bride, he does not recognize her, though an older generation
would have put it that she has sacrificed "all," even life itself, for
him.

There is no irony in the telling. All the irony is reserved for the
meaning: the irony and the pathos of fate. Even the man who
leaves the woman to die in the desert is not treated as having made
a questionable moral choice: all, he as well as she, are victims. And
victims not of their choices but of "the way things are," of the

universe, acting in this instance through a disease. The story begins in irony and culminates in despair. Like Melville's story of the Chola widow in *The Encantadas,* it is emotionally univocal, speaking a language in which all the words point finally to one referent, a generalized pity. Its only act of moral judgment is directed against the universe: in this kind of world this is what we can all expect.

It is not relevant that the woman's suffering resulted from two human choices, her own decision to leave her husband and children to go to her lover, and his later decision to leave her. The story implies that choice is irrelevant or illusory. It suggests important aspects of the treatment of Popeye in *Sanctuary* and Joe Christmas in *Light in August* as well as the despairing pity that at times threatens to destroy those novels. The irony of *Idyll in the Desert* is not the same as that of *As I Lay Dying;* it is closer to the romantic irony sometimes apparent in Melville. The story makes a drastic simplification of experience.

2

SANCTUARY HAS often been called sensational, and Faulkner himself once referred to his original conception of it as a "cheap idea." But he has also told us how he rewrote it after the first version was already in proof, to make it a work of which he would not be ashamed.[1] Certainly the novel as we know it is a serious work of art. Yet if we need not concern ourselves further with the idea that it is cheap, I think we shall have to grant that the term *sensational* is not wholly inappropriate. A novel so violent and so despairing could hardly fail to strike us as sensational; but to say "sensational" is to describe rather than to evaluate. The significant questions for evaluation remain to be asked. If life itself is the outrage it seems in *Sanctuary,* if the will is always impotent and the intelligence baffled, if all our values must in the end lie "prone and vanquished in the embrace of the season of rain and death," then to call the novel sensational in such a tone as to imply a dismissal of it is merely to reveal the tameness and timidity of our own vision of life. The question to ask first about the sensationalism of *Sanctuary* is how cheaply or dearly it is bought.

The despair may be sensed immediately in the style. Several of Faulkner's favorite words, especially *furious, outrage, profound, tragic, terrific,* are here sometimes used idiosyncratically, without full contextual justification. In a sense the notes of the bird that sings as Horace and Popeye face each other across the spring could be called "profound," though we are not likely to be able to see how until after we have finished the novel and gone back to the opening scene; but the same adjective applied to the ruined house—"lightless, desolate, and profound"—surely seems a little forced, as though what is about to take place here were already exerting an irresistible pull toward tragedy. When the bootleggers' truck gets under way and grinds "terrifically" up the slope of the side road toward the highroad and Memphis, we are likely to feel that even the noisy, clashing gears of a truck of the 1920's would hardly make a sound deserving to be called "terrific." The feeling seems somewhat in excess of the facts.

But in most of the book the emotional style is justified by the horror of the objects it delineates. The picture of Goodwin's father eating, the eager blind old man so close to nothing at all, so pitiful, so disgusting: here is an outrage that casts a terrible light on the human situation. "Then Benbow quit looking." The paragraph is one of the most vivid evocations of mingled disgust and pity in modern writing, almost too vivid to be borne, and it is a clue to the atmosphere of the work as a whole.

Or again, consider the scene of Temple in the corn crib with the rats. There is a gruesome, macabre horror about this scene that makes us want to call it Gothic and reminds us of Poe, though I think it is more horrible than anything Poe ever wrote, perhaps because it is behavioristic, not cerebral. In its extreme vividness, its nightmarish intensity, its factual veracity (their faces "not twelve inches apart"), it subjects us to an experience that we feel it would be no exaggeration to call "terrific" and an "outrage."

Finally, Red's funeral. The whole scene is an outrage, even

before the coffin is tipped over, but what happens then would justify adjectives expressive of grotesque horror:

> The corpse tumbled slowly and sedately out and came to rest with its face in the center of a wreath.
> "Play something!" the proprietor bawled, waving his arms; "play! Play!"
> When they raised the corpse the wreath came too, attached to him by a hidden end of a wire driven into his cheek. He had worn a cap which, tumbling off, exposed a small blue hole in the center of his forehead. It had been neatly plugged with wax and was painted, but the wax had been jarred out and lost. They couldn't find it, but by unfastening the snap in the peak, they could draw the cap down to his eyes.

Like the holes bored by Vardaman in Ma's face, this wreath fastened to the face by its hidden wire is a violent reminder of our mortality. (It is suggestive of the difference in quality between *Sanctuary* and *As I Lay Dying* that here the incident is less closely tied in with character and theme than in the earlier novel.) It is hardly possible to go beyond this in the direction of macabre horror and emotional violence. This is the ultimate and climactic outrage. The lynching of Goodwin that follows occurs "off stage"; it could not increase the pure horror of Red's funeral and might adulterate the purity of the horror with admiration for Goodwin's stoical courage or a moral judgment of the action of the mob. The center of *Sanctuary* does not lie in social criticism or in moral judgment but in horror and despair. After Red's funeral the action moves rapidly to its close.

The reasons for the despair are clear enough and easier to state than Quentin's reasons. The bird by the spring that "sang three notes and ceased" first announces the loss that Horace Benbow and thoughtful people like him have suffered. The bird sings three times, three notes each time. Its song may not literally, but does symbolically, justify Faulkner's "profound":

> Behind him the bird sang again, three bars in monotonous repetition: a sound meaningless and profound out of

a suspirant and peaceful following silence which seemed to
isolate the spot . . .

The song of the bird suggests the loss of a meaningful relation
to nature and, in a more extended sense, of the meaningful relation
to an ultimate reality symbolized in the hope of heaven. I think we
are not over-reading when we see it as foreshadowing the many
later references to the "heaven tree." Negroes sing spirituals in
"the ragged shadow of the heaven tree" which grows before the
jail. Horace Benbow is very much aware of the tree but he neither
sings spirituals nor stands in its shadow for any other purpose; he
finds it cloying:

> The last trumpet-shaped bloom had fallen from the
> heaven tree at the corner of the jail yard. They lay thick,
> viscid underfoot, sweet and over-sweet in the nostrils with
> a sweetness surfeitive and moribund, and at night now the
> ragged shadow of full-fledged leaves pulsed upon the bar-
> red window in shabby rise and fall.

When the Negro murderer sings on the last night before his
execution, "clinging to the bars, gorilla-like . . . while upon his
shadow, upon the checkered orifice of the window, the ragged grief
of the heaven tree would pulse and change, the last bloom fallen
now," Horace thinks "They ought to clean that damn mess off the
sidewalk."

Horace is the Quentin of this novel, as Popeye is a Jason further
dehumanized by "modernism," but there is no Dilsey to counteract
Popeye and complement Horace. When he thinks of the suffering
people he is unable to help, Horace imagines them already dead,
"removed, cauterized out of the old and tragic flank of the world."
He too, he thinks, might better be dead, though he does not seriously
consider Quentin's way of asserting his freedom; he thinks, instead,
"of lying beneath a low cozy roof under the long sound of the rain:
the evil, the injustice, the tears." And no remedy, no relief:

> Perhaps it is upon the instant that we realize, admit, that
> there is a logical pattern to evil, that we die, he thought,

thinking of the expression he had once seen in the eyes of a dead child, and of other dead: the cooling indignation, the shocked despair fading, leaving two empty globes in which the motionless world lurked profoundly in miniature.

Horace is Prufrock once again: he can see, he knows, but he is barred from any effective action. He is Tiresias too, blind seer. And he is presented as a wholly sympathetic character. We must attend closely to his thoughts, even when their apparent subject is a matter of casual observation of the progression of the seasons:

> There was still a little snow of locust blooms on the mounting drive. "It does last," Horace said. "Spring does. You'd almost think there was some purpose to it."

Piety wears many expressions in the novel, but none of them have the quality of Dilsey's Easter service or Vardaman's revealing delusion. Temple in her extremity prays, but since she cannot think of any name for God, she prays "My father's a judge." The Negroes before the jail and the condemned man sing their spirituals, but Horace does not stop "to listen to those who were sure to die and him who was already dead singing about heaven and being tired." The singers remain on the edge of his and our consciousness, picturesque, meaningless, a little irritating, like the mess on the sidewalk left by the fallen blooms of the heaven tree. The Baptist minister exhibits another face of piety: he takes Goodwin as the subject of a sermon, finding him "a polluter of the free Democratico-Protestant atmosphere of Yoknapatawpha county." Horace reports to Miss Jenny the essence of the sermon:

> I gathered that his idea was that Goodwin and the woman should both be burned as a sole example to that child; the child to be reared and taught the English language for the sole end of being taught that it was begot in sin by two people who suffered by fire for having begot it. . . .

To which Miss Jenny makes a reply that, in this context, seems wholly sufficient: "'They're just Baptists,' Miss Jenny said."

A committee of Baptists force Ruby, a woman who has been

"taken in sin," to leave the hotel. "Christians," Horace comments, "Christians." The expressions on the faces of the committee as they went about their work are not recorded, but we can imagine the grim and rigid piety of them. Flem Snopes is a Baptist too, though of a more relaxed kind. When Horace asks him "Are you a Baptist, by any chance?" he answers: "My folks is. I'm pretty liberal, myself. I ain't hidebound in no sense, as you'll find when you know me better."

In *Sanctuary,* Southern fundamentalist Protestantism is pictured as self-righteous moralism, "Puritan" as the populace in the opening scenes of *The Scarlet Letter* is Puritan. The religious conscience, thus portrayed, is the immediate antagonist, though the universe itself is man's ultimate antagonist. In *The Sound and the Fury,* in contrast, what Jason stands for is the antagonist: Quentin can ignore Baptists while he concentrates on the challenge presented by Jason's image of the world, and the omniscient observer of the last section can present Dilsey (who is probably a Baptist, and certainly a fundamentalist) without satire or the distance created by a sense of superiority.

What is left of the Christian tradition in *Sanctuary* is negative, perverted, and corrupt. It is not simply a belief we are unable to accept (we were not asked literally to believe with Dilsey) but one which we are compelled, with intelligent Miss Jenny and visionary Horace, to spurn and reject. There is a complex irony in Temple's name: the temple has been violated, the Sanctuary broken into; but whether the temple ever held anything sacred that could properly speaking be "violated" is open to question. There is, at any rate, no sanctuary left anywhere now except that offered by Miss Reba's house.

Traditional meanings are gone, traditional codes emptied of meaning. Though the annual rebirth of spring might make us "almost think there was some purpose" to life, there clearly is none for educated, thoughtful, intelligent men like Horace. The breaking of the image of man foreseen by Quentin is now complete. The peace and beauty of nature mock and torment us: this is the source

of the terrible tension and irony of *Sanctuary*. It is not Temple herself, not even Horace, but the objective narrator who describes
Temple, frantic and agonized, as she watches the old man go
through the barn: "She opened the door and peered out, at the
house in the bright May sunshine, the sabbath peace. . . ." This
image of human agony and frustration against the backdrop of the
"sabbath peace" of nature is at the very center of the work. We do
not need the reminder of Temple's thinking "about the bells in cool
steeples against the blue, and pigeons crooning about the belfries
like echoes of the organ's bass."

In the end Temple sits with her father in Paris, not listening to
the band playing its stale romantic and heroic music, music that is
given the lie by the cold gray light, but yawning and powdering her
face. Like the woman in Eliot's "Sweeney Among the Nightingales"
who "yawned and drew her stocking up," she seems to "dissolve"
with the waves of music

> into the dying brasses, across the pool and the opposite
> semicircle of trees where at sombre intervals the dead tran-
> quil queens in stained marble mused, and on into the sky
> lying prone and vanquished in the embrace of the season
> of rain and death.

There is another way of looking at the despair that permeates the
novel, a way that is closer, I suspect, to what Faulkner would now
indicate as the meaning he intended. Faulkner is quoted by William
Van O'Connor as having said of Popeye that "he was symbolical of
evil. I just gave him two eyes, a nose, a mouth, and a black suit.
It was all allegory."[2] Allegorically, then, evil modernism has brought
us to the situation that motivates Horace's despair. *Because* the
temple has been violated, because the sanctuary has been destroyed
or degraded, the image of man has been destroyed. This may in
fact be the intended meaning, but I shall give some reasons for not
thinking it fully achieved.

Popeye, the mechanical man, impotent for life's purposes and
furiously active for death, with his eyes like rubber knobs and his
appearance of being stamped from tin, is, by implication, a dis-

tinctively modern product. In Horace's dualism of "nature" and "progress," he is the product of "progress": he spits into the spring.

Temple, "with her high delicate head and her bold painted mouth and soft chin, her eyes blankly right and left looking, cool, predatory, and discreet," is much like him. He is compared repeatedly to a doll, she to "one of those *papier-mâché* Easter toys filled with candy." But whereas Popeye is finally seen from inside, in terms of the causes that produced him, as a victim, she is utterly rejected, portrayed with cold fury. Like Popeye, she is somehow typical of a new generation and a new world, but unlike him she is finally seen, paradoxically, as doer, not victim, of evil.

The implication that she and Popeye are to be seen as typical is strengthened by the portrayal of her admirers. They look from a distance very much like Popeye and are cut from similar material:

> Stooping they would drink from flasks and light cigarettes, then erect again, motionless against the light, the upturned collars, the hatted heads, would be like a row of hatted and muffled busts cut from black tin and nailed to the window sills.

Popeye once cut up live birds with scissors: they spread broken glass across the road. When Horace rides on the train with the group from the university, he finds that Snopesism is not limited to Flem and his tribe; it is becoming the way of life of the younger generation. When, some twenty years later, Faulkner continued in *Requiem for a Nun* the story of Temple Drake he had begun in *Sanctuary,* he made it very clear that Temple and her kind were to be held accountable for the suffering in the earlier novel: Temple would have to learn to ask forgiveness as well as to forgive.

But in *Sanctuary* the element of social criticism and moral judgment does not come to much.[3] Faulkner's later interpretation of Temple's history may or may not have been the one he intended twenty years before; but whether or not intended, it was certainly not consistently achieved. To read it back into *Sanctuary* now, because of what *Requiem* has shown us, would be critically irresponsible. What we find when we look at *Sanctuary* itself, without keeping *Requiem* in mind, is an "outrage" for which there is no real solution, moral or otherwise. Though Horace is repelled by Snopes and Snopesism, by Popeye and modernism, by Temple and her amoral young men, he is never tempted to interpret the essential tragedy as caused primarily by the qualities that repel him in these people. Rather, as we have seen, he finds the ultimate outrage in the discovery that there is a "logical pattern" to evil. The meaning here is, I submit, obscure; but it seems to be connected with his feeling that there is no meaning in nature, outside of man. ("You'd almost think there was some purpose to it.") If this is so, then the source of the evil is not moral but metaphysical. Gangsterism and bad manners in the young are only symptoms, and symptoms not of a falling away from the truth but of a discovery of it, natural concomitants of the "neutralization of nature."

If Horace's words about the "logical pattern" mean that the evil springs from the motivation and behavior shared by Popeye, Temple, Snopes, and Temple's young men, then the book suffers by the lack of a character effective for right as these are effective for wrong. If this is the meaning, the book needs a Dilsey, or at least a Dr. Mahon or a Cash, a Lena or a Byron Bunch. Because there is no such character, because even Narcissa sides at the crucial moment against Horace and his futile effort for justice and mercy, because the Baptists are summed up with apparent adequacy by Miss Jenny as those from whom no real charity or understanding can be expected, we have in fact a novel of pure despair whether or not it was so intended. The moral evils and social failings are finally seen as merely exacerbating an outrage already unbearable for fully conscious and sensitive men.

What is left, so far as the effectively achieved meaning is concerned, is pity and horror. Pity: here is a significant difference between the poem and the novel that draws upon it for its conclusion. Sweeney and his "friends" are seen without pity in the poem, assimilated to the lower animals their actions resemble. Nothing mars the sharpness of the satire. Here our view of Popeye undergoes a drastic shift at the very end. In the last chapter we are made to see Popeye as he presumably sees himself, or perhaps as God in His infinite mercy may see him: like Joe Christmas (and Popeye was born on Christmas day) a victim driven to a sado-masochistic denial of life and search for death: a victim perhaps more than he is a doer of evil. By the time we have followed Popeye through his childhood the effectiveness of the opening portrayal of him has been destroyed. He has become as much a victim as Goodwin, not of Temple's moral viciousness and Southern mores and the bungling of the processes of justice but of "fate" working through venereal disease and fire and accident.

The pity that is extended to Popeye reaches not only Horace but Goodwin and Ruby. It is withheld most notably from Temple, with the implication that she exercises more choice than Popeye and can be held accountable for her choices; but it is withheld from all who refuse pity for whatever reason. The Baptist general public, with their cruel piety, and Narcissa, with her religion of propriety, are alike rejected. Pity shapes the novel, and horror: the wreath on the face, the rats in the crib, the cold gray light.

The pity and the horror create the irony. Popeye was arrested on his way to visit his mother, not for the murder of Tommy or Red whom he had killed but for the murder of a man he had never seen in a town where he had never been. He finds the situation grimly appropriate in the world he has come to know and hate. The reader has been prepared to agree. The heaven tree prepared him, the sabbath peace at the time of Temple's ordeal prepared him, Horace's impotence and frustration prepared him. The ending, with Temple sitting "sullen and discontented and sad," is one of the finest pieces of ironical writing in all fiction. The sense of horror here is too great for anything but understatement, and the tragedy is the more terrible because it is not Temple's but man's. The music of Massenet and Scriabine and Berlioz, "like a thin coating of tortured Tschaikowsky on a slice of stale bread," impotently and irrelevantly asserts the possibility of tragedy, of Quentin's "honor" and "sin," but Temple is only bored and cold and empty. The irony is epitomized even in the order of the adjectives applied to her: she is "sullen" and "discontented" before she is "sad," so that any element of the tragic or heroic in her sadness has already been discounted before it comes. The music might be playing in another world.

The wonderful humor of the scenes when the Snopes brothers take lodgings at Miss Reba's and when Miss Reba entertains her friends after the funeral is in a sense "comic relief" from the tension of the deeper irony, but in another sense it extends that irony into another range, changing the key but not dropping the theme. In the perspective afforded by Miss Reba's place, we may see that there has been the potentiality of a grotesque humor in Temple's misadventures all along, but of humor withheld and denied by the predominance of the pity and the horror. Now the irony moves from the tragic to the comic, is pitched differently, but is never entirely lost as irony. Virgil's supposition that the women in Miss Reba's house are all married—"Aint you heard them?"—is pure folk humor, but Miss Reba's judgment of Flem Snopes—who came in and "sat around the dining-room blowing his head off and feeling the girls' behinds, but if he ever spent a cent I don't know it"—as "Just a cheap, vulgar man, honey" is not far from the irony expressed in the description of Narcissa and the Baptist committee.

When Miss Reba and her two friends refresh themselves after the funeral they "talk politely, in decorous half-completed sentences, with little gasps of agreement." This is a world in which words, and the standards they represent, have lost all real meaning and continue their existence quite apart from, and even in opposition to, reality—a world we have already come to know in the funeral itself, in Narcissa's dedication to the standards of decency, and in the Negroes singing by the jail. Miss Reba and her friends are responding to a code which has very little connection with the situation. "'Miss Reba's the perfect hostess,' the thin one said." The fact that she is a "hostess" in a sense not intended in her friend's statement is the basis not only of the obvious humor but of an irony never very far from the surface. Miss Reba's disapproval of Popeye's introduction of unusual pleasures into her house—and "Me trying to run a respectable house"—certainly suggests, and may very possibly have been suggested by, the speaker's complaint in Eliot's "Sweeney Erect"—"It does the house no sort of good." The quality of the irony is the same in the poem and in this scene of the novel. In both places it springs from a sense that the image of man is lost and continues to exist only in language now grotesquely inappropriate. This is also the idea which inverts the story of the betrayed girl to make it the story of her betrayal of Goodwin and Red, a story sardonic, always on the verge of macabre humor, and violently ironic.

This suggests that the "comic relief" of the scenes at Miss Reba's is not wholly discontinuous with the rest of the work, though it is not so closely integrated as is the humor of As I Lay Dying. Though Sanctuary seems to me one of the finest novels in modern literature, when we compare it with Faulkner's best—with The Sound and the Fury and As I Lay Dying and Absalom, Absalom!—we note a comparative lack of connection and development. The symbolism is, comparatively—but only comparatively—superficial, "flashy." The heaven tree has more obvious force and less meaning and relevance than Vardaman's fish. Popeye's mechanical appearance never leads into anything like Jason's mechanical philosophy. At times we may feel that here violence does not so much embody and motivate judgment as serve in its absence. Perhaps the trouble is that there is so little hope in the novel that thinking lacks motive. At any rate it is clear that the tension is at times almost—but never quite—destroyed by being weighted on the side of despair. The result is a distinguished novel that is less an implicit judgment of experience than a compelling and almost unbearable subjection to it.

3

IN ONE OF Gail Hightower's final meditations he pronounces an often quoted judgment on Southern Protestant Christianity. The music he hears coming from the church seems to him to have "a quality stern and implacable, deliberate and without passion so much as immolation, pleading, asking, for not love, not life, forbidding it to others, demanding in sonorous tones death, as though death were the boon, like all Protestant music." "Puritanism," or punitive religious moralism, is perhaps the chief intended antagonist in *Light in August*, as it is the immediate antagonist in *Sanctuary*.

"Pleasure, ecstasy," Hightower thinks, "they cannot seem to bear." Hines and McEachern could be his illustrations, the two most obviously pious people in the story and the two most responsible for the fate of Joe Christmas. He does not think of them because he does not know what we know about Christmas's past, but we, reading, supply them for him. And when we have finished the novel we feel that events have proved Hightower right when he pictures a crucifixion inflicted not despite but because of the religion of his fellow townsmen:

> *And so why should not their religion drive them to cruci-*
> *fixion of themselves and one another?* . . . It seems to him
> that the past week has rushed like a torrent and that the
> week to come, which will begin tomorrow, is the abyss, and
> that now on the brink of the cataract the stream has raised
> a single blended and sonorous and austere cry, not for justi-
> fication but as a dying salute before its own plunge, and not
> to any god but to the doomed man in the barred cell within
> hearing of them and of the two other churches, and in
> whose crucifixion they too will raise a cross. 'And they will
> do it gladly,' he says, in the dark window.

Hightower's thoughts constitute a terrible indictment of Southern Christianity, charging that it has become so distorted that it leads men toward hatred and destruction and death, crucifying Christ all over again, and "gladly." A great deal of the substance of the book has the effect of leading us to accept this judgment, and *Light in August* is Faulkner's most fully documented statement on what he sees as the religious errors and the racist guilt of his region. The grim fanatical fundamentalism of McEachern and the mad fundamentalist racism of Hines are judged in negative terms and without any shadow of qualification.

But a recognition of this theme of the book, necessary as it is, will not alone take us to an understanding of the whole novel. We may get at a further meaning by going on with Hightower's meditation to a passage which, unlike the negative judgment of the Southern Protestant churches, has not been quoted by the critics. Hightower has thought that the people would crucify "gladly." Now he thinks why they will have to do it gladly:

> 'Since to pity him would be to admit self-doubt and to hope for and need pity themselves. They will do it gladly, gladly. That's why it is so terrible . . .'

They will do it as Percy Grimm commits his murder and mutilation, secure in the confidence that they are doing their duty, without the least shadow of self-doubt, with perfect confidence in their own rectitude; like Percy Grimm, whose face "above the blunt, cold rake of the automatic . . . had that serene, unearthly luminousness of angels in church windows."

But the whole strategy of the book is designed to prevent the reader not only from sharing their sense of their rectitude—this would be easy—but from resting confident in his sense of his own rectitude, his superiority to Joe Christmas, the warped sadist and murderer, and to Christmas's bigoted and cruel tormentors. Faulkner has said that a writer should be judged partly in terms of the difficulty of what he attempts, and that those writers who lack courage and so continue to do only what they know they can do well perhaps have earned less of our respect than those who attempt more and fail. In *Light in August* Faulkner attempts a task difficult enough to be a challenge to any novelist, too difficult perhaps to be perfectly accomplished. He attempts to make us pity, identify ourselves with and even, in the religious sense of the word, love, a man who would be rejected not only by Southern mores with their racial bias but by any humane standard. He tries to awaken compassion for "one of the least of these" based on a recognition of universal guilt and mutual responsibility, not so that we may suspend judgment entirely but so that we may judge with love. *Light in August* is addressed not only to the conscience of the South but to the conscience of all readers anywhere. It has never to my knowledge been called a tract, but if it were not so powerful as a work of art it might well justify that designation. The moral feeling in it is intense. It demands nothing less than a withholding of self-righteous negative moral judgments and a substitution of unlimited compassion. If it shows us how and why "faith without deeds is dead," it shows us equally why we must "repent" before we "believe."

The novel moves toward this end the hard way, aesthetically and morally. It never makes Joe Christmas attractive. With the exception of a few passages on which I shall comment later, it does not picture him as "good at heart," forced into bad actions by circumstances. It shows us a man of whom we might say that it is surprising not that he commits one murder but that he has not committed more, a man apparently capable of any violent and repulsive deed, a man who hates not *even* those who love him but *especially* those who love him. It asks us to consider this man's death as parallel to the crucifixion of Christ.

The Joe Christmas—Jesus Christ analogy is prominent and consistent throughout the novel, and not simply, as the introduction to the Modern Library edition would have it, begun and then forgotten. It has nothing to do with any resemblance in character or outlook between Christmas and Jesus: indeed, this is precisely the point, that we are asked to see Christmas's death as a crucifixion despite the fact that Christmas is in every imaginable way different from Jesus. To make us pity a Christ-like figure would be easy, but the novel never attempts to do this. It asks pity for Christmas by making us see that the terrible things we do and become are all finally in self defense. We are asked to feel not that Christmas is really good or nice but that he epitomizes the human situation. To do this is difficult for precisely the reason given by Hightower: it must be preceded by a personal confession of sin and a felt need for pity, forgiveness.

When we first see Joe Christmas it is through Byron Bunch.

Bunch refuses to judge him but we are not likely to make the same refusal. Christmas's hat is "cocked at an angle arrogant and baleful above his still face." And there is nothing superficial or deceptive about the appearance of arrogance. All the men in the mill note his "air of cold and quiet contempt." The foreman speaks the general mind when he says "We ought to run him through the planer. Maybe that will take that look off his face." Christmas is later run through a planer of suffering, but "that look" comes off his face only at the moment of his death. The foreman is right, in a way, but his judgment is that of the reader at this point, lacking compassion.

After we have seen Christmas at his baleful and repellent worst we are taken back into the childhood that produced the man. The homicidal maniac who now thinks in fantasy "God loves me too" is the product of a complete absence of love in his earliest formative years. The experiences in the orphanage beyond present conscious memory were the formative ones in Christmas's life, and they all lead to one multiple impression: rejection, self-hatred, hatred of others.

> Memory believes before knowing remembers. Believes longer than recollects, longer than knowing even wonders. Knows remembers believes a corridor in a big long garbled cold echoing building of dark red brick sootbleakened by more chimneys than its own . . . the bleak windows where in rain soot from the yearly adjacenting chimneys streaked like black tears.

By the time the McEacherns take the boy he is already shaped to reject love and respond only to hatred. It is unnecessary to qualify the description of McEachern as a "ruthless and bigoted man," a man cold, hard, and cruel, to recognize that he was faced with a virtually hopeless task in his efforts to transform Joe into an acceptable Presbyterian foster-son. We learn that though the man beat him and the wife attempted to be kind and was unfailingly sympathetic, the boy hated the woman more than the man:

> It was the woman: that soft kindness which he believed himself doomed to be forever victim of and which he hated worse than he did the hard and ruthless justice of men.

When we remember his response to Mrs. McEachern's attempts to befriend him and his kicking of the Negro girl in the shed, we see that his finally murdering the woman who had loved him and was trying to help him was predictable, in character, true to form psychologically. Unable to accept himself, Joe Christmas seeks punishment and death throughout his life as, earlier, he had forced McEachern to beat him. Psychologists might describe his character as "sado-masochistic." His aggressiveness is turned in upon himself as well as out toward others: he seeks to hurt and be hurt. Only when he has suffered the final pain and outrage inflicted by Percy Grimm does a look of peace come into his eyes. He had been waiting for this since the dietician offered him fifty cents instead of beating him.

Joe Christmas wants justice, not kindness—law, not mercy. The dietician should have punished him to preserve life's moral clarity. Christmas would be justified by keeping the Law, not by declaring himself a sinner and throwing himself on the Grace of God. To be able to accept kindness is implicitly to acknowledge one's self in need of it: Christmas is like his persecutors in having no humility, for all his "inferiority complex." He is like them too, even like mad old Doc Hines, in being an absolutist and a legalist. This is the quality which creates the curious kinship between him and Mc-Eachern even while they oppose each other with all their strength. For both of them right and wrong must be clear and definite; only so may a system of rewards and punishments ensure justice. McEachern seeks to enforce his, and God's, commandments, Christmas to violate them. The two are more alike than different.

All his life Christmas demands to know whether he is black or white. What he feels he cannot endure and will not accept is the not knowing, the ambiguity of his situation. Like many another Faulkner character, he is Ahab-like in his scorn of all petty satisfactions and his determination to "strike through the mask" to get at absolute truth, ultimate certainty and clarity, for good or for ill. He must know the truth, and for truth kindness is no substitute. In this sense his very "idealism" drives him to every degradation and finally to his destruction.

But there is still another light in which we may look at him. We have seen him as doubly victimized, first by circumstance and a loveless society, which together have made him what he is, second by his own need for the kind of justice and certainty not to be found (the novel implies) in life. But now, as we think of the final events of his life, we see him becoming society's victim in still a further sense—its scapegoat. Society heaps on him all the sins which it cannot, will not, see in itself. Hightower has understood this too: "to pity him would be to admit self-doubt and to hope for and need pity themselves." A scapegoat is needed not by the innocent but by the guilty. Joe Christmas makes it possible for his persecutors never to recognize their guilt. Hines, McEachern, and Grimm are all, in their several ways, "believers," but they have never repented and their actions are unconsciously calculated to protect them from the need to repent. To concentrate on this aspect of the portrait of Christmas leads one to feel the religious profundity of *Light in August,* and to realize that the work is deeply Christian in its meaning, despite its excoriation of the exemplars of piety.

This is the man, then—debased murderer, victim, scapegoat— whom we are forced, by the frequent symbolic pointers, to think of in terms of Christ. Readers have generally taken the parallel either as pure irony—everything so much the same, and yet the two figures so utterly different as to be quite incomparable—or as an ironically expressed insight into a likeness that remains real despite the irony. For the latter reading, which seems much better able to account for all the facts of a highly complex portrait than the former, a passage of Scripture is helpful:

> Then shall they also answer him, saying, Lord, when saw we thee an hungered, or athirst, or a stranger, or naked, or sick, or in prison, and did not minister unto thee?
> Then shall he answer them, saying, Verily I say unto you, Inasmuch as ye did it not to one of the least of these, ye did it not to me. (Matthew 25:44-45).

Joe Christmas is surely "one of the least of these." When the novel opens he is soon to be captured and put in prison; early in the book we see him naked beside the road; during his flight he suffers from hunger and thirst and is sick: every item in the catalogue of the unfortunate is paralleled in the book. The irony lies partly in the fact that he rejects or strikes down those who do try to "minister unto" him—Mrs. McEachern, Miss Burden, Gail Hightower. But we are invited to believe that by the time these attempts to help him came he was beyond being able to respond to them except with rejection.

The motif of Christmas's adult life takes its pattern in part from the *Agnus dei* of the service of Holy Communion. In the *Agnus dei* the worshipper calls upon the "lamb of God" first to have mercy and then, in culmination, to "grant us thy peace." "All I wanted was peace," Christmas thinks after he has killed Miss Burden; and on another occasion, though the word used here is the close synonym "quiet": "That was all I wanted . . . That was all, for thirty years." In his boyhood he had slain a sheep and dipped his hands in the blood, thus in fantasy and symbol being "washed in the blood of the lamb." When he is killed and his own blood flows he seems to find peace at last.

> For a long moment he looked up at them with peaceful and unfathomable and unbearable eyes. Then his face, body, all, seemed to collapse, to fall in upon itself and from out the slashed garments about his hips and loins the pent black blood seemed to rush like a released breath. It seemed to rush out of his pale body like the rush of sparks from a rising rocket; upon that black blast the man seemed to rise soaring into their memories forever and ever.

It is perhaps the last irony of Joe Christmas's life that at his death there is a kind of metaphoric ascension. There is a sense in which he himself has become "the slain sheep, the price paid for immunity," to use a phrase applied earlier to his taking Bobbie Allen into the fields. Those who witnessed his death, into whose memories his blood has "ascended," are never to lose this memory

> in whatever peaceful valleys, beside whatever placid and reassuring streams of old age, in the mirroring faces of

whatever children they will contemplate old disasters and newer hopes. It will be there, musing, quiet, steadfast, not fading and not particularly threatful, but of itself alone serene, of itself alone triumphant.

The career of Joe Christmas constitutes a rebuke to the community, a measure of its sin of racial arrogance and of its corruption of Christianity from a religion of love and life to one of hatred and death, from Jesus to Doc Hines and McEachern. But Christmas is not the only source of the rebuke. The novel opens with Lena, an "unconscious Christian"; it moves, except in the sections on Christmas's childhood, largely through the minds of Byron Bunch and Gail Hightower, Christians of two different kinds; and it closes with Byron and Lena. The story of Christmas is thus framed and illuminated by the stories of several kinds of practicing Christians. McEachern and Hines, it would appear, do not give us the whole picture. Each is true to those aspects of religion under condemnation, but taken alone they would constitute a caricature. The force of the criticism comes from the recognition that they are so typical, their errors of practice or doctrine so widespread.

Meanwhile there is Lena to suggest a Christianity different from that of McEachern or Hines. She is not only a kind of nature or fertility goddess,[4] but also a witness to the efficacy of the three theological virtues, faith, hope, and love. Her trust is in the Lord, as Armstid recognizes when he recalls how "she told Martha last night about how the Lord will see that what is right will get done." She may have been created with a passage from St. Paul in mind; at any rate she suffers long, and is kind, does not envy and is not (like Joe Christmas) too proud to accept help, is never unseemly in her conduct, and (to shift to the Revised Standard Version) "is not irritable or resentful"; she "bears all things, believes all things, hopes all things, endures all things." Considering that she is so saintly an image, it is remarkable that she seems so real to us. Novelists have seldom been successful in portraying saints. No wonder there is what has been called a "pastoral" quality in the Lena episodes. No wonder she moves "with the untroubled unhaste of a change of season." Unlike Christmas she is not in flight.

And Byron Bunch. He is the portrait of the unlettered practicing Christian. He works alone at the mill on Saturday afternoon to avoid any occasion of sin, thus following good Catholic precept. (He finds that even so he cannot avoid temptation.) Only Hightower knows that he "rides thirty miles into the country and spends Sunday leading the choir in a country church—a service which lasts all day long." He immediately offers Christmas a part of his lunch when they first meet (the reply is typical: "I aint hungry. Keep your muck.") and refuses to pass judgment on him when he is told that Brown and Christmas are bootleggers. He holds himself responsible for having listened to the gossip: "And so I reckon I aint no better than nobody else." He thinks of Miss Burden and her reputation and the negative judgment the town makes of her; he makes no such judgment. He is a friend of the ruined outcast minister Hightower, not simply "befriending" him, refusing to share the town's harsh judgment, but recognizing in him a kindred spirit, seeking him out for advice, paying him the compliment of putting burdens upon him that he would ask no one else to bear. He pities and tries to help not only Lena and Hightower but Christmas's grandparents, bringing them to Hightower for advice. He extends his compassion to Christmas himself and might have been effective in his intended aid if Hightower had not refused until too late to accept the responsibility Byron tried to get him to see was his.

Byron Bunch has learned to bear the burden of being human. Generally inarticulate, he yet manages several times to define that burden for Hightower:

> I mind how I said to you once that there is a price for being good the same as for being bad; a cost to pay. And it's the good men that cant deny the bill when it comes around.

What Byron knows, he has had to learn in painful experience. We see him repeatedly tempted to deny the bill. No man, he often feels, should have to bear what he has to bear. But in the end he discovers that he can bear even the thought that all his efforts have succeeded only in getting Lena married to Burch. "It seems like a man can just about bear anything. He can even bear what he never done." His burden, finally, is total recognition of the impurity, the injustice, the unresolvable irony of life itself. When he has learned this, he knows not to ask for justice but for mercy and the strength to persevere. Like Lena, Byron is travelling the road recommended by the saints.[5]

And Hightower. Here the picture is more complicated, so complicated that many readers have had difficulty putting the pieces together. Fundamentally, Hightower is a romantic idealist who, confronted with a reality less pure and heroic than his dreams, has retreated to a spot where he hopes life cannot reach him to hurt him again. His master symbol is the galloping horsemen; he cannot steadily face the fact that the horsemen were engaged in raiding a chicken house. When he sits at his window at sunset waiting for the dusk and the image of the galloping horsemen, a part of him knows that he is really waiting only for death,

> waiting for that instant when all light has failed out of the sky and it would be night save for that faint light which daygranaried leaf and grass blade reluctant suspire, making still a little light on earth though night itself has come.

"Daygranaried": the natural light imagery here cannot be freed of its religious associations. The light of his religious faith has gone from Hightower and he has nothing to wait for now but the little light reflected, stored up perhaps from the source, but now coming, or seeming to come, from the earth itself,[6] before the final coming of night. When he is about to die he thinks he should try to pray, but he does not try.

> "With all air, all heaven, filled with the lost and unheeded crying of all the living who ever lived, wailing still like lost children among the cold and terrible stars."

Yet he finally atones for whatever sin has been his by trying to protect Christmas from his pursuers, at a terrible cost to any pride he has left. Like Joe Christmas, Hightower thinks on one occasion that all he has ever really desired was peace; thinking too that it should rightly be his now, that he has earned it through suffering endured. It is Byron Bunch who teaches him that peace is not to be had by retreat, by taking no chances, that the purity achieved by denying the bill, refusing the risks of his humanity, is more like death than like life. As Hightower explicitly recognizes when he thinks Byron has left town without saying goodbye, Byron has restored him to life, or life to him. And so at the end he acts for once not like the romantic idealist and absolutist he has always been but like Byron, the practising Christian, the doer of the word who can submit to unreason and persevere in good works. Telling the pursuing men that Christmas was with him on the night of the murder, Hightower takes on himself the opprobrium of the town's worst surmise.

Before his death Hightower has learned that he is not simply a victim, that in some degree at least he has brought his martyrdom on himself. He sees that he has been "wild too in the pulpit, using religion as though it were a dream," getting religion and his romantic idolization of the past all mixed up together, using perhaps, he suspects, even his wife as a means to the end of his self-inflicted martyrdom. If he could pray at the end of his life he would pray not simply for peace but for mercy, as a sinner. He learns late what Byron Bunch has known all along. Before this when he and Byron sit together he looks "like an awkward beast tricked and befooled of the need for flight. . . . Byron alone seems to possess life." Yet at the end if he has neither faith nor hope he has shown himself capable in the supreme test of acting in terms of love, "the greatest of these." Hightower too is finally a redeemed and potentially redemptive character.

Joanna Burden is more complex than Byron Bunch and perhaps more perfectly realized than Hightower. Faulkner's critics have generally passed over her in silence, leaving her unrelated to the central themes of the book. But I think that if we consider the clue offered by her name, we shall find a key to at least the most significant aspect of her symbolic role. To do so seems not to be capricious in considering a book filled with suggestive names:

Hightower, who spends most of his life *above* the battle and only at the end of his life comes down into the common life of man; Bunch, whose name suggests something common and solid and unromantic; Grimm; Christmas. Miss Burden, then, may be seen in a preliminary way as one who has taken the opposite road from the one followed by Hightower during his years of isolation. She accepts the burden of working for human betterment and the other, often painful, burdens it entails. Her isolation in a hostile community has been the price *she* has had to pay, in Byron's terms, for working for the cause of Negroes. For her, the white man's burden is her own burden.

But her conscience is not just sensitive, it is sensitive in a special way, the way of her grandfather the abolitionist. Though she has responded to life by commitment instead of flight, she is fundamentally as "idealistic" and "absolutist" in her reactions as Hightower. She accepts Joe Christmas, paradoxically, because he is, or she thinks he is, a Negro, not because he is a human being. The crisis in their relationship comes when she tells him her plan to send him to a Negro college. Her very idealism forces her to *place* him, in black or white. Thus she ends by reinforcing for him the terrible need that has driven him all his life, the need to know what he is. He has become her world, and she cannot accept a mixed, impure, ambiguous world, any more than Joe himself can, or Hightower before Byron teaches him. Like Melville's Pierre, she finds "the ambiguities" intolerable, just because she is so much an idealist. Her cause is finally more important to her even than Joe, and in her inflexible conscientiousness she drives him to murder her.

She is not, of course, an obvious sinner like Doc Hines and the other "righteous" characters in the story. There is real nobility in her that sets her quite apart from all the "idealists" but Hightower. She pays the price of goodness unflinchingly. But she can function only in a world of black and white; gray leaves her baffled, helpless. There is one burden, then, she cannot bear: precisely Byron Bunch's burden, the perception of essential irony. She is murdered by a man neither white nor black, but in a deeper sense she is destroyed by her abolitionist grandfather, for whom moral issues were perfectly clear and unambiguous.

In these people and their relationships the theme of the novel finds whatever expression it gets. There are no author's intrusions, no pointing fingers to tell us what it means. The meditations of Hightower come closer than anything else in the book to the voice of Faulkner the moralist but Hightower is portrayed as so clearly the victim of his own delusions that we are left to make our own decision as to which of his ideas are sound and which mere symptoms of his spiritual sickness. Byron Bunch is nearly as inarticulate as Lena, and we are given every opportunity to dismiss them both as essentially creatures of tender comedy in a pastoral idyl. The only characters of whom we may say that a definite and single judgment is required are McEachern, Hines, and Grimm; these are the only important characters approached wholly from outside, without any sympathetic identification with them on Faulkner's part.

Yet the novel "says" some things clearly enough. To the region in which it is laid it says that its racial injustice is a sin of the most terrible proportions and consequences (not merely a mistake or an accident—there is no moral relativism here or anywhere else in Faulkner) but also an opportunity for moral action. It says that suffering is the universal lot of mankind: in every man's death, even in that of a Joe Christmas, there is a kind of crucifixion. It says that the test of character is the individual's response to suffering: the hatred of Joe Christmas, the flight from responsibility of Hightower, the humble engagement of Lena and Byron.

The fact that these two open and close the novel seems to me crucial and not to have been given sufficient weight in most interpretations. It is not enough to say that the beginning and end are comic relief from the pure tragedy of the major part of the work. Lena and Byron *are* comic, of course, and the ending is an anticlimax, but it is also an affirmation of the possibilities of life. The voice of the travelling man from Memphis is the voice of sanity which makes no excessive demands on life, the voice of "realism" if you will, but a realism capable of seeing two people of precisely Byron's and Lena's qualities as those who offer hope. That only Byron and Lena, in the end, are capable of carrying on is to be expected. We have been prepared for this kind of affirmation by Dilsey and Cash. Certainly one meaning of the ending is that though knowledge of absolutes is not granted to man, yet what he is given to know is enough, if he has the moral and religious quali- ties of Byron and Lena. If this is the central meaning of the ending, the final implication of the book is a kind of Christian existentialism which could be explicated in terms of the theology of a Tillich or a Bultmann. Byron and Lena have the courage and the faith to *be* in a world where man does not see God face to face and any localizing of the absolute is a mark of pride.

This much is tolerably clear, but there is a good deal that is not, and even this is likely to seem most plausible if we keep our attention centered on the contrast between Byron and Lena, on the one hand, and Hightower, Christmas, and Joanna Burden, on the other—as of course the structure of the book in the largest sense suggests that we should. There is a theological ambiguity and a moral one, each of which tends in some degree to run counter to what I have described as the implication of the ending. The theological seems not crucial in the context which the story itself has created. Whether ultimate meaning here should be thought of in a humanist or in a Christian sense, in Hightower's way or in Byron's way, it is perfectly clear that the humble commitment of Byron and Lena is presented as the only alternative to suicide or destruction. If God exists, and cares, he demands this of us; if He does not we must live, if we are to live at all, by the old virtues anyway. Humanists may be living only by "daygranaried" light, light stored up from a higher source that now only *seems* to seep up from below; or the light may really come from below, from the earth. In either case, the "old truths of the heart" are valid. The theological ambiguity is not crucial to an interpretation of the main thrust of the novel.

But the moral ambiguity is not so easily disposed of. It concerns, as so often in Faulkner, the problem of freedom and responsibility.

We have seen Hightower as one who has demanded purity and, not finding it, has tried to isolate himself from an impure world; in this sense he is a victim of his own delusion and so in another sense not a victim at all but a man who has been mistaken. But most of the time during his years of seclusion he sees himself, and Faulkner seems to see him, as an innocent victim of other people or of life. His parishioners, the townspeople, the church, his wife, God, all seem to him to have failed him; and since we see them from his point of view, it is not entirely clear that he is wrong. Or at least it is not until toward the end. Then he thinks, "After all, there must be some things for which God cannot be accused by man and held responsible. There must be." Presumably there must, but it is not entirely clear to Hightower or to the reader what they are. It is significant, I think, that after Hightower achieves this insight and the reader comes to see him in terms of what it implies, the man himself becomes clear and believable to us at last. His dying meditation is one of the most powerful passages in all of Faulkner.

The same ambiguity is more troublesome in the portrait of Christmas. We see him chiefly as a "bad" man who cannot help being what he is. Living and dead he is a condemnation of an unjust society and a perverted religious conscience. But it is difficult if not impossible for us to picture a man as *simply* a victim. We may withhold judgment, refusing to try to decide what he can be held responsible for in the Last, and true, Judgment, but we must assume that he has some degree of moral responsibility if we are to see him as fully human. Apparently Faulkner must, too. Though the chapters on Christmas's childhood and boyhood, constituting a kind of case history of the growth of a sadomasochist, seems to remove from him all responsibility for what he later becomes, there are passages in which choice is imputed to Christmas. There are others in which, choice being denied but felt by the reader, the effect is sentimental. A couple of examples will serve to illustrate the point sufficiently.

When, after striking McEachern in the dance hall, Christmas runs away, there is a definite imputation of choice:

> The youth . . . rode lightly . . . exulting perhaps at the moment as Faustus had, of having put behind now at once and for all the Shalt Not, of being free at last of honor and Law.

But the point of the Faustus myth is that Faustus, with full knowledge and acceptance of responsibility, made a choice. Most of the portrait of Christmas has the effect of suggesting that he was simply a victim, made no choices.

Again, and in contrast to the Faustus passage, the treatment of Christmas's experience with Bobbie Allen culminates in an apparent acceptance by Faulkner of Christmas's own view of the experience, a view which makes this the final betrayal, the last bitter blow of fate. "Why, I committed murder for her. I even stole for her," Christmas thinks. But that is not quite the way it was. As for the stealing, he had been stealing for some time before, and this particular "theft"—he took Mrs. McEachern's money in her presence, knowing well that she would have given it to him gladly—was not so much a theft as a final premeditated blow to the woman who had tried to help him. As for the "murder," whether or not McEachern died from the blow we are not told, but we do know that the boy had been waiting for the opportunity to deliver it for a long time and "exulted" when the opportunity came to "get even." It was not then in any real sense a murder committed "for her." Yet there is no indication in the writing at this point that these rationalizations of the boy's are not to be accepted at face value. The effect of the passage is sentimental.

A final example. As a part of the summary of Christmas's years between the time when he ran away from the McEacherns and the time when he came to Jefferson we are told of the effect on him of his first experience of sexual relations with a white woman.

> He was sick after that. He did not know until then that there were white women who would take a man with a black skin. He stayed sick for two years.

I am afraid I shall have to say that this seems to me just plain nonsense. The implication that he was sick for two years not simply "after that" but because of "that" is wrong from several points of view. Would this amazing discovery make a well man sick, and for two years? Anyway, he does not have a "black skin." It is already perfectly clear, and even explicit, that he was very sick indeed psychologically long before this discovery, and is sick long after the two years are up. The passage is melodramatic in its imputation of too great an effect to too little a cause, and it is sentimental in its implication, once again, of innocence betrayed. It tells us more about Faulkner's own mixed racial feelings than it does about Joe Christmas.

No doubt this was how Christmas remembered the incident, but the passage could be effective only if there were some indication that Faulkner himself did not accept Christmas's sick notion of cause and effect. Faulkner's submergence of himself in his characters, which accounts for some of his greatest triumphs, also sometimes accounts for his failures. Here he has become Joe Christmas, sickness and all, as he thinks "back down the street, past all the imperceptible corners of bitter defeats and more bitter victories."[7]

It seems to me, finally, that all the street and corridor imagery, applied chiefly to Christmas but also, less conspicuously, to several of the others, comes to less than it should. Perhaps its chief effect is to imply that for a person with (possibly) mixed blood life is a one-way street with no exit, no escape, leading inevitably to defeat and death. This at least is the effect of the passage in which Christmas finds that the street has turned into a circle, that he is inside it, and that there is still no escape. But this idea is both banal and untrue, or true only in a sense that needs just the kind of qualification a novel could give it. Only one aspect of this too prominent image pattern seems to me interesting, and that one only partially justifies the elaborate and repeated treatment of the pattern. There is some indication that Lena is in a street or a corridor too, as in the passage which begins

> Behind her the four weeks, the evocation of *far*, is a peaceful corridor paved with unflagging and tranquil faith and peopled with kind and nameless faces and voices . . .

or in the description of Armstid's wagon as "a shabby bead upon the mild red string of the road." It depends, apparently, how we *take* our corridor, whether it is "peaceful" or bitter, a string of beads, each bead intrinsically valuable, or an avenue of flight. Percy Grimm too has his corridor and to him it means an escape from the necessity of choice: "his life opening before him, uncomplex and inescapable as a barren corridor." With her face lighted by the "unreason" of her faith, Lena finds friendly and helpful people everywhere, while Christmas finds only hatred and frustration.

These technical failings have the cumulative effect of creating an undeniable element of obscurity in a work nevertheless distinguished by its passion and immediacy and the seriousness of its imaginative grasp of reality. The obscurity here is quite different from the intentional ambiguity of *The Sound and the Fury* or *As I Lay Dying,* and different from the ultimately functional obscurity of *Absalom, Absalom!* This obscurity must be seen as an aesthetic weakness. I have suggested that it may be related to the mood of despair that dominates *Sanctuary.* But perhaps we should say only that *Light in August* attempts more than Faulkner could perfectly accomplish.

4

A DEBATE on the comparative merits of *Sanctuary* and *Light in August* would be likely to reveal, and in the end to be decided in terms of, fundamental differences in approach to works of fiction. We may imagine the argument going something like this: *Sanctuary* is a finer novel because it shows greater evidence of artistic control; it is neater and tighter, with fewer loose ends; it moves more inevitably toward its conclusion; it is never obscure. *Light in August* is a finer novel because it is richer, more various, has more compassion, and does not over-simplify experience as *Sanctuary* does; its obscurity is a reflection of the irreducible opaqueness of life itself and could not be eliminated except by the kind of aesthetic sleight-of-hand that we see at work in that more unified but less meaningful work, *Sanctuary*. Overhearing such a debate, we might suspect that it would settle nothing except the incompatibility of the premises on which it was conducted, and we might suggest the irenic conclusion that both novels rank very high among Faulkner's works and in the whole body of modern fiction.

More to the point than any such attempt to establish a hierarchy of merit would be to note similarities and differences and to try to see what these imply for these novels and for Faulkner's career. That both are related to the kind of tragic vision expressed in *Idyll in the Desert* seems clear enough, but that they end by making somewhat different comments on the outrage that is life is also clear. *Sanctuary* seems to me to express no hope at all of any meaning, any achievement. Many of Faulkner's works have been called negative and despairing when in fact a more perceptive comment would call them tragic, but *Sanctuary* really is negative and despairing: only the Snopes boys find any satisfaction in this world; the sensitive and intelligent find the outrage too terrible to bear.

Light in August offers hope, but only by shifting levels, changing perspectives. The central story of Joe Christmas is unrelieved tragedy; the story of Lena and Byron is tender comedy. The hope is real, but inevitably qualified by our feeling that we must smile at Lena and Byron even as we admire them: *we* are more like Hightower or Miss Burden, or even Joe Christmas. I have argued that we must not undervalue Lena and Byron, that certainly we must not dismiss them as bumpkins before we see their moral and religious implications; but I should certainly not want to imply that we can take them in the same way that we take Hightower or Christmas.

Hope may be found in *Light in August* only by giving up the intellectual and emotional struggle for ultimate certainty embodied in Hightower and Christmas and turning to the humble and unselfconscious engagement of Lena and Byron. Because this means, in effect, turning to what is likely to strike us as a lower level of apprehension, the novel is perhaps in its final effect more unrelievedly tragic than *The Sound and the Fury*. If we agree that Dilsey has truly heroic qualities we may say that redemptive hope in *The Sound and the Fury* lies within the tragedy itself. Because we feel Dilsey's nobility, we feel that we move upward to identify with her and to achieve her view of life. But because we smile at Lena and Byron, though by an act of judgment appreciating their virtues, we must in a sense move down to a vision less serious than the tragic to reach the hope which they alone offer in *Light in August*. As we sit with Hightower in the twilight, we are likely to feel that the darkness is more powerful than the light.

CHAPTER 6

New World

PYLON

THE WILD PALMS

IN THE MIDDLE THIRTIES Faulkner wrote two novels that have yet to be adequately appreciated. Both *Pylon* and *The Wild Palms* seem to me works of real brilliance, but that has not been the usual opinion. No early Faulkner novels have been more consistently written off as failures by the critics than these two.

Most readers today have probably never read *The Wild Palms* in the form in which it was published and intended to be read. Since Malcolm Cowley some years ago characterized the two stories that make up *The Wild Palms* as "unrelated,"[1] the novel has generally been reprinted as two separate works. More recently it has been reissued with both parts within the same set of covers, but without alternating chapters. Read separately, neither story has very much meaning. The separated parts have continued to sell in the drug stores and to be pretty much ignored by the critics.

Pylon and *The Wild Palms* have a good deal in common besides being written within a few years of each other, dealing with the contemporary period, and eschewing Yoknapatawpha. Both of them are directly concerned with describing and assessing certain distinctive features of the contemporary world: they are not simply laid in a setting of the present but are attempts to get at the very essence of what distinguishes the present from the past, our society from traditional society. They carry on from where Quentin left off in his attempt to understand and come to terms with the present world.

2

FAULKNER HAS said of *Pylon* that his intention was to write a book which would be the expression of pure speed and to people it with a new race, dedicated to speed. Like the majority of the critics, Faulkner "was disappointed in this book":

> I had expected, hoped that it would be a kind of new trend, a literature or blundering at self expression, not of a man, but of this whole new business of speed just to be moving fast.[2]

Pylon does convey, with terrifying vividness, a sense of great speed mechanically contrived and mechanically continued quite apart from ordinary or familiar human motivations and needs; but it does much more than that. It implicitly judges, by describing, a whole culture and civilization. If it does not accomplish what Faulkner had hoped to accomplish, it accomplishes something better. It is in effect, whatever Faulkner intended, a picture, not painted in oils but made with a camera with the lens in sharp focus, of our times, of the conditions that characterize contemporary urban-industrial mass society.

The imagery of the opening pages conveys the sense of a kind of nightmare world, intensely present, yet unreal. Natural objects are seen in "gargantuan irrelation" or disguised as something else. As Jiggs stands looking in the store window, admiring the boots, he sees them in an artificial light that is like "an unearthly day-colored substance," palpable but unbelievable, falling on "drinking tools shaped like boots and barnyard fowls and the minute impedimenta for wear on ties and vestchains shaped like bits and spurs," resembling "biologic specimens" held in the light as in a preservative. The lighting is indirect: it has no apparent source, and it is as unnatural as the objects and relations it reveals. The store window introduces us to a world in which both relationships and identities have been altered beyond casual recognition. The scene is what Eliseo Vivas would call the constitutive symbol of the novel.

After Jiggs (a man who looks like a horse, as the objects in the store window look like other objects) gets on the bus for the airport we learn that he is not from anywhere in particular, that the place he is "staying away from right now" is Kansas. "I got two kids there; I guess I still got the wife too." Now the moving bus reveals a landscape as miragelike, hallucinatory, as the store window. The bus

> ran now upon a flat plain of sawgrass and of cypress and oak stumps . . . a pocked desolation of some terrific and apparently purposeless reclamation across which the shell road ran ribbonblanched toward something low and dead ahead of it—something low, unnatural: a chimera quality which for the moment prevented one from comprehending that it has been built by man and for a purpose.

Earth and water appear to blend here, to lose all distinction, as the bus rushes toward the "chimerashape" of the airport which seems

> to float lightly like the apocryphal turreted and battlemented cities in the colored Sunday sections, where beneath sill-less and floorless arches people with yellow and blue flesh pass and repass: myriad, purposeless, and free from gravity.

The airport building when they arrive looks "like a mammoth terminal for some species of machine of a yet unvisioned tomorrow, to which air earth and water will be as one." The airplanes resemble insects and dead animals; the reporter who now appears looks like a walking corpse; and Jiggs' legs move with "pistonlike thrusts." The music of the band that starts playing is amplified through multiple loudspeakers, so that it is heard fractured, multiplied, and distorted. When the music stops a voice speaks through the amplifiers, "talking of creatures imbued with motion though not with life," "the voice too almost as sourceless as light," talking between "erupted snatched blares of ghostlike and ubiquitous sound" of the air-meet celebrating the opening of the airport, a voice impersonal, disembodied, mechanical, hired. The light in the airport building is like that in the store window:

> The rotunda, filled with dusk, was lighted now, with a soft sourceless wash of no earthly color or substance and which cast no shadow . . .

The airport has been built on made land, on a part of the lake which has been filled in with rubbish from the city: it is a product wholly of man's ingenuity, his mechanical triumphs. Its lights around the plaza look like "bloomed bloodless grapes on their cast stalks." Dedicated to machines, it is dominated by the mechanical voice of the announcer, "inhuman, ubiquitous and beyond weariness or fatigue." Here all ties with the past are cut and time and space have new names suited to their new dimensions: ". . . the first day of a meet is the one they call Monday." The family of fliers that fascinates the reporter has no more permanent relation to place than to the traditional measurements of time. It has neither home to leave or return to nor purposeful destination: it follows the meets, living as best it can in makeshift pragmatic adjustment to the machines by which and for which it exists.

This is the brave new world of a thoroughly mechanized, traditionless, and "purposeless" culture. The reporter in the phone booth thinks of "love"—"of eternal electrodeitch and bottom-hope"—before he hears the voice of the operator:

> "Deposit five cents for three minutes please," the bland machinevoice chanted. The metal stalk sweatclutched, the guttapercha bloom cupping his breath back at him, he listened, fumbled, counting as the discreet clock and cling died into wirehum.

The cadaverous reporter who thinks of the physics and chemistry of love as he waits to report the achievements of man's mastery of the physics and chemistry of flight is identified by Jiggs as Lazarus, a fitting reporter of the doings of a world beyond the dead or dying older world. He lives in a room vaguely bohemian, "filled with objects whose desiccated and fragile inutility" made the room seem "exhumed intact from one month to the next." He has no father, or rather, a constant succession of new and unknown "fathers" as his mother remarries again and again. He is nearly anonymous: even Hagood, the editor, knows only his last name and the one initial he uses. Yet, because he is so close to nothing at all, being Lazarus who has died—many times—and come back, he has sympathy: "he stood there without impatience or design: patron (even if no guardian) saint of all waifs, all the homeless the desperate and the starved." Ignored, beaten, laughed at, and robbed by the flying family, he is yet compelled to try to help them by an inseparable mixture of eros and agape, desiring the woman and pitying them all.

The days and nights through which he moves are blended and indistinguishable, like the landscape in which the distinction between earth and water has been eradicated. Only the time indicated by the watch on the pile of newspapers in the elevator, which he looks at every time he enters or leaves the building, has any significance for him; and this time has lost all connection with ordinary human purposes. In this new time-dimension life and death are almost as indistinguishable and scrambled as day and night have become for the reporter, like

> the Franciana spring which emerges out of the Indian summer of fall almost, like a mistimed stage resurrection which takes the curtain even before rigor mortis has made its bow . . .

Time as he now experiences it is not connected with seasons and cycles, not divided and measured by rite and function, but abstract, alien, compulsive:

> When the reporter entered the twin glass doors and the elevator cage clashed behind him this time, stooping to lift the facedown watch alone and look at it, he would contemplate the inexplicable and fading fury of the past twenty-four hours circled back to itself and become whole and in-

tact and objective and already vanishing slowly like the
damp print of a lifted glass on a bar.

Time for him has become motion, and motion itself, because
unconnected with discernible human purposes, unreal: "now the
room's last long instant of illimitable unforgetting seemed to draw
in quietly in a long immobility of fleeing."

The reporter, who is compared in the book not only to Lazarus
but to Prufrock, who thought himself a kind of Lazarus, sees the
death of Roger Shumann in the lake as a "death by water" in terms
that suggest both the fourth section of *The Waste Land* and the
closing lines of "Prufrock." It has been said that the relationship
between the corpse-like reporter and Eliot's Prufrock is obscure or
non-existent, despite the explicit parallel enforced by the title of
one of the chapters, "The Love Song of J. A. Prufrock." But it seems
to me that the parallels between the novel and the poem, especially
the ending of the poem, are quite close. In the opening lines of the
poem Prufrock has seen nature as dead, sick, alien—or "neutralized,"
as I. A. Richards called it a little later in *Science and Poetry.* But
in the last six lines his thoughts turn to a vision out of the past, his
own past perhaps, his culture's certainly. Now for a moment he sees
nature not as alien but as created and purposive like man himself.
The beauty and mystery of the natural world for man's imagination
is embodied in the vision of mermaids rising from the teeming
depths of the sea. But in the last line Prufrock's mind is once more
and finally conquered by the contemporary world, which no longer
believes in mermaids or gods in nature, which sees nature as
essentially lifeless and meaningless. The sea, source of both life
and death, now suggests only death: "Till human voices wake us
and we drown."

The "Death by Water" section of *The Waste Land* and the
ending of "The Love Song of J. Alfred Prufrock" are as relevant
here as they were in Quentin's death by water in *The Sound and the
Fury.* In both scenes Faulkner has paralleled, and almost certainly
been influenced by, Eliot's contrast of a "scientific" (that is, materialistic and positivistic) view with the religious one that is

identified equally with the pre-Christian fertility religions and with the rite of Christian baptism. In *Pylon* water has lost its ambivalence, its suggestion of both life and death, and has come to suggest death alone. The voices of modern reason rule out the hope of a resurrection. Tangled in the refuse of a scientific and technological civilization, Shumann's body cannot be raised. We have already heard the "human voices" of the new age blaring through the loudspeakers, and we have found them both inhuman and meaningless, as measured by traditional or religious standards. No wonder the reporter sees Shumann's death as he does.

But long before Shumann dies we have been reminded of the parallels between the novel and the poem. When the reporter first appears on the scene our view of him is influenced immediately by two allusions to Eliot's poem, as he is called an "etherized patient" who looks as though he might have "escaped into the living world." Later allusions keep us reminded of the parallel, so that we are not surprised when, after Shumann's death, he thinks of the reasons why the body cannot be recovered, in terms that ironically echo Prufrock's final vision. The inescapable voices of the amplifiers have prepared the reporter, and the reader, for the realization that the plane and the body in it have become inextricable from

> a sunken mole composed of refuse from the city itself— shards of condemned paving and masses of fallen walls and even discarded automobile bodies—any and all the refuse of man's twentieth century clotting into communities large enough to pay a mayor's salary—dumped into the lake.

Like Prufrock too, he has a vision, as he waits in the cold and wind on the shore with the headlights of the parked cars piercing the darkness, of water blown by the wind, as the ending of the poem has it, "white and black," water holding not "mermaids" but the body of Shumann. The brilliant artificial lights do not penetrate but only glare

> down upon the disturbed and ceaseless dark water which seemed to surge and fall and fall and surge as though in travail of amazement and outrage.

The whole section describing the anguished hours the reporter spends by the shore is a nightmarish montage of black and white. Darkness and glare succeed each other and intermingle, interpenetrate, but the object beneath the water which gives purpose to the search remains hidden:

> Now (the searchlight on the shore was black and only the one on the dredge stared as before downward into the water) the police boat lay to and there was not one of the small boats in sight and he saw that most of the cars were gone too . . . as he looked upward the dark seawall overhead came into abrupt sharp relief and then simultaneous with the recognition of the glow as floodlights he heard the displacing of air and saw the navigation lights of the transport as it slid, quite low, across the black angle and onto the field.

Having learned what is called "the taste not of despair but of Nothing," the reporter knows, like Prufrock, "not only not to hope, not even to wait: just to endure."

I have quoted so much because it seems to me that almost the whole value of *Pylon* lies in its quality as a kind of lyric poem, an evocation, largely through the imagery, of what cannot be said successfully in the abstract language of paraphrase. But what does it all come to, what meanings are here that analysis can handle without shattering?

What it comes to first of all is a magnificently vivid and sustained distillation of a world, not a world satirized by caricature as in Huxley's *Brave New World* or created by the selection and projection of certain present political realities as in *1984,* but a world we already know in all its aspects, though we may also know or remember another, an older, world too. Some of the features of the new world described by Faulkner in 1935 have since been described and measured and analyzed by sociologists; by David Riesman, for instance, in *Faces in the Crowd* and *The Lonely Crowd.* The loss of true community; the dwindling significance of the traditional family and home; the relaxing grip or embrace of institutions that embodied and supplied meaning and a sense of stability and permanence; the increasing mobility—rootlessness it might be called —of a people one fifth of whom moved to a new place of residence in a single recent year and an increasing fraction of whom have never known any "permanent" home at all but live always in trailers or motels—all these and other distinctive features of our time, of technological and cultural revolution, with their as yet unknown effects on human experience and personality, are stated in symbolic form in *Pylon*.

No one reading Riesman or Karl Mannheim could think of *Pylon* as simply fantasy.[3] The symbolic distortions in it are not only revealing of their object: they partake of the quality of their object. *Pylon* shows us a world from which the reporter, despite his sympathy and interest, is effectively shut out. It pictures and holds up for our judgment a world in almost all essentials the opposite of that which Quentin mourned the loss of in *The Sound and the Fury*.

The most curious thing about *Pylon*, in view of Faulkner's reputation as a simple Yoknapatawpha traditionalist, is the fact that the book passes conditional, limited judgments but no final, sweeping judgment on what it describes. Most of the conditions and outward features of the age which boasts that it has "annihilated space" it describes with obvious distaste—the ubiquitous venal mechanical voice, for instance, which could well be the voice of the TV in our living room. But the people of the new age, however different their manner and relationships may be from ours, from the known and familiar and approved, are presented with sympathy. The reporter speculates that perhaps "They aint human like us," but Faulkner presents them as human:

> Why don't you let the guy rest? Let them all rest. They were trying to do what they had to do, with what they had to do it with, the same as all of us . . .

Though they live by a different code from the one the reporter, from beyond the grave of hope, recognizes as the traditional one, their code is perhaps not of their choice but a product of new conditions. There is at least one indication that the woman, if not her men, would like a different manner of existence: "And all I want is just a house, a room . . . where I can know that next Monday and the Monday after that . . ." If these people seem cold, mechanical, dehumanized, so that even their sex life is isolated, mechanized, devoid of tenderness and unrelated to consequences, it is perhaps because they have taken on a protective coloration.[4] Roger Shumann exercises the essential and distinguishing human prerogative at the moment of his death: he makes "a choice." Choosing to guide his falling plane into the lake where its crash would kill no one but him, he gives the lie to the reporter's earlier suspicion that he and his family are not "human." Before the jumper and the woman and child leave the city the jumper attempts to pay their debt to the reporter and to arrange to have Shumann's body, if discovered, sent back to the one place on earth with which it has any humanly meaningful connection.

When the woman leaves the little boy with the elder Shumanns, who may or may not be his grandparents, a final bit of conversation points up this whole matter of the way in which the flying family is treated.

> "You are going to leave him like this?" Dr. Shumann said. "You are going to leave him asleep and go away?"
> "Can you think of a better way?" she said.
> "No, That's true."

We are likely at this point I think to feel that Dr. Shumann is agreeing too easily, that *we* can think of a better way, or several better ways, including the rather drastic but certainly not impossible one of Laverne's so changing her way of life that she could care for her child and not abandon him, sleeping or otherwise. The reader, in other words, is likely to be less sympathetic with these people than Faulkner seems to be. Since it is not clear that they have honestly explored all the possibilities, we may doubt that they are doing only "what they had to do." The question of the reality of choice is as relevant here as it was in the portraits of Popeye and Joe Christmas.

Here, as in *Sanctuary* and *Light in August,* pure compassion, love without any judgment, would assume that there has been no choice: and here, as potentially in those novels, charity overrides judgment, is seen as an alternative to it. This is the source of the noticeable ambivalence in the portrayal of the flying family. Creatures of a world despised and rejected, they themselves are pitied and accepted. They are finally pictured as victims, not agents.

The result is a certain ambiguity that cannot be wholly resolved by an analysis of the work that refuses to ignore any of the evidence. When the reporter, early in the book, looks at the bunting hung in the streets for Mardi gras, part of what he sees is described this way:

> And here also the cryptic shield caught (i n r i) loops of bunting giving an appearance temporary and tentlike to [the] interminable long corridor of machine blush and gilded synthetic plaster . . .

That "i n r i," the initials of the Latin words for "Jesus of Nazareth, King of the Jews," a title mockingly given to Christ at his crucifixion, measures the distance between the scene being portrayed and the religious meaning of Lent, as Ash Wednesday follows Mardi gras or fat Tuesday. It measures too the distance between the new world of the fliers, in which "the Light of the World" has diminished to a "daycolored substance," and the old, so that if we were to stop here in our reading we should believe we had found clarity of meaning in the work: straight-line decline into a kind of neopaganism and dehumanization in which human relationships have become merely fortuitous, mechanical, and man's relation to nature and to God has been obscured or destroyed. But this meaning has been qualified or rendered somewhat ambiguous by the time we reach the end: the fliers are still "human," despite the inhuman conditions of their lives.

As a result, *Pylon* is certainly ambiguous and perhaps ambivalent. It reads as though Faulkner, when he wrote it, was of two minds about his subject. The traditionalist in him, the Quentin, looked with horror on the loss of community and of a truly human image of man implicit in the mechanization of culture and of thought; but the Mr. Wiseman aspect, the critical reason, accepted the new world as inevitable, perhaps only strange, not terrible. Nevertheless, *Pylon* is both vividly and solidly created. To reject it completely as a work of art, as many have done, seems to me to imply that clarity of symbolic implication in a work of art is all-important. It is important, and *Pylon* falls short of the achievement of Faulkner's very finest works. But since the imaginative richness of it never fails, even when judgment falters, it deserves and rewards our closest attention.

3

AS ORIGINALLY published, *The Wild Palms* consisted of ten chapters, five of them telling the story now called *The Wild Palms* and five telling the story of the convict in the flood, now called *Old Man*. Faulkner thought of the two stories as connected, complementary, properly making up one book, and arranged them so that we would read first a chapter in one, then a chapter in the other. As he has recently said in answer to an inquiry on this matter, he wrote the story of the convict to bring the story of the two lovers "back to pitch" by contrast with its "antithesis."[5]

Faulkner has constantly experimented with the creation of new forms in his writing, and this was one more experiment—making a "novel" out of two separate and different stories, not connected in plot or overlapping in characters but arranged so that they had to be read together. The general view has been that the attempt was ill-judged, the experiment a failure. Whether that opinion is correct or not depends on a judgment of how close and significant the connections are between the two stories and of what new values emerge when we try to hold the two of them in mind at once. We may have to decide in the end that the work is a failure, but we shall not be in a position to judge it until we have undone recent critical and publishing history and put the parts back together again. If we had never tried to read *The Sound and the Fury* in the form in which it was published but only as four separately published short stories we should not know what aesthetic whole would emerge from those disjointed parts until we tried reading them as Faulkner arranged them.

The connections between the two stories are not literal but basically thematic, though these thematic connections are reflected in tone, setting, imagery, even in a sense in plot, when these are given their natural and inevitable symbolic extensions. Faulkner himself has said of *The Wild Palms* that it was his intention in the book to try to express "two types of love,"[6] and we may take this as our starting point and see what happens when we explore the book with this in mind.

The doctor and his paramour give up everything for love, make it their only concern and their only basis of a continuing relationship, break all ties and connections and obligations, fleeing from family and society and work to keep their love pure, unmixed, unconnected. She leaves her husband and children, he gives up his career, for love. The convict does his duty toward the young woman with whom he is isolated in the boat, caring for her as best he can but refusing to become personally involved. Though he cares for the woman in his charge more effectively, in the end, than the doctor in the other story, his is a depersonalized, a grim and dogged and abstract charity. He does his duty to society and to the woman, but his only effort is to have done with it, get rid of his terrible responsibility, and get back to the prison.

The doctor and his lover eschew society to find the perfect freedom in which to hold and keep love. The convict seeks escape not from but to the prison, which offers security in an alien and hostile environment; he has no time for love. The doctor and his lover magnify personality, the convict minimizes it. The lyrics of many popular love songs express, on their own cultural level, the conviction and the effort of the doctor and the woman; Eric Fromm's *Escape From Freedom,* offering a psychological analysis of the personal origins of totalitarian submergence of personality, is relevant to the convict's story. Together, the two stories say that we make "romantic love" in our time, with all that it implies about freedom and personality, either all or nothing, that we either magnify it and make it bear more than it can bear or deny it entirely.

This I think is the most general thematic implication of the two stories when they are considered together. Far from being trivial or unworthy of consideration, this theme seems to me not only insightful but prophetic. It could be and has in fact been explored from different points of view by psychologists and sociologists. The crisis arising from changing patterns of marriage and family, we are told, arises in large part from the decay of the economic and other functions of the family unit, so that the family comes to exist solely for and because of the fragile tie of personal love and loyalty: love becomes the only reason for the existence of the group, as the doctor and his lover tried to make it. Hemingway's love stories—*A Farewell to Arms,* for instance—have this ideal and this necessity (it is not only Hemingway who makes an ideal out of a necessity) at their very center: all other ties, functions, and group relationships are severed and denied to keep love pure, central, all in all. Frederick and Catherine go to Switzerland where they can be wholly free of everything but love. D. H. Lawrence and some popular interpretations of Freudianism in the recent past offer equally relevant illustrations of the same tendency in our culture.

On the other hand the explaining away of love in biological or other terms, the "reductionism" of those who, especially in the twenties and thirties, could believe that "love" was real only insofar as they could identify it with a glandular secretion, a chemical, is one of our ways of denying love. In another dimension the same denial of the personalistic values of love is made by the materialist ideologies and social patterns of half the world: freedom for the individual, without which love is meaningless, is minimized or destroyed, and love, along with all other "ideal" values, is explained as a mere by-product of economic and social "realities." Thus "realism" and "scientific socialism" in our time agree in denying status to the values of "romantic love."

If, as I have tried to suggest, there is a basis in present social and cultural trends for the thematic implication of *The Wild Palms*, which says that today we tend to make love all or nothing, then it remains to be seen how this theme is embodied in the novel with its two stories. This attempt to define and "justify" by reference to social conditions a theme most abstractly conceived, before any detailed examination of the novel, may seem an odd critical procedure—as it does to me. But it should be recalled that in the final analysis theme alone holds these two stories together, and that a failure to recognize this theme, or a denial of its significance, was responsible for taking the novel apart, denying its existence as a novel.

Early in the story of the doctor and the woman there is a passage that provides a clue to the rationale of their effort. The doctor thinks:

> "*It's not the romance of illicit love which draws them, [women] not the passionate idea of two damned and doomed isolated forever against the world and God and the irrevocable which draws men; it's because the idea of illicit love is a challenge to them, because they have an irresistible desire to . . . take the illicit love and make it respectable . . .*

Despite his theories about the difference between men and women, it is not Charlotte but Wilbourne himself who feels the impulse to make their love "respectable," to integrate it with the rest of normal existence. Charlotte will permit nothing to dilute the pure emotion, the unconnected experience, not even personal tenderness: her yellow eyes are "hard," even when she looks at Wilbourne, her manner rough, self-absorbed, demanding. "*There's a part of her that doesn't love anybody, anything,*" Wilbourne finally realizes. "*Why, she's alone. Not lonely, alone.*"

> She grasped his hair again, hurting him again though now he knew she knew she was hurting him. "Listen; it's got to be all honeymoon, always. Forever and ever, until one of us dies. It can't be anything else. Either heaven, or

hell: no comfortable safe peaceful purgatory between for
you and me to wait in until good behavior or forbearance
or shame or repentance overtakes us."

"So it's not me you believe in, put trust in; it's love."
She looked at him. "Not just me; any man."

"Yes. It's love. They say love dies between two people.
That's wrong. It doesn't die. It just leaves you, goes away,
if you are not good enough, worthy enough."

One of the reasons we cannot imagine any happy ending for *A
Farewell to Arms* is that we cannot imagine Frederick and Catherine
normally married, earning a living, rearing children. If Catherine
had not died, presumably their love would have gone away, left
them. Their love is pure as well as intense: it has no connections,
no relevance to anything but itself. Similarly in *The Wild Palms;*
their love will not leave them, as Charlotte says on another occasion,
if they are "good enough, strong enough." Love as she understands
it is not essentially a product of, a reality to be found only in,
personal relations, but something in the final analysis outside either
of them. Her point of view is that which was once expressed in the
conviction that "marriages are made in heaven" and which glorified
"love at first sight." She and Wilbourne fall in love, if not at first
sight then literally at second sight, at their second meeting; and
what happens after that is something she feels neither of them can
do anything about.

She eventually wins Wilbourne around to something like her point
of view, so that he comes to see society as the antagonist, the force
that makes love impossible: "Because this Anno Domini 1938 has
no place in it for love." But he has ceased to be "vulnerable" to
society's expectations. They go to a deserted mine in Utah in the
winter, where they hope to devote themselves entirely to love. But
Wilbourne comes to believe that society is not the only antagonist:
that hostility to love is embodied in the very nature of things, in
the natural universe itself, trapping and defeating those who love
—by pregnancy, infection, death. Charlotte dies of an abortion
bungled by Wilbourne and he decides against suicide, decides to

continue to cherish the memory of their love in prison: "Between grief and nothing I will take grief."

It is not easy to make parallel quotations from the story of the convict because he is not thoughtful or articulate. His motives must be judged largely from his actions, but the essential meaning his story embodies is clear enough; it may even be partially suggested by quotation:

> He wanted so little. He wanted nothing for himself. He just wanted to get rid of the woman, the belly . . .

Charlotte too wanted, she thought, very little:

> "I like bitching and making things with my hands. I don't think that's too much to be permitted to like, to want to have and keep."

The convict wants only to be rid of "the woman, the belly": responsibility for the continuance of life. Charlotte wants, and finally forces Wilbourne to perform, an abortion. Both "types of love" shed responsibility, deny or try to prevent consequences and connections. Both kinds are a flight, one into pure intensity of love experience, the other into a denial of personal relations. As the convict does his duty, thinking of his "responsibility" and his "honor," he reminds us of the old doctor and his wife in the first chapter of Wilbourne's story. Like them, he is "charitable" in the modern, depersonalized sense of the word, the sense that suggests money or effort given without any personal involvement with the recipient; but, like them again, his dutiful response lacks *caritas* or true compassion. Love romanticized, love avoided: both lead to death or imprisonment. So much, in bald and banal summary, we may say of the meaning that holds these two stories together, justifies their being considered as one work of art, and is created only by their interrelationships.

This theme is expressed, and qualified, enriched, in many aspects of the two stories but most clearly in the symbolic extensions of the settings. The river for the convict is alien (he has never seen it before; though he grew up within a few miles of it, he knows nothing of it), frustrating, seemingly malevolent: like the stormy sea in Stephen Crane's story, "The Open Boat," its maliciousness seems conscious, willful, directed at frustrating him. He knows the impulse of Crane's correspondent to throw bricks at the temple. The river is the "alien universe," a universe not created for man's good or comfort, which the convict did not know existed until now. The same feeling is expressed in the doctor's story by the wind in the wild palms. Wind, waste, wildness, desolation: the setting in both stories expresses, through flood or the tail end of a hurricane, the same lonely and precarious and doomed situation of man, tossed, swept, overwhelmed by forces hostile to the values man thinks he alone conceives and cherishes.

In the plots, too, though they are not literally connected, there are parallels. In both stories the characters endure terrible hardships and frustrations to be free—from love or for love. The convict paddles frenziedly and interminably to get

> where there would be people, houses, something, anything he might reach and surrender his charge to and turn his back on her forever, on all pregnant and female life forever and return to that monastic existence of shotguns and shackles where he would be secure from it.

Wilbourne and Charlotte struggle to be free from society's compulsions so that there may be nothing in their lives but love:

> You are born submerged in anonymous lockstep with the teeming and anonymous myriads of your time and generation . . .

Only by breaking free of the lockstep, they feel, can they achieve the fullness of love.

In both stories the characters feel that they are trapped, controlled by circumstances, by fate. Though the doctor's and Charlotte's primary antagonist is society, it soon turns out, when they have shed all social obligations and concerns, that there is a more formidable antagonist behind society. Accident governs, frustrating human purposes in both stories. Wilbourne meets Charlotte by accident and accidentally finds the money that enables them to go away; he thinks of Charlotte's pregnancy as an unlucky accident and her fatal sickness as another. This is the way the malignancy in things, symbolized for him in the sound of the wind in the palms, gets at you and destroys you. The convict felt the same way:

> It seemed to him that he had accidentally been caught in a situation in which time and environment, not himself, was mesmerized; he was being toyed with by a current of water going nowhere . . .

Both men, like Jason before them, come to feel that *time* is the key to success in their fight with circumstance. The convict battles the waters with almost incredible endurance and courage to get where there are people before the baby is born; Wilbourne races against the time when their money will be gone, the time when it will be too late to do an abortion, the time when Charlotte will be dead. For the convict: "Time: that was his itch now, so his only chance was to stay ahead of it as long as he could and hope to reach something before it struck." For Wilbourne, remembering Charlotte after her death: "the body, the broad thighs and the hands that liked bitching and making things. It seemed so little, so little to want, to ask. *With all the old graveward-creeping, the old wrinkled withered defeat . . .*"

Finally, it is not insignificant, trivial, as it has been suggested, that both plots end with the man in the state prison. Both men *choose* to go to prison, the convict when he was already free and would never have been searched for, having been listed as dead in the flood; the doctor after the means of suicide has been offered him. The one chooses prison to be free of entanglements, the other to keep love alive a little while longer by remembering. The convict expresses his reason for preferring prison to life outside in the final words of his story: " 'Women—!' the tall convict said." Wilbourne wonders about the possibility of survival after death but decides that it would, if it existed, not provide for survival of the kind of love to which he and Charlotte have dedicated themselves:

Because if memory exists outside of the flesh it wont be
memory because it wont know what it remembers so when
she became not then half of memory became not and if I
become not then all of remembering will cease to be.—Yes,
he thought, between grief and nothing I will take grief.

The stories end in antithetical parallelism with a thematic implication that is clear enough. The image of imprisonment not endured
but desired suggests a negative judgment of both men.

The atmosphere of the parallel stories is conspicuously similar.
One image in the story of the convict, when they see a burning
plantation house, epitomizes the atmosphere in both stories, in the
integral novel: "Juxtaposed to nowhere and neighbored by nothing
it stood, a clear steady pyre-like flame rigidly fleeing its own reflection, burning in the dusk above the watery desolation with a quality
paradoxical, outrageous and bizarre." The road on which the truck
travels at first dips below the water "like a flat thin blade slipped
obliquely into flesh by a delicate hand": the death and frustration
brought by the river appear before the river itself is seen.

The story of the doctor opens with Charlotte lying in the new
beach chair on the beach all day long, listening to the unceasing
wind and "watching the palm fronds clashing with their wild dry
bitter sound against the bright glitter of the water." Wilbourne, at
night, "could hear the black wind again, risible, jeering, constant,
inattentive, and it even seemed to him that he could hear the wild
dry clashing of the palms in it." Imagery of storm and flood, of
wild palms and wild waste waters, creates the atmosphere and
expresses a part of the theme in each story: "the smell and taste
and sense of wet and boundless desolation."

Once we have discerned some of the larger parallels between the
two stories, we may be tempted to look for more specific ones,
particularly in the two plots. If we look closely, we shall certainly
find some, though where just perception leaves off and sheer ingenuity takes over in such a search is a question that each reader
must answer for himself. Certainly there is a notable parallel between the doctor's performing an abortion and the convict's deliver-

ing a baby, and an antithesis between the doctor's flight from
society to the lake and later to the mine, and the convict's search
for signs of human habitation. And there are a good many other
analogous incidents of the sort, though I must confess I find them
in most cases of doubtful thematic significance.

But one final parallel, of clear symbolic import, must be men-
tioned. There is a striking similarity in the nature of the two men,
the doctor and the convict. Both are portrayed as innocents, trapped, taken in, because of their ignorance and naivete. If only the
convict had not believed the pulp magazines he would not have
tried to rob the train. He was taken in by robbery made to seem
both easy and romantic; his failure started the chain of circumstances that led to his choice of prison over freedom. If Wilbourne
had not been forced by his poverty to lead so narrow and monastic
a life in medical school, if he had had any experience at all with
women, he might not have become the fool of love; he might

> have discovered that love no more exists just at one spot
> and in one moment and in one body out of all the earth
> and all time and all the teeming breathed, than sunlight
> does.

Both are trapped by their lack of knowledge of the world.

The tones of the two stories are quite different. The story of the
doctor is told throughout in a tone immediate, compelling, realistic.
The antithetical story of the convict opens in a manner suggestive
of the recital of a legend, a tale remote and possibly fabulous:
"Once (it was in Mississippi, in May, in the flood year of 1927)
there were two convicts." The convict is referred to throughout
simply as "the convict," or, when he is with the other convicts, as
"the tall convict." One thinks of another realistic fable, *The Red
Badge of Courage.* The effect is to counter-balance the immediacy
with a kind of remoteness. *The Wild Palms* is written in counter-
point.

If this is so, it is not surprising that the deepest meaning of each
story emerges only as it is thought of in connection with the other.
Images of flight and search dominate the one work made from two

stories. The convict's struggle with and attempted flight from the river and the doctor's wish to escape from the sound of the wind in the palms suggest two different modern reactions to the concept of man's ultimate loneliness, the concept of the alien universe. He flees into romantic exaggeration both of personal emotion conceived as a wholly subjective value, and of freedom; or he flees into totalitarian security where there is no freedom and none of the agonizing responsibility which freedom entails.

The convict's effort to achieve a situation in which he cannot be disillusioned again, hurt again, is one with the primitivistic tendencies of Hemingway's stories, which, as Edmund Wilson said long ago, are true barometric indicators of the atmosphere of our times as well as, at their best, great works of art. The effort is essentially to reduce one's hopes and expectations, that one may not be disappointed: to adjust to a hard, a shrunken and threatening reality. This is why Hemingway's "aware" characters do not talk or think of "love" while they make love, or concern themselves with "ideal" values but fight and hunt and fish. They feel that they can cultivate well, "truly," what is left to them only by shrinking the area of their concern. Their effort is the same as that of the inarticulate convict who seeks inward peace and control by turning away from what he cannot control.

The doctor and Charlotte take another way, very different yet like in that it involves a sloughing off of responsibilities. They want to "burn with a hard, gem-like flame" in love. The romantic search for intensity of experience finds its culmination in their story. There is no time, they think, for the lesser values—children, the prosaic. They too, like the convict, are in flight from man's lonely and desperate situation in the world as he believes he has discovered it to be; but not only fleeing, searching too, searching for identity, integrity, real value.

There are perhaps reasons in the book why these themes—or any themes, any meanings—have not been recognized. I have tried to show that there are many connections between the two stories that have not generally been recognized, so that there is good reason

for reading the work as Faulkner intended we should. But I shall
not attempt to deny that there is a certain obscurity in the work as a
whole.

Whatever obscurity there is here springs in the first place I think
from a partial failure to achieve aesthetic distance in the chapters
telling the doctor's story. In the convict's story the distance comes
from the legendary tone more or less consistently maintained, but
in the doctor's story we sometimes feel that we are being asked to
identify very closely, with only intermittent reservations, with the
doctor and Charlotte. The reservations are there, as in the passage
I have already quoted about what the doctor might have recognized
about the nature of love if he had not been tricked by the poverty
of his experience; but on the whole he and Charlotte are treated so
sympathetically, so much from within their own point of view, that
we tend to feel that they must be wholly "sympathetic characters."
That they are not, that however much we may sympathize with
them in their suffering, we must hold to the judgment that their
effort has been misguided, doomed from the start and calculated to
bring just this kind of end to themselves and suffering to others, is
finally but by no means consistently clear.

The opening in particular renders this meaning obscure. The contrast between the lovers and the older doctor and his wife from
whom Wilbourne and Charlotte have rented the shore cottage is
calculated to put the reader's sympathy wholly on the side of the
lovers. Perhaps Faulkner thought that he had to do this to over-
come a conventional prejudgment against Charlotte and Wilbourne,
the sort of judgment that would condemn them for their selfishness
and their folly without ever examining their situation sympathetically to see what good reasons they might have for their actions.
But if so, I think the hand of the artist faltered here, by overemphasis, perhaps because while the head drew back from the
lovers' way, the heart was with them. At any rate, the old doctor
and his wife, who embody and represent society, convention, are
so unattractive that we feel immediately that the lovers *must* be
right if this is the only alternative, this puritanical fear of love and

life, this utter conventionality, this "provincial protestant" hostility to everything but a grimly conceived duty. There is no love at all here, illicit or otherwise, personal commitment or true *caritas*, only a dour puritanism. When the doctor's wife sends over the food to the lovers, the doctor knows that the action is an "uncompromising Christian deed performed not with sincerity or pity but through duty."

We may feel in this opening chapter that the contrast is too sharp and somehow false, the alternatives not comprehensive or complex enough. We do not really need to choose, we feel, between the old doctor and his wife's varicose-veined repression and the lovers' wild doomed romance. Of course, as I have tried to show, the novel does not finally mean that we should. On the contrary, it means that we in fact falsely do. But meanwhile we may have been misled, thrown off the track of meaning. Backwoods puritanical protestantism bulks too large as the alternative to personal enjoyment and beauty. Faulkner's Southern background occasionally works against him, as it usually works for him.

If we were really being asked to identify without significant reservations with Wilbourne and Charlotte, as the first chapter may make it seem, we should have to conclude that their story is intolerably romantic and sentimental. If there is a crucial weakness in the work it is here; and it springs, once again, from the difficulty Faulkner sometimes has in achieving distance from his characters. As Faulkner has said of the work, it was intended as

> One story—the story of Charlotte Rittenmeyer and Harry Wilbourne, who sacrificed everything for love, and then lost that. I did not know it would be two separate stories until after I had started the book. When I reached the end of what is now the first section of *The Wild Palms*, I realized suddenly that something was missing, it needed emphasis, something to lift it like counterpoint in music. So I wrote on the Old Man story until *The Wild Palms* story rose back to pitch.[7]

The story of Charlotte and Harry could rise "back to pitch" only with the achievement of greater aesthetic distance, which is certainly lacking in the first chapter. But it may be doubted that Faulkner's expedient was the best solution of this felt difficulty. The obscurity of the first chapter remains. Speculation may remove it, particularly if the speculation centers on what both internal and external evidence suggests is the intended meaning. But feeling continues to find it. We may conclude, I think, that only by making changes in the first chapter itself, not simply by writing a balancing chapter, could Faulkner have removed it. If one strand of a two-strand work is defective, the work as a whole must suffer.

To read *The Wild Palms* as it was written, then, is to discover sufficient unity to justify our speaking of it as one work, whether we want to call it one "novel" or not. But it is also to discover that the unity is primarily unity of theme, expressed chiefly, though not solely, through subtle parallels and contrasts that emerge from the imagery. The two distinct stories offer implied comments on each other; yet, since they never meet except at the end, there remains a sense in which we must say that the theme of the whole work is expressed without benefit of localized embodiment—except once and finally. Perhaps this means that the reader must here do part of the work which the novelist normally does for him. If so, the common opinion that the work as a whole is a failure is justified—provided we understand "failure" here to mean failure only by the highest standard of aesthetic achievement. This failure is more interesting, more alive, more rewarding in the whole complex experience we get from works of art, than most ordinary successes.

4

BOTH PYLON and *The Wild Palms* may profitably be thought of in connection with the work of Hemingway. In *Pylon* the fliers are like Hemingway's tough, laconic, hard-boiled, unconventional heroes and heroines, with the significant difference that they are seen from a distance, through the eyes of the reporter, whose first response is amazement. They are not caricatured, but they are certainly judged: they are different from us. After a while we discover, with the reporter, that they are "human," but we never see them as ideal. Faulkner's vision of life is a more social vision than Hemingway's. The negative judgment of the fliers, qualified but not cancelled by the sympathy felt for them, presupposes the importance of tradition and community. The fliers belong to no place, to no group except people like themselves who have cut all ties; in the sense that they measure time only by the demands of the air meets, they belong even to no time, no traditional, natural, seasonal, human time. They are man reduced to essentials, stripped of connections, without history. They are what many of Hemingway's early characters would look like if the power of his art, and the integrity and completeness in its own terms of his vision, did not compel us to look at them differently.

The more social nature of Faulkner's vision is as apparent in *The Wild Palms* as it is in *Pylon*. The doctor and Charlotte might be Frederick and Catherine, cutting all ties with a dishonest society, living two against the world, finding in love that which alone makes life worthwhile; they even try to find, in Utah, their clean cold place, their Switzerland. In contrast with the old doctor and his wife of the first chapter, they are Hemingway's "aware" characters, their courage and honesty growing precisely from their sense of the danger, the loneliness of man's situation, the lack of time for anything but the essential values. The sound of the wind in the wild palms reminds them, as the ants on the log reminded Frederick, that man is utterly lost unless he can *create* values in a world in which nothing is guaranteed except death. As we have seen, if the first chapter were all of the novel, something very like the Hemingway vision would take over and control the story, without the justification Hemingway gives it in his best work. But as we gain the perspective offered by the later chapters we come to see the doctor and Charlotte as heroic only in a misguided way, as "romantic" in a sense that carries overtones of negative judgment. They are finally no more idealized than is the convict, who, like a caricature of a Hemingway hero, chooses to give up much in order to be sure of something, to give up life and love in the threatening and apparently meaningless world so that he may enjoy his cigar and the quiet conversations in the evening in prison, "the cigar burning smoothly and richly in his clean steady hand, the smoke wreathing upward across his face saturnine, humorless, and calm."

Both *Pylon* and *The Wild Palms* deal with the threat of meaninglessness, in society and in nature itself, and with ways of meeting the threat. What amounts finally to dehumanization is one way, but not a way Faulkner asks us to admire. The comments on the modern world implied in *Pylon* and *The Wild Palms* help us to become more aware of what is admirable in the past of Yoknapatawpha and why it is that in the world of Faulkner's imagination there is finally no adequate substitute for "the old virtues."

CHAPTER 7

Past as Present

ABSALOM, ABSALOM!

ABSALOM, ABSALOM! HAS no close precedent, even in Faulkner's own works. Hindsight suggests now that much in modern fiction, and in modern opinion, should have prepared us for it, but it is not really surprising that most of the early reviewers were bewildered. Like *The Waste Land*, *Absalom* has many voices but no official, sanctioned Voice. The voices in it speak from many points of view, none of them removed from the criticism of irony. *Absalom* demonstrated once more Faulkner's artistic courage.

Compared with *Absalom*, *The Sound and the Fury* seems almost traditional. It shocks us at first by asking us to see the Compson world through the mind of an idiot for whom the present has reality chiefly as it reminds him of the past, and it takes us through two subsequent limited views of many of the same events before, in the last section, we come back again to the present to stay. Yet everything in the first three sections prepares us for the last, which corrects and completes them by centering on Dilsey. Nothing in what has preceded the last section, and nothing within it, undermines Dilsey's authority. Aesthetically, we are compelled to accept her and the criticism of the others which her character and actions imply.

In *Absalom* there is no Dilsey, or anything corresponding to her.

There is only Quentin, who speaks with no special authority, mostly in the words of others, and who does not act at all; and Shreve, who speaks as one amazed, even outraged, by a tale hard to credit and almost impossible to understand, and who, when he is not repeating what Quentin has told him, invents a version based on no uniquely privileged knowledge of the facts. Quentin and Shreve together finally imagine a version of Sutpen's story that has both plausibility and meaning, but the plausibility rests upon our willingness to accept as correct certain speculations of theirs for which they can offer no solid proof, and the meaning is left implicit, without even such partial dramatic statement as Dilsey gives to the meaning of the Compson story in her section of *The Sound and the Fury*.

Quentin has grown up with the Sutpen legend. He does not have to listen very closely to Miss Rosa Coldfield's retelling: he already knows not only the main plot but many of the sub-climaxes and lesser actors:

> His childhood was full of them; his very body was an empty
> hall echoing with sonorous defeated names; he was not a
> being, an entity, he was a commonwealth. He was a bar-
> racks filled with stubborn back-looking ghosts. . . .

Quentin has heard it before—and he will hear it again, from his father later on this same afternoon and later still from Shreve. He lacks only the sense of reality and meaning that neither Miss Rosa, with the bias created by her hatred of Sutpen, nor his father, with his surmises that are sometimes shrewd but sometimes wide of the mark, can give him. The fact about Sutpen's story that will not let Quentin rest is that everything is known about it except what is most important to know.

As Quentin tells his college roommate what he has been told and what he discovered for himself the night a few months before when he went to the ruined house with Miss Rosa, the two of them imaginatively recreate and relive Sutpen's story. The novel that emerges from their cooperative retelling has seemed to many readers best defined as a lyric evocation of the Southern past: the novel as poem. Quentin and Shreve retell the facts about Sutpen and his children in order to discover the feelings that can make the facts credible, rehearsing the deeds to discover the motives. The result is a kind of poem on time and death and the presentness of the past which seems so remote when we know only the "facts," a poem on the failure of the old order in the South, created by an evocation of the "ghosts" that have haunted Quentin's life. Quentin and Shreve are young, imaginative, easily moved to sympathetic identification. The joint product of their efforts, as they work with memory and imagination, evokes, in a style of sustained intensity of pitch, a feeling of the mystery and a sense of the pain and defeat of human life. It conveys its impressions through some of the most sharply realized images in modern writing in a rhetoric strained almost to the breaking point by an agony of identification with the suffering of the characters.

But *Absalom* cannot be completely understood in terms of this analogy with a lyric poem. The insight is useful in its pointing to pure evocation achieved through a strategy of indirection, but it leaves the central fact of the form of *Absalom*—its multiple retellings of what is in one sense already known and in another sense eludes knowing—unrelated to the feelings evoked and the meanings created by the form. Much of Faulkner's fiction may be called lyrical, and criticism today forces on us a recognition of the fact that all success-ful novels are in some sense like poems. The uniqueness of *Absalom* is not to be found here, so much as in the fact that it takes its form from its search for the truth about human life as that truth may be discovered by understanding the past, in which actions are com-plete, whole, so that we may put motive, deed, and consequence all into one picture.

Early in the book, as Quentin listens to Miss Coldfield, there is a passage which takes us some distance toward a recognition of the central theme and intent of the novel and suggests its strategy:

> Quentin seemed to see them, the four of them arranged into the conventional family group of the period, with formal and lifeless decorum, and seen now as the fading and ancient photograph itself would have been seen en-

larged and of whose presence there the voice's owner was
not even aware, as if she (Miss Coldfield) had never seen
this room before—a picture, a group which even to Quentin
had a quality strange, contradictory and bizarre; not quite
comprehensible. . . .

The whole effort of Quentin and Shreve, who end by becoming
twin narrators, is to comprehend what is "not quite comprehensible."
There is something in the picture "not (even to twenty) quite
right": they try to get it right, correcting each other's "faultings,"
sometimes supplying alternative explanations, imagining alternative
motives and actions, sometimes agreeing, as on Bon. What was true
for Quentin's father as he talked on the porch on that September
evening before Quentin went out to the old house with Miss Rosa
is only a little less true for Quentin and Shreve:

> It's just incredible. It does not explain. Or perhaps that's
> it: they don't explain and we are not supposed to know.
> We have a few old mouth-to-mouth tales; we exhume from
> trunks and boxes and drawers letters without salutation or
> signature, in which men and women who once lived and
> breathed are now merely initials or nicknames out of some
> now incomprehensible affection which sound to us like
> Sanskrit or Chocktaw; we see dimly people, the people in
> whose living blood and seed we ourselves lay dormant and
> waiting, in this shadowy attenuation of time possessing
> now heroic proportions, performing their acts of simple
> passion and simple violence, impervious to time and in-
> explicable. . . .

Quentin and Shreve think they know the answer to the question
that baffled Quentin's father at this point in his narration, but other
questions remain for them to speculate on. Their difficulty is not
in any paucity of "evidence"—of massed anecdote, belief, interpretation, even "facts," such as the letter Quentin has before him as they
talk and his memory of what he saw and heard on his trip with Miss
Rosa. Their difficulty lies in making the leap from facts, or what
they or someone else can only suppose to be facts, to understanding,
to insight, to meaning.

The story they finally put together is a product of their imagination working as best it can toward truth with the over-abundant, conflicting, and enigmatic material at hand. As bias is balanced against bias and distorted views give way to views with different distortions, fragmented and overlapping pictures of people and actions emerge from the multiple mirrors and screens of the telling. Then the fragments begin to fall into place for us and at last they cohere in a story possessing an immediacy, a distinctness of outline, and an evocativeness almost unparalleled in modern fiction. The dim ghosts evoked by Miss Rosa out of the distant past take on flesh and their actions finally take on meaning as we move from Miss Rosa's memories to Shreve's and Quentin's imaginings. A story is told, and a meaning expressed, despite a technique seemingly designed to delay the telling and withhold meaning.

There is a curious and significant relation between immediacy and meaning, on the one hand, and the number and complexity of the reflectors and screens, the "difficulties," on the other. "Then he thought *No. If I had been there I could not have seen it this plain.*" Quentin and Shreve are both troubled by the impossibility of checking in some incontrovertible way the correctness of their interpretations. All their reconstructions are prefaced by "as if," spoken or unspoken. Yet for the reader there is more lifelikeness in what Quentin and Shreve partly imagine than in what is "known" —as a comparison of Chapter Eight, presenting Bon from his own point of view as imagined by Shreve and Quentin, with Quentin's retelling of Miss Rosa's initial presentation of Sutpen, whom she had "known" very well indeed, will show. The implication is clear. An act of imagination is needed if we are to get at lifelike, humanly meaningful, truth; but to gain the lifelikeness we sacrifice the certainty of the publicly demonstrable. " 'Wait. You don't know whether what you see is what you are looking at or what you believe. Wait.' "

In the language of science, the experimenter is not passive in his experiment; his nature and purposes not irrelevant to his results. Shreve and Quentin supplement and correct each other; and Shreve,

Quentin, and the reader join with Miss Rosa and Quentin's father and grandfather in a joint effort to understand Sutpen and search out what is hidden. Sutpen cannot be questioned, and Quentin's experience in the house has to be understood in relation to matters that cannot be known with certainty; and then it becomes hardly distinguishable from what has been posited, imagined. The tale that finally takes shape in the mind of the reader of *Absalom* is in several senses a cooperative construct—not a figment or a fantasy but something creatively discovered.

As it may be said of the naturalistic novel that it attempted to probe behind conventional interpretations and values to get at "fact," so it may be said of *Absalom* that it tries to get behind not only received interpretations but the public facts themselves to get at what Faulkner has called in the introduction to "Monk" in *Knight's Gambit,* "credibility and verisimilitude." One of the meanings of *Absalom* is that the central effort of the naturalistic novel, to transfer a "slice of life" onto the printed page without any shaping act of imagination, interpretation, and judgment, is impossible. It is impossible not because the sacrifice of art to truth is too great a price to pay but because without the kind of imaginative effort and creation we find always at the center of art, there is not only no art but no truth.

2

THE COMPLICATIONS of the telling can be clarified somewhat if we think of the basic story—Sutpen, from his early youth through the death of his remaining son and half-Negro daughter—as having not one but several narrative frames. The telling of the story by Quentin to Shreve—and partly later by Shreve to Quentin—makes the frame which encloses all the others. But this telling and retelling is based on versions of the same story, or of parts of it, given to Quentin by Miss Rosa and father; and father's version is based in large part on a version given him by his father, who got it in part from Sutpen himself. Since in Quentin's version each of these people speaks in his own voice, often at great length and circumstantially, with unintended revelation of himself in the process, what we have in effect is a series of frames, one within the other, like the picture of a picture containing a picture, and so on.

The outer frame, the telling of the story within the present of the novel—not the present of the first chapter, which is a memory of a day some four months before—takes place in Quentin's college room at Harvard in January, 1910. At first Quentin is alone, reliving in memory that afternoon in Miss Rosa's house and the later talk of Sutpen by his father. Then Shreve comes in and together they go over the story once more, with Shreve doing much of the talking, basing his version on what Quentin has already told him and using his imagination to fill the gaps. When they come to Bon's part of the story they are in perfect agreement, though about Bon and his motives and character they know less than about anyone else. Finally they go to bed and Quentin relives in memory once more the evening with Miss Rosa at the Sutpen house of which he has already told Shreve. This Shreve-Quentin frame is the largest and most distant of the frames.

In the first chapter then we begin where memory intersects the past at a point very close to the present, with Quentin becoming actively involved in the story whose general outline he has known for as long as he can remember. Almost at once we move back into the more distant past with Miss Rosa, without however being allowed to forget the present (now already past) in which Quentin sits in the stifling room and listens. Then this frame, this telling, is replaced by a frame supplied by father's account of Sutpen and his speculations on the meaning of the letter he gives Quentin. Again we move back and forth between past and present—the present of the telling, which is already past by the time we are able to identify it. Then the absoluteness of this frame too is destroyed and we see father's telling of the story as only another version, and not without its distortions. Shreve and Quentin talking in their college dormitory room now supply the frame to replace Miss Rosa in her "office" and father on the gallery. Miss Rosa's inadequacy as interpreter—her bias—has been apparent all along, and now it becomes clear that some of father's interpretations and speculations too are unacceptable: ". . . neither Shreve nor Quentin believed that the visit affected Henry as Mr. Compson seemed to think . . ." But on another matter, " 'maybe this was one place where your old man was right.' " As the frames are shifted and the implicit distortions discovered, we see the motive for the continual retelling. Each new version is a part of the search in which Quentin and Shreve involve the reader, the search for a truth beyond and behind distortion.

So the past has to be continually reinterpreted; and each reinterpretation becomes a part of the accumulating past; a part even of the past which it attempts to interpret. A knowledge of the end supplies the motive for the search for the beginning: the earliest part of the story—Sutpen's boyhood and young manhood before he came to Jefferson—is retold by Quentin, as his father had told him, in response to Shreve's reaction to Miss Rosa's completed story of the "demon." Perhaps the demon could be understood if we knew what made him as he was. So the telling circles in on the story from a different angle—Sutpen's own account, multiply filtered, of his past and his intentions. The motive for the retellings, the reinterpretations, each of which adds new facts as well as a new perspective and makes necessary a reinterpretation of the facts already known, is constant, and it supplies the organizing principle of the novel.

3

SHREVE'S ROLE as interpretive listener and finally as partial narrator is crucial. By the time we discover his presence we are more than halfway through the book and we realize now that both Miss Rosa's telling and father's retelling are part of the past which Shreve and Quentin have rehearsed. Now a new frame, more distant from Sutpen, comes into focus. As father had been less intimately involved in the Sutpen story than Miss Rosa, so Shreve the Canadian is less involved than father. The movement is one of progressive disengagement, a moving outward from the center. Yet the parts of the story that Shreve retells are among the most vivid and circumstantial in the whole book. Shreve's imagination moves freely. His presence in the story makes possible the widest of the circling movements through which the subject is approached.

In one of his recapitulations, Shreve calls Sutpen, in a caricature of Miss Rosa's own words, "this Faustus, this demon, this Beelzebub . . . who appeared suddenly one Sunday with two pistols and twenty subsidiary demons," thus reducing Sutpen to ordinary size by his humorous exaggeration and offering an implicit comment on Miss Rosa's "demonizing." His humorous summary follows immediately after a recital calculated to make us feel the weight and at least the partial justice of Miss Rosa's terms. Shreve's presence in the book is one of the ways in which the tone is controlled.

Shreve puts Sutpen's whole story in another kind of perspective when he says, toward the end, " 'So he just wanted a grandson . . . That was all he was after. Jesus, the South is fine, isn't it. It's better than the theater, isn't it. It's better than Ben Hur, isn't it.' " *Absalom* has been called Gothic and obsessive, but true Gothic cannot survive irony, and obsession does not admit criticism. Here the irony and the criticism are central. When Shreve speaks of "the money, the jack, that he (the demon) has voluntarily surrendered" his very language, even when he is not offering any explicit comment, provides a perspective that can come only with distance and that could not come from Quentin, who is part and product of what he is telling.

As Quentin and Shreve sit "in the now tomblike air,"

> the two of them creating between them, out of the rag-tag and bob-ends of old tales and talking, people who perhaps had never existed at all anywhere . . .

what emerges is substantially different from what would have
emerged had there been no Shreve for Quentin to talk and listen to.
In the context of the passage I have just quoted we don't know for
sure that there *was* a dishonest lawyer who had private reasons for
wanting Bon to come in contact with his father, Sutpen, much less
that the reasons Shreve is giving for the posited lawyer's actions
are the true ones. But we are ready now, prepared by the inter-
change between Quentin and Shreve, to speculate with them, to
invent probable characters and fill in details to make the story, the
given incomprehensible facts, plausible. This is one of the most
extreme examples of the conjectural method of the whole search that
Quentin and Shreve are engaged in; and it is made to seem natural,
right, because Shreve, who cannot be accused of excessive closeness
to the material, offers the speculation.

In the last chapter Shreve's presence becomes decisive. He speaks
for most readers when he says

> We don't live among defeated grandfathers and freed
> slaves . . . and bullets in the dining room table and such, to
> be always reminding us to never forget . . . a kind of en-
> tailed birthright father and son and father and son of never
> forgiving General Sherman . . .

This would be a peculiar sort of comment for one of the two narrators to make at a climactic point if there were as little aesthetic
distance in *Absalom* as some have said. In Shreve's definition of
the difference between his own Canadian background and Quentin's
Southern one there is an implied comment on Sutpen's story that
Quentin would have been incapable of making. Not that Shreve
is right and Quentin wrong, but that Shreve's is another, and clarify-
ing, point of view. "You cant understand it," Quentin tells Shreve.
"You would have to be born there." To which a comment Shreve
makes later, on another matter, could serve as a partial reply: "The
South. Jesus. No wonder you folks all outlive yourselves by years
and years and years."

And it is Shreve who at the end offers the prediction that "the
Jim Bonds are going to conquer the western hemisphere" and asks

Quentin why he hates the South. Shreve adds distance, controlling
irony, to a story that otherwise might be obsessive or too shrill. If
his final question to Quentin is, perhaps, somewhat unprepared for,
so that we may find the ironic effect a little forced at this point,
nevertheless he discharges his crucial function in the story with
wonderful economy. His point of view is not the final one because
there is no final one explicitly stated anywhere in the book. There
are only other points of view and the implications of the form of
the whole.

4

IN THE ABSENCE of chronologically related plot as the controlling
factor, the relations of points of view govern the order of the
chapters. Chapter One is Miss Rosa's. Miss Rosa lives in the past,
in the cherishing of her hatred and her frustration. Quentin is
restive as he listens, not only because of the heat, and partly dis-
counts what she tells him. Her view of the past is simple, moralistic,
and, to Quentin, quite incredible. For her Sutpen was an evil man,
satanic, with no redeeming qualities.

The next three chapters are Quentin's father's. His point of view
is that of the interested but emotionally uninvolved rational observer. Unlike Miss Rosa, father is impressed by the mystery of
human action and frequently confesses himself baffled in his search
for understanding. If he is biased in any way it is slightly in Sutpen's
favor, partly because the town condemned Sutpen and father is an
iconoclast who has little respect for conventional opinion, partly
because much of his information he got from his father, who was
Sutpen's one friend in the community, the only one willing to
defend him against outraged public opinion.

Chapter Five is Miss Rosa's again. We are now prepared for a
verbatim report of a part of what she said to Quentin that afternoon.
Miss Rosa, it is clearer now, not only hates Sutpen but judges him
from a point of view not wholly distinct from his own. Sutpen's

actions destroyed not only his "design"—his plan for his life, his purpose—but hers. She shares, it begins to appear, both his racial and his class prejudices, and she hates him chiefly because he destroyed for her that social eminence, respectability, and security which it was the aim of his design to secure for himself and his posterity. Yet though we recognize and allow for her obsessive hatred, we learn much from her account that we should not otherwise know, and we cannot entirely discount her judgment.

Chapter Six is Shreve's retelling of what Quentin has told him of what Quentin's father has told Quentin. Shreve keeps calling Miss Rosa "Aunt Rosa": he does not quite understand, and he is not concerned to try to master, the details of Southern kinship ties and class etiquette. He sees "this old dame," Miss Rosa, and her tale without any of Quentin's painfully mixed feelings, simply with astonishment verging on incredulity. The snow on Shreve's overcoat sleeve suggests the distance from which he views this tale which began for us in the "long still hot weary" afternoon when Quentin sat with Miss Rosa. And Shreve himself, with his ruddy vitality, contrasts sharply with the other narrators—with the passive Quentin and with Miss Rosa herself, whose very existence seems a mere "disturbance" of the dust of that "dead September afternoon."

Parts of Sutpen's story have been told and retold now from points of view both hostile and friendly or neutral, by narrators within his own culture, and again from a point of view entirely external. How did he view himself? What would be added to our knowledge of him and his motivations if we could share his own self-awareness? Chapter Seven gives us Sutpen's story, the first part of it largely in a paraphrase of his own statements and some of it in his own words, as he told it to Quentin's grandfather—and as grandfather told it to father and father told it to Quentin and Quentin told it to Shreve: there is no certainty even in *ipsissima verba*, no possibility of getting back to "the thing in itself" of Sutpen's consciousness.

Sutpen saw himself alternately in the role of innocence betrayed and the role of a man who had made some mistake in adding a row of figures. Grandfather does not question his self-evaluation, simply passes it on. We are given almost no reason and very little opportunity, within the early part of this chapter, to question Sutpen or to step outside his frame of reference. The poor child who had been turned away from the door of the rich man's house conceived a design for his life calculated to put him in a position where he could never again be humiliated by anyone. Since he could see that the rewards in life went to the "courageous and shrewd" and since, though he felt sure he had courage, he had failed in his design, he must have made a mistake, a miscalculation somewhere. What could it be?

Toward the end of the chapter there is, not negative moral judgment and certainly not Miss Rosa's hatred of Sutpen, but a kind of neutral clarification of Sutpen's own story offered in the comments of Quentin prompted by the interruptions of Shreve. Quentin interprets the "design" as essentially "getting richer and richer" and the innocence as a kind of moral obtuseness:

> that innocence which believed that the ingredients of morality were like the ingredients of pie or cake and once you had measured them and balanced them and mixed them and put them into the oven it was all finished and nothing but pie or cake could come out.

Quentin's father, on whose report Quentin is drawing here, sees Sutpen as "fogbound by his own private embattlement of personal morality" but he seems to accept Sutpen's idea that his design was created solely for the "vindication" of "that little boy who approached that door fifty years ago and was turned away." He gives us Sutpen's climactic question to grandfather without indicating that he thinks we should have to redesign it to make it ask another question, with different assumptions in it, before we could answer it:

> 'You see, I had a design in my mind. Whether it was a good or a bad design is beside the point; the question is, Where did I make the mistake in it. . . .'

Most of the material of this chapter comes ultimately from grandfather, who was not only Sutpen's "advocate" but the only one in

Jefferson who knew about the past which had shaped him to be what he was. Since this report of Sutpen's history has the additional advantage, if "inside knowledge" is an advantage, of resting on Sutpen's own self-awareness, it constitutes an effective foil to the "demonizing" of Miss Rosa, through whom we first met Sutpen.

Chapter Eight is Bon's chapter, his story (and Henry's, but chiefly his) as interpreted sympathetically by Shreve and Quentin. Shreve is no longer amused, ironic. He has been drawn into the tale now: this is a part he can feel, thinks he can understand. And for the first time he and Quentin are in complete agreement in their interpretive reconstructions. It no longer matters who is speaking: each is capable of taking up where the other left off, completing the other's thought. This is the most direct and circumstantial segment of the whole tale. It might be called interpretation by immersion, or by empathy. It penetrates Bon's consciousness to discover his point of view, reporting his experiences in detail, complete with imaginary conversations for which there is no warrant in the literally known facts. In place of Miss Rosa's bald summaries of Sutpen's whole career, mingled with moral judgments, we have here a detailed "realistic" rendering of the qualitative aspects of a few of Bon's experiences. There is no certainty, of course, that Shreve and Quentin are right in the details of their reconstruction. They are biased, for one thing, being young like Bon and easily aroused to sympathy by the spectacle which the idea of him presents. And they are relatively uninformed, for another thing; there are some very crucial facts that they cannot know for sure, such as when Bon told Henry, if in fact he did tell him, that he was not only his half brother but was part Negro. Yet the reader is led by the circumstantial solidity of this chapter to feel more certain that this sympathetic account of Bon is correct than he is of any other interpretation he has encountered so far in the book.

Chapter Nine presents what might be called a general perspective on the whole tale. We are beyond the uniquely biased views of those who were closest to Sutpen. Two things happen at this point. First, Quentin and Shreve come into the foreground of the picture explicitly as narrators. No longer merely voices speaking to us in the words of the past, chiefly through direct and indirect quotation, they now appear as preservers of a past which must in some degree be created in order to be perserved. We are told more of Quentin's immediate sensations than we have been told before. The afternoon in Miss Rosa's house when she talked to Quentin in the office seems far away, as though it were as remote in time as in space. Miss Rosa is dead, and we recall from her tale chiefly a sense of the "victorious dust" that her recital made Quentin think of at the time. All those able to speak from direct knowledge of Sutpen are now gone; all that remains is the mutual creative remembering of Quentin and Shreve.

The second thing that happens is that as the appearance of objectivity evaporates the "facts" come back into focus and we move out again from subjective to objective. We learn for the first time in this last chapter what Quentin experienced that night when he went with Miss Rosa to Sutpen's decaying mansion. Everything before this has been hearsay, rumor, conjecture, hypothesis, or, at best, biased accounts of matters of fact. Here we are in the presence of something that we know "really happened," the terrible culmination of the Sutpen story. We are in a position to understand and to respond emotionally and imaginatively. Quentin does not need to theorize, or even create an atmosphere. The bare, elliptical, subjective record, the fragmentary memory, of what happened that night is enough. Without what has preceded the record would be meaningless. We now see that Quentin had to prepare Shreve for this direct confrontation with the living past; that any literal-minded insistence on "sticking to the facts," would have made it impossible for these facts, the only ones connected with Sutpen that Quentin can be absolutely sure of from personal experience, to convey any meaning.

Though Quentin's meeting with Henry is the one thing in the novel which may conceivably justify a charge of pointless mystification—why are we not told what Quentin learns from Henry?—yet I think the bareness of this climactic episode suggests its own justification. This meeting was a confrontation with a flesh-and-blood ghost. Here is proof that the past is "real" (though not yet, for Quentin at the time, explicable). This is the shock that motivates the search for understanding. In giving us the incident only in the barest outline, Faulkner is following the Jamesian formula of making the reader imagine. By the time we come to the episode in the book we have plenty of material for the imagination to work with. We discover, better than if we were told, that the past is still alive, still with us, demanding to be understood.

We end, in this last chapter, sharing Quentin's and Shreve's certainty about just two other matters of the first importance: that Sutpen brought his destruction upon himself, and that Bon asked only for recognition. But the first of these certainties rests upon the second, and the second is itself "certain" only if we either decide to trust Quentin and Shreve to be right or if we have so far shared their imaginative adventure as to arrive with them at the same conclusion. It is, at any rate, beyond proof. The whole meaning of Sutpen's history hangs on this leap of the imagination.

5

BUT ABSALOM, ABSALOM! is not an exercise in perspectivist history, it is a novel; it tells a story. Each chapter contributes something to our knowledge of the action. It is true that we know something of the end of the story before we know the beginning, but what we know of the end is tantalizingly incomplete until we get to the end of the book; and what we know of the beginning of Sutpen's story, by the end of the book, could not have been understood earlier. If tricks are being played with time here, if the form is less conspicuously temporal than spatial or conceptual, it is not in the interest of obscuring the story but of making possible an existential understanding of it.

The versions of the Southern past that Quention has grown up with he recognizes as inadequate, but he is not interested in adding to them one more subjective version, his own. What he is interested in is "the truth." But the truth, he discovers, and we discover with him, is no rabbit to be pulled out of the hat by some sleight of hand. The traditional novelist's pretense of omniscience could be kept up only so long as Miss Rosa's view of life obtained. Just because Quentin is interested in truth he must reject too simple a view of it. The "spatial" form of the novel *is*, from one point of view, *symbolizes*, from another, Quentin's probing beyond and behind appearances to get at reality. *Absalom* is conspicuously an orderly book, but the order in it springs from within, from the human need and effort to understand, not from anything external to itself. It substitutes an aesthetic and human order for temporal order. The result is a story inseparable from its meanings.

But the screens, the baffles that keep us from getting directly at the facts, are not only thematically expressive, they serve a more elementary, but indispensable, need of fiction. They do not lessen but increase the suspense. We learn in the first chapter, for instance, that Sutpen must have said or done something outrageously shocking to Miss Rosa to precipitate her departure from his house. We do not learn what it was until much later, but meanwhile we have never been allowed entirely to forget it. Again, we hear of Wash Jones early as an ill-mannered "poor white" who brought Miss Rosa the news of Bon's death. We learn later that he was responsible for Sutpen's death, but not how. We find out later still something of the manner of the death, hearing of the rusty scythe. But only toward the end do we witness the death itself, one of the great scenes in literature. Meanwhile our conception of Jones has been growing so that by the time we see him kill Sutpen we are prepared to see the action of this grim and silent avenger as both psychologically motivated and far-reaching in its symbolic implications. Our knowing ahead of time something of what would happen—as though we had a premonition at once certain and indistinct—has not lessened but actually increased the impact of the scene.

The characters of *Absalom* grow, emerge and develop, as we catch glimpses of them from different angles. When we finally confront

Judith directly, after we already know the outline of her life, we are prepared to feel her few words and actions reverberating in areas that would have been closed to us without the preparation. She has become a figure of tragic proportions. The fluid and subjective quality of *Absalom's* sifting of memory implies no diminution or beclouding of the world of significant action.

6

IF SHREVE and Quentin are right in their sympathetic estimate of Bon, then the immediate cause of the tragic events that resulted in the failure of Sutpen's design was his refusal to recognize his part-Negro son. Bon, Shreve and Quentin both believe, would have given up Judith and gone away if he had had any sign at all from his father, even the most private and minimal acknowledgment of their relationship. Shreve and Quentin cannot be sure that they are right. If they are wrong and Bon was a conscienceless extortioner, then the failure of Sutpen's design was caused, not by moral failure but as he himself thought, by ignorance, by the simple fact of his not knowing when he married her that Bon's mother was part Negro.

The title of the book, with its Biblical allusion, supports the hypothesis of Shreve and Quentin. Sutpen would not say "My son" to Bon as David said it to Absalom even after Absalom's rebellion. And different as he was from his father, Henry acted in the end on the same racist principle, killing Bon finally to prevent not incest but miscegenation. One meaning of *Absalom* then is that when the Old South was faced with a choice it could not avoid, it chose to destroy itself rather than admit brotherhood across racial lines.

But the theme is broader and deeper than the race problem which serves as its vehicle and embodiment. Sutpen was a cold and ruthless man motivated by a driving ambition to be his own god. His intelligence and courage won him a measure of success, but his pride destroyed him. In Martin Buber's contemporary terminology, for Sutpen other people were objects to be manipulated, related to him in an "I-it" relation. He not only never achieves, he never once even approaches, an "I-Thou" relation. Sutpen was the new man, the post-Machiavellian man consciously living by power-knowledge alone, refusing to acknowledge the validity of principles that he cannot or will not live by and granting reality to nothing that cannot be known with abstract rational clarity. He lives by a calculated expediency.

Sutpen the rationalist and positivist would have agreed with a pronouncement in a recent book-length attack on the Christianity of Eliot and other modern writers, that "Progress for the whole human race would be, if not inevitable, at least highly probable, if a sufficient majority of people were trained to use their reasoning power on their general experience, as a scientist is trained to use his reasoning power on his special experience."[1] Sutpen of course was not so much interested in the progress of "the whole human race" as he was in the progress of Sutpen, but there the difference ends. When he came to grandfather to review his life he was concerned to discover not which of his actions had been morally right and which wrong but where he had made the mistake which kept them from being, as modern scienteers would say, "effective." "Whether it was a good or a bad design is beside the point." When he put away Bon's mother, his first wife, on discovering her taint of Negro blood, he did so, he told grandfather later, because he found her "unsuitable to his purpose"—that is, ineffective for the forwarding of his intelligently conceived plan. Later he could calculate no advantage to be gained by recognizing Bon as his son, and he was not one to be moved by the incalculable. There is point as well as humor in Shreve's characterization of him as Faustus. He is also related to Ahab and Ethan Brand.

The total form of the novel implies the ultimate reason for the failure of Sutpen's design.[2] Considered as an integral symbol the form of *Absalom* says that reality is unknowable in Sutpen's way, by weighing, measuring, and calculating. It says that without an "unscientific" act of imagination and even of faith—like Shreve's and

Quentin's faith in Bon—we cannot know the things which are most worth knowing. Naturally Sutpen failed in his design, and naturally he could not imagine where his error had been. His error had been ultimately, of course, in the moral sense, that he had always treated people as things. Even Bon falls into the same error when he tries to use Judith as a lever to move Sutpen, to get recognition.

Absalom also has implications about the nature and role of history that are worthy of further thought. Quentin's effort to understand Sutpen is an attempt to interpret all history, man's history. Quentin encounters two conflicting modes of interpretation, is satisfied by neither, and creates, with Shreve, a third that has some of the features of both.

Miss Rosa's interpretation epitomizes the traditional views with which Quentin has grown up. This "demonizing," this interpretation in terms of inflexible moral judgment, does not, to his mind, explain: the past remains incredible and unreal. Nor is he satisfied by his father's view that there is no meaning at all in history, that the only proper response is to call it a mystery that we are "not meant to understand." Father is as close to nihilism here as he was in *The Sound and the Fury*. Between Miss Rosa's belief that Southern history was God's punishment of the South, and of herself in particular—precisely for *what* she is unable to imagine—and father's denial of any intelligibility, Quentin is unable to choose.

The view that he and Shreve together work out has in common with these two views more than its tragic cast. Implicitly—and unlike Miss Rosa's and father's views the final one in the book is wholly implicit—they find room for moral judgment: Sutpen's *hubris*, his narrow rationalism, his lack of love, all these are descriptions that imply the relevance of moral judgment. But Quentin and Shreve do not categorize Sutpen as simply a "bad" man: they know that to do so is to substitute judgment for explanation. With father they feel the mystery of human life, but they are not satisfied cynically to give up the effort to understand. The view in terms of which they operate is that of classical-Christian tragedy, at once Greek and Biblical: history contains both God's judgment and man's decision, both necessity and freedom, and it has sufficient intelligibility for our human purposes. But its meaning is neither given nor entirely withheld. It must be achieved, created by imagination and faith. Historical meaning is a construct.

Such a view of history contrasts sharply with Marxist and "scientific" theories of history, but it has much in common with the best historiography of the thirties and of our own time. It has in it something of the historical relativism of the school of Beard and Becker. Becker's presidential address to the American Historical Association in 1931 criticized simplistic notions of historical "fact." Robinson's "new history," more than a decade older than *Absalom,* had been an attack on "scientific" history. More recently, Herbert Butterfield's essays on the philosophy of history, in *History and Human Relations* and *Christianity and History,* are written in terms of assumptions perfectly consistent with those that are operative in *Absalom.* Oscar Handlin's recent *Chance or Destiny: Turning Points in American History* brilliantly displays the interpretive possibilities which a creative search like that of Quentin and Shreve may offer. As a novel built from the clash of conflicting views of history, *Absalom* seems to me as relevant now as when it was written.

No doubt *Absalom* gets its chief effect as a novel from our sense that we are participating in its search for the truth. *Absalom* draws us in, makes us share its creative discovery, as few novels do. The lack of an authoritative voice puts a greater burden on us as readers than we may want to bear. Faulkner ran this risk when he wrote it. He has had to wait long for a just appreciation of its greatness. Few readers were ready for it in the thirties. But if we can and will bear our proper burden as readers we shall find the rewards correspondingly great.

Absalom is the novel not denying its status as fiction but positively enlarging and capitalizing upon it. It appropriately closes Faulkner's period of most rapid and successful productivity with a full-scale thematic exploration of what had been implied in all the major works so far: that fiction is neither lie nor document but a kind of knowledge which has no substitute and to which there is no unimaginative shortcut. Adding to this the implication that fiction is not unique in its dependence upon imagination and the necessary deviousness of its strategy, it suggests a view of life that Faulkner was to make increasingly explicit in later works.

CHAPTER 8

Present as Past

THE UNVANQUISHED
THE HAMLET

FAULKNER'S CRITICS HAVE NOT liked *The Unvanquished*. Seeing the book only as "a group of stories" without essential unity except that given it by its closeness to "the romancing of popular Southern fiction," they have found it of slight consequence, "the least serious" of Faulkner's works.[1] What they take to be its presentation of "the Southern myth" without criticism makes them uneasy; only in the last story of the book does Faulkner seem even to his most sympathetic critics to have moved beyond "slick magazine stereotypes."

But it may be not that the book lacks unity but that we have failed to see the unity, not that it presents the Southern past uncritically but that we have failed to identify the criticism, not that it is weakly romantic and heroic but that we have failed to see the function of the romantic and heroic in a unified work. The minority report that follows will argue that *The Unvanquished* deserves to be called a "novel" as much as *The Hamlet* does, that it develops a serious theme throughout, not just in its last story, and that it has been seriously misunderstood and consequently undervalued.[2]

2

SOME OF Faulkner's critics seem happy only when he is most critical of the Southern past: they like "An Odor of Verbena," which shows young Bayard Sartoris becoming critical.[3] But the point of Bayard's criticism of the code rests upon a perception of what that code is and what value it has. For Bayard's criticism was more a reinterpretation leading to a reaffirmation than it was a flat rejection. The young Bayard who became the old banker of *Sartoris* did not reject the South, the past, or the Southern past. He modified a code to bring it into better relationship with living conditions. By so doing he effectively, for himself at least, preserved it.

The Unvanquished begins as a record, taking the form of objective memory, a reliving without criticism or interpretation, with only a sense of urgency, of poignance, imparted by the fact that all this is *remembered,* a reliving of a boy's experiences as he grows up during and just after the Civil War. What he discovers when he is grown up, a student in college—that there is something false about the heroics of Drusilla, for instance—is not read back into the memories of earlier, boyhood experiences. It could not be without falsifying the character of the boy, destroying the very innocence of his experiences which is the necessary basis for the book's theme. It could of course have been done in a different book, with a critically mature reflector as narrator, but it could not have been done from within the mind and experience of young Bayard in any other way but this. To complain that there are different points of view in *The Unvanquished,* and that the point of view of the early stories is uncritical, is rather like complaining that in Hemingway's *In Our Time* there is a difference between the points of view of "Indian Camp" and that of "Big Two-Hearted River," the first presenting Nick as a child, the last as a young man returning to the home country with his memories.

Like *In Our Time, The Unvanquished* gives us a boy's discovery of his world, and his reaction to it and criticism of it. Nick Addams discovers chiefly violence and chaos and death and a failure of courage and of meaning, except insofar as he himself can learn how to impose or create meaning. Bayard discovers a unified conception of man and a code of action, a conception and a code that can be criticized just because they are coherent and meaningful even if, ultimately, partially unacceptable. The code puts a high value on personal honor, on integrity, especially on courage; it breeds violence, but not uncontrolled or merely meaningless violence. As Drusilla says to Bayard, "There are worse things than being killed." Where Nick Addams finds no code, unless hypocrisy be called a code, and seeks to make one for himself, Bayard grows up with one that is at first merely experienced and later criticized.

Bayard as a small boy lives with the code without recognizing it as a code, seeing his father as the embodiment of heroism and accepting and depending upon the courage and integrity and unflinching sense of duty of Granny, Rosa Millard. In her the code is presented as functional, though finally corrupted. Then he stands off and looks at the code in operation, recognizing it as a standard embodied in the actions of both his father and Drusilla, a standard which is implicitly criticized by the act of mere recognition: it is not inevitable, but a possible way of acting. Finally, he dissociates himself from the decadence of the code—Drusilla handing him the pistols—but only to be true to its reinterpreted essence in a way that Drusilla's uncritical theatricality is not. Walking into Redmond's office unarmed, he at once proves his courage—the value most prized by the code of Drusilla—and his sense of reality, his awareness of new times and conditions and of the demands of other values.

With the help of Miss Jenny, Bayard has come to see that the courage so highly prized by the old code would not always stand up under close inspection. Like the daring of the blockade runners Miss Jenny tells him about, it often depended on there being "no bloody moon." Bayard wants to exhibit a courage that can stand the light of greater awareness and broader and deeper sympathies.

He does what he thinks is called for by such a conception of courage and thus keeps the old code, fructified by new insight, alive. The early stories in the book do not indicate Faulkner's "acceptance" of the romance of the old South, nor does the last story indicate his rejection. The book is not so simple, either way.

In a sort of shorthand notation, we may say that the general thematic movement in the stories is from a presentation of the code in its functional integrity (Granny confronting the Union officer while hiding the boys) to a presentation of the beginning of its corruption (Granny moving from stealing the mules of the enemy to trying to steal the horses of Grumby) to a presentation of its extravagant and unintelligent application (Drusilla on the steps in a yellow gown with the light behind her) to a critical disengagement of its meaning from its forms (Bayard going to Redmond). Granny Millard personified, at first, the best in the code. Drusilla caricatures and corrupts it by her very insistence on preserving its forms without criticism. Bayard, disenchanted, purifies it. We could not very well understand "An Odor of Verbena" without understanding in some degree all that is recalled to Bayard by the fragrance that becomes for him so powerful a stimulus to memory, so poignant a natural sign; and neither Drusilla's undoubted courage nor her violation of the code in her invitation to Bayard to adultery with his father's wife would be understandable in their full significance without the earlier stories.

Naturally, then, the early stories have about them a kind of romantic air. They are told not only from within the mind of a boy but in terms of what Bayard once calls "a boy's affinity for smoke and fury and thunder and speed." In them, Bayard still identifies the code with the image of his idolized father. Some of them, notably "Raid," have something of the character of "tall tales"—or perhaps of a family legend retold many times and exaggerated in the telling. They sometimes carry an air of fiction, of make-believe, that is usually rare in Faulkner, even when more bizarre or improbable things are being related than are pictured here. But unless we insist on a realistic tone everywhere, regardless of what is going on formally and thematically, we shall not jump to the conclusion that these early stories are inferior because "romantic."

A part of their meaning is contributed by this "romantic"—or, perhaps better, idyllic—atmosphere. These are memories of the long-ago, old glamorous times before reason and criticism did their work. Perhaps the code—with its conception of an unfragmented, undissipated man—was once adequate, perhaps not. Bayard cannot know, for by the time he was called upon to act responsibly in its terms and found it necessary to act differently from the way Drusilla and Wyatt expected, he could not be sure whether Drusilla and Wyatt were adequate interpreters of the old code. But though he cannot be sure that he is right, he increasingly suspects that the glamour is based on injustice, the heroism mixed and sometimes primitive, the romance the result of distance and a child's perspective. Just to what extent these corrosive suspicions are justified is precisely what Bayard cannot discover: he knows now that actually his father was a small man, and that he once *seemed* heroically large, but just how far to push this discovery he does not know. He only knows that he too wants to be true to the personal values his elders proclaimed, whether they exemplified them adequately or not.

It may be, Bayard suspects, that in the old days, as Quentin's father speculated in *Absalom,* men were victims, as we are, of circumstance but a circumstance

> simpler and therefore, integer for integer, larger, more heroic and the figures therefore more heroic too, not dwarfed and involved but distinct, uncomplex who had the gift of loving once or dying once instead of being diffused and scattered creatures drawn blindly limb from limb from a grab bag and assembled . . .

But if so, if there was some reality behind Bayard's childhood impression of their simplicity of outline and their heroic size, he cannot now be sure. He knows that Rosa Millard was always courageous, but also knows that her courage was finally directed

to a questionable end, that she was corrupted in her dealings with
Ab Snopes. He knows that she met her death courageously, but he
also knows that the action which precipitated it lacks the justification that had formerly applied—that the mules she was stealing
were stolen from the enemy, and that anyway she was giving most
of them away. Actions are not justified by daring alone.

Again, in the bloody personal feud of "Vendee," Bayard and
Ringo display their loyalty and their courage and win the admiration of the spokesmen for the old order, but when, a few years later,
Ringo joins with the others in urging similar violently direct action,
Bayard does not answer. He does not simply repudiate nor does he
simply reaffirm the past. He goes his own way, satisfies his own
conscience, summoning all his courage to repudiate violence without
dishonor. And we note that Ringo misinterprets the past in his
effort to prompt Bayard to what he thinks is right action: "We could
bushwhack him," he said. "Like we done Grumby that day." But
they did not bushwhack Grumby, Grumby's men bushwhacked,
ambushed, them; so that Ringo's memory of this episode is like
Bayard's childhood memory of his father: father was not large, the
boys not quite so heroic—or fortunate—as Ringo remembers them.
The "romantic" atmosphere of the early stories in *The Unvanquished*
is clearly functional. It expresses a part of the meaning.

3

"AMBUSCADE" introduces all the themes that are to be developed,
even the criticism of the code that is the subject of "An Odor of
Verbena." The story opens with Bayard and Ringo re-enacting
the battle of Vicksburg. Their childish model of the city and river,
made with chips and scratched in the dust, "lived" for them in their
play. It lives for us, too, in this magnificently vivid evocation of a
child's innocent awareness of things vaguely portentous but not
understood:

it (river, city, and terrain) lived, possessing even in miniature that ponderable though passive recalcitrance of topog-
raphy which outweighs artillery, against which the most
brilliant of victories and the most tragic of defeats are
but the loud noises of a moment.

Their miniature Vicksburg is an artifact, laboriously constructed
and laboriously maintained (the dry earth drinking up the water
with which they made their river as fast as they could carry it)
which has no less reality to them because the real battle of Vicksburg
has already been lost by the South. Loosh, sullen with drink and
with what he knows of the defeat of Vicksburg, sweeps the chips
aside. " 'There's your Vicksburg,' he said." But Loosh is not thinking
of "their" Vicksburg at all, but of the real Vicksburg, lost, fallen,
before its model was even created for the purposes of their sham
battle, their reenactment, by which

> we could engender between us and hold intact the pattern
> of recapitulant mimic furious victory like a cloth, a shield
> between ourselves and reality, between us and fact and
> doom.

Through the reenactment of their childish game, the art of their
play, they have "stopped" time for a moment ("the two of us needing
first to join forces and spend ourselves against a common enemy,
time") and held Vicksburg up to view as something having a form
and meaning that they are able to grasp. They are, for the moment,
artists; Loosh, the literalist. Their art interprets and makes available, but does not quite reproduce, "the real thing." The "romantic"
air of *The Unvanquished* is not unconnected with this opening scene
of the mimic battle that is like "a shield between ourselves and
reality." Bayard later comes consciously to wonder what the reality
is that is so ambiguously hidden and revealed by the imaginative
act.

He knows later, after these early experiences have become fused
in memory, that only gradually did he discover that father was not
actually large ("He was not big; it was just the things he did, that

we knew he was doing . . .") and that his ability to give the impression of heroic stature rested upon his power to command ("Father was everywhere . . . standing still and saying 'Do this or that' to the ones who are doing . . ."). The implication here is clear enough, though never made explicit—it could not be without distortion of Bayard's experience: the system which made it possible for father to seem to possess heroic proportions was a caste system with the injustices that such a system entails. All the references to the subtle caste line drawn between Bayard and Ringo, who was, according to father, "more intelligent" than Bayard and who was the initiator in many of their activities, have this same effect. The childish sense of companionship and equality, like their mimic battle, was partly a make-believe, valuable but not perfectly in harmony with the facts. This matter, too, like the question of father's size, gives us some insight into the functional character of the "romanticism" of the book.

The last sentence of the story defines all this. Bayard and Ringo have rinsed and spit the last of the soapsuds after having had to wash out their mouths with soap for telling a lie—a punishment imposed by Granny, who was so inflexible in her demand for truth yet who was soon to make a fine art of systematic lying—and they look at the cloud bank in the north which Ringo takes to be literally and Bayard symbolically the mountains of Tennessee where they supposed that father was fighting. "But it"—the cloud bank, the illusion it represented, the sense of meaning; and also the last bubble made by the rinsing—"But it was gone now—the suds, the glassy weightless iridescent bubbles; even the taste of it." The bubbles, the cloud bank resembling mountains, the sham battle—all are gone now except as held in memory through a deliberate effort to recapture them, to hold them up above the rush of time and the destructiveness of Loosh. "Romanticism" as conscious as this is not self-deception but an effort at definition.

The uneasy relation between fact and value in our memories of the past is a theme introduced in the first story and developed in the later ones in the history of Granny's fall. She is very punctilious in keeping to the code she lives by, but she loses the meaning as she preserves the forms. She will not let Bayard drive the "borrowed" horses and she kneels to pray for forgiveness for the lies she has to tell; but it becomes harder and harder to conceive of the horses and mules as "borrowed" or confiscated as a justifiable act of war, or of the lies as necessary. When, against the advice of Bayard and Ringo, she listens to Ab Snopes with his scheme for recouping a part of the family losses, she loses her integrity. She meets her death bravely, but the death is unnecessary and meaningless: the courage is now all that is left, existing in isolation from other values, a proximate value become final. The life of the code died with Rosa Millard. Afterwards there is Drusilla. In her the courage is undiminished, but the principles the courage should serve are even more obscure than they became with Granny.

The decay of the code into empty formalism is convincing enough, but the positive value before the decay set in is not so clear or convincing. The old order created a code of personal relations in which loyalty and courage were conspicious virtues and a sense of personal honor an indefinable superstructure, but the whole thing rested on narrow, perhaps deliberately narrowed, sympathies. "Vendee," in which Ringo and Bayard avenge Granny's death in a prolonged demonstration of their loyalty, courage, and sense of family "honor," ends in an act of barbarous mutilation that defines for us well enough the weakness of the old code but not its strength. "Aint I told you he is John Sartoris' boy?" Uncle Buck asks triumphantly, and we may feel, yes, and Granny's too, culturally if not by physical inheritance.

For Granny is not as attractive as, apparently, she was meant to be. Unless the code had a wider and deeper purpose than a defense of Sartoris "honor" and privilege in a world in which most people were not fortunate enough to be Sartorises, it can hardly recommend itself to us seriously as something in the loss of which there is genuine pathos. The old code is not presented, here or elsewhere in Faulkner, as a religious, more specifically as a Christian, code. The old order he "defends"—or presents with *both* negative judgment and a feeling of sympathy—seems more feudal than Christian, more conspicuously related to caste than to the two great commandments.

Granny is presented as religious, a devout Episcopalian, faithful in her observances. But there are two ways to take this aspect of the characterization of her. Either the empty formalism of her religious habit, the utter gap between her religious words and acts on the one hand and her deeds and even her intentions on the other, is a part of the *intended* meaning in the portrait, in which case the old code was empty even before her fall from virtue; or this formalism of hers is not a part of the intended meaning, and she is supposed to appear to us as a person whose religious belief and experience at first is fruitfully expressed in her life but later becomes "dead" faith.

Though we might suspect from some of Faulkner's other works, "The Bear" for instance, that we ought to choose the first of these alternatives as more typically Faulknerian, I can find no evidence here for such a reading. Granny seems intended to be wholly admirable before she succumbs to Snopesism. But if so, the portrait of Granny is partly spoiled for us by the influence of that side of Faulkner which, especially in the works of the middle and later thirties, speaks sometimes in very ambivalent accents about historic Christianity. When Granny takes the boys to the empty church to pray, the form is Christian but the spirit and intention are something else, an expression of her "indomitable" spirit perhaps but certainly not of any really felt or understood Christian piety. There is nothing of repentance or humility in her "confession." She argues with God subtly, proving to Him that her opening statement, "I have sinned," does not really mean what it says. "I defy You," she says, thus proving herself a true Sartoris but hardly a Christian. But it is not at all clear that this is the effect intended. Bayard remembers her as consistently devout, and nothing that he later discovers as he matures qualifies this description. Yet as we see her through him, we can only judge that at best, before any corruption set in, her religion consisted of a rigid, more pharisaical than Christian, moral code, which she can neither adhere to nor interpret and modify, and a set of devotional habits apparently empty of inner meaning. When we think of this aspect of Granny, we feel that we hardly need Drusilla to demonstrate the emptiness of the code. If in Drusilla the code becomes theatrical, in Granny it had already become divorced from either a broad or a deep sense of reality.

But this defect, though it is probably serious enough to prevent our ever comparing *The Unvanquished* with Faulkner's greatest things, still seems to me quite insufficient to destroy a work of such power and beauty. After all, the central theme does not undertake so much a defense of the old order as an evocation leading to a criticism. Faulkner has protected himself cunningly against any demand that he justify the felt sympathy for the order and the code: he has presented the glamour and the heroism through the mind of a child, and made even that child, as he matures, aware of the thin line between heroism and heroics. This is a very different strategy from that which he employed in the ending of *Sartoris*, though the *feeling* for the past, or at least the Sartoris past, is similar. Perhaps we should dismiss as irrelevant the suspicion that, on the evidence here before us, the Sartoris dream was not so very different in essentials from Sutpen's design—not different enough at least to justify the extreme difference in attitude toward them.

To press any further with this sort of objection, demanding as it were that Faulkner make more plausible to us what is felt here and elsewhere in his work as the glamour of the Sartorises, would be to ask for a different book from the one he has written in *The Unvanquished*. The form of the work effectively cuts off the possibility of critical speculation, except that which the form itself motivates and directs. When Bayard, at the death of his father, becomes "the Sartoris," he is expected to carry on the code, unchanged. Whether he will do so, and if so, how he will do it, are the questions in the minds of Wyatt and Drusilla and Ringo and the others, and they take us in the direction of the central theme. Will Bayard have the courage to *not* kill, yet to acquit himself well, as the Sartorises defined *well*, honorably, courageously? He thinks, in his crisis, "*Who lives by the sword shall die by it* just as Granny would have thought" (but not acted); and also

> how if there was anything at all in the Book, anything of hope and peace for His blind and bewildered spawn which He had chosen above all others to offer immortality, *Thou shalt not kill* must be it . . .

For Bayard in his situation, expected by everyone apparently except Aunt Jenny to kill the man who had killed his father, this is perhaps dramatically right, granting a combined skepticism and religious ignorance that may safely be assumed for all Sartorises except ancient aunts and legendary great-grandmothers. But it may be noted in passing that only for a primitive and violent people would this be "it," the one thing meaningful and valid in "the Book." It is not surprising, in view of so simplistic a theology, that though Bayard noted the discrepancy between Granny's moral principles and her actions, he was not aware of any discrepancy between form and meaning in her worship. In several of his best works Faulkner has presented the religious issues that are central in the crisis of our time with full, magnificently definitive embodiment. It is no reflection on the achievement of these works to note that the artist sometimes works better than the man knows. In *The Unvanquished* there is a hint of that peculiar combination of theological muddle and ignorance that may be detected in *A Fable*.

Meanwhile, however obscure the connections between the limited Sartoris code and any larger scheme of meaning, the immediate problem before Bayard is clear enough. Is he to carry on in the old expected way, symbolized by the vengeance he and Ringo took on Grumby, or to deepen the meaning of the code, make it more truly itself by denying it where it is out of harmony with its own inner meaning—to realize it by breaking with it? The difference between the Sartoris dream and the Sutpen dream is essential if Bayard is to reinterpret the code truly. Bayard and Drusilla's talk of the difference between Sartoris and Sutpen gives Bayard the clue he needs. John Sartoris, it seems, had a somewhat broader area of social concern than Sutpen; his "good" was not so exclusively his own. His dream centered on preserving the system which put and kept the Sartorises on the top of the heap, but he was not wholly unconcerned with the cost to others of Sartoris well-being. He may have been "immoral" but he was not "amoral": his dream was qualified by his acceptance of the old moral code as he understood it. Sutpen's dream was qualified by no code at all except his "private morality," which was more primitive and inadequate and self-centered than John Sartoris'.

In resisting the pressures to "remember Grumby," then, Bayard is proving that his loyalty to the code is as real as Drusilla's, and his understanding of its essence more acute than hers. He takes the action which indicates at once his growth in moral awareness and his loyalty to the older, pre-Sutpen, ideal. He acts responsibly, on principle, having counted the possible cost but also acknowledging the incalculable. Though his action out of context may seem theatrical or even stereotyped, it is it seems to me a more convincing embodiment of the value everywhere imputed to the Sartoris way in Faulkner's books than anything we ever see Granny do. The Sartorises at their best rose in crises to morally responsible action.

But the moral theme is not the only one in the book, despite its centrality and its function as the unifying theme that binds all the stories together. A moral code, any code, is like art in that it imposes a pattern on the otherwise formless—or elicits a pattern from it. Any code is "artificial," something made and followed by choice, not existing "in nature." A part of the meaning of *The Unvanquished* is that the Sartoris moral code, like the mimic battle of the boys in the opening, momentarily arrests the rush of time to doom—arrests it long enough for human choice to be exercised. Yet, though it is an instrument of control, it is not beyond time, not timeless. Loosh comes and destroys Bayard's artifact. The art and the code which partially and momentarily arrest the flow of events must not falsify.

When a code or an art becomes too artificial, it becomes an instrument of the very death it is its proper function to inhibit.

4

THE HAMLET contrasts sharply with *The Unvanquished* in mood, tone, manner, and the type of people dealt with; it complements it in theme. Thematically, the two should always be considered together, for they make together one statement. *The Unvanquished* pictures the beginning of the decay of the old Sartoris order as it is corrupted by Snopesism. The fact that Snopes was foreshadowed by Sutpen, a man ahead of his time in the development toward what Faulkner identifies as modernism, and the fact that the distinction between Sutpen and Sartoris was not so sharp as Drusilla wanted Bayard to think, remain merely qualifications of the central moral theme of *The Unvanquished*. Granny's loss of purity of motive in her conniving with Ab Snopes represents the beginning of the end of the old order.

The Hamlet completes the process. Flem Snopes, Ab's son, now takes over and proves more effective than his father in the work of corruption. He demoralizes not one indomitable old woman in time of crisis but a whole community, until in the end, when he has exhausted the community's possibilities for exploitation, even Ratliff, reflector become participant, is digging for gold in a frenzy of avarice. Then Flem moves on to larger opportunities in Jefferson. For an understanding of the "world" Faulkner has created, the structure of meaning and value in Yoknapatawpha, *The Unvanquished* and *The Hamlet* are equally indispensable keys.[4] In them both the viable tradition and all that threatens it in the present are traced in the past. In Yoknapatawpha there is very little that is new under the sun.

But in everything but theme, the two books complement each other by contrast. *The Unvanquished* is more single in purpose, tone, and vision, to be sure, so that any contrast of it with the richer and looser work must fail to be neat and decisive; but a contrast is possible, nevertheless. While *The Unvanquished* is romantic in incident and mood, *The Hamlet* is predominantly realistic—and sometimes extravagant. *The Unvanquished* is nostalgic-sympathetic, *The Hamlet* (again predominantly) humorous-satirical. *The Unvanquished* pictures a period somewhat more distant in time than *The Hamlet,* but in it the past comes very close and the aesthetic distance is often as slight as it can be, without the collapse of judgment; in *The Hamlet,* except in the Houston and Ike Snopes episodes, the aesthetic distance is greater. Finally, as I have already suggested, *The Hamlet* has more variety, ranging from the savage satire of the picture of Flem Snopes to the delicate lyricism of the treatment of his cousin Ike, from the Melvillean irony and despair of the Houston story to the tall tale in the tradition of Western humor of the spotted horses section. There is I think a sufficient unity in *The Hamlet's* richness, but it is not so pronounced as the unity of *The Unvanquished,* despite the common characterization of that work as "a group of stories."

The unity that *The Hamlet* has, which is certainly enough to make it proper to call it a novel, is a product less of its presentation of the stories of related characters in a single community than of its treatment of the nature and effects of Snopesism. Snopesism is avarice married to pure animality. Flem is moved only by greed, and Eula, his wife, is moved by nothing at all except the processes of her own organic chemistry. Flem is a clod whose constantly chewing jaw deceptively suggests the ruminant animals, but he is brought at least partially within the human orbit, within range of negative moral judgment at any rate, by his ability to sin—to connive and scheme to lay hands on everything of any monetary value in Frenchman's Bend. Eula in contrast is a mere eruption, a beautiful, passive eruption, of animal process; so passively beautiful indeed as to seem more vegetable than animal. She is not only incapable of sin, she is incapable even of desire; she is safe with Labove because she cannot even imagine the possibility of danger.

Flem himself is broad, squat, soft, with his predatoriness built upon a bovine base; very different from his cousin Mink, with his fierce, "indomitable" face. Flem could never be driven to murder. He is at once too shrewd and too soft, soft not in pity but in adaptability. When he marries Eula he is reinforcing that side of him which is merely animal; in his human attribute he neither wants nor needs any reinforcement and will tolerate no rival. He defrauds other Snopeses as placidly as he defrauds the rest of Frenchman's Bend. He will find Eula a useful adjunct.

The analysis of Snopesism in *The Hamlet* is Faulkner's most effective attack on modern popular culture. It is quaintly amusing only if we assume that Snopeses live only in Yoknapatawpha. If we take it without defensive cutting of the lines of relevance, we shall find it as savage as any satire in Mark Twain, and probably on the whole more effective. Flem Snopes is a Horatio Alger hero, rising by shrewd attention to business from rags to riches. He parodies the American dream, caricatures the American success myth. He has ambition, go-ahead, gumption, a head for figures: everything deemed necessary for success in the Ben Franklin-Dale Carnegie popular philosophy. He is cautious, discreet, self-controlled, soft-spoken. He never loses his temper, is never driven to self-forgetful rashness or violence by any lust, passion, need. He keeps his eye on the main chance and looks out for number one. He is rewarded by riches, as Franklin's Poor Richard had prophesied.

His cousin, I. O. Snopes, makes Flem's significance as the paradigm of the ideal self-made man clearer than it might otherwise be. The jumbled proverbs I.O. quotes are mostly out of Poor Richard— and before they were polished by Poor Richard they were in the popular mind. Snopesism is prudential morality rendered down to purity, presented in its essence. Flem is a combination of the mythical Yankee pedlar and Poor Richard, with the latter's unthinking, foundationless benevolence worn away, with only the calculation of expediency in the interest of self left.

Flem measures all things by a single, simple standard that

involves no metaphysical nonsense, no unknowns. Though he has no "friends" in the sense of the word in which friendship has moral connotations, he has an apparently inexhaustible supply of "friends," most of whom are related to him at least by marriage, ready to serve his purposes in each new scheme. He is always able to "win friends and influence people" when there is need to. Flem never fails, because as I. O. Snopes reminds us, God helps those who help themselves. Flem goes early to bed, and no man ever caught him napping. He has hitched his wagon to a star and knows that the word *can't* is not in the dictionary. "Just give him time," as I. O. says; "a penny on the waters pays interest when the flood turns." For Flem, as for Poor Richard, time is money.

I. O.'s proverbs take the words of the Judeo-Christian religious vision and give them practical, down-to-earth meaning by suggesting that morality after all *pays,* is not visionary. Snopesism as Faulkner presents it did not arise full-grown in Yoknapatawpha in the late nineteenth century. It has a distinguished ancestry, including the secularization of Christian morality of the eighteenth century, with its resultant shopkeeper's ethics. Snopesism could be documented by reference to Defoe (Robinson Crusoe as the first self-made man) and Richardson (for Pamela chastity is an asset because she knows how to make it *pay*), as well as Franklin. Snopesism is democratic opportunism with everything vestigial cut away.

Not all the Snopeses of course illustrate the nature of Snopesism. Many of them do not get ahead at all. They lack initiative, drive, intelligence, or self-control. Eck, the blacksmith, is stupid; he can be used not only by Flem but even by I. O. (He is also the only Snopes in the book who ever expresses pity for anyone, even another Snopes: he gives the idiot Snopes a toy cow, stating as his reason simply "I felt sorry for him."). I. O. is ineffectual, scattered and without concentration: he does not rise in the world. Ike, the idiot who is in love with a cow, is the only Snopes, so far as we know, capable of love: he will not get ahead either. Mink is a murderer, stupid enough, as his cousin tells him, to get caught.

The Snopeses are a varied clan, united chiefly by their admiration for and dependence upon Flem. He is the successful one, the one who made good.

5

THE PORTRAITS of Ike the idiot and Mink the murderer deserve special attention. Except for Eck, these two are the only Snopeses sympathetically drawn; and Eck closely approaches Ike in stupidity. He is not smart enough to achieve even Lump's or I. O.'s degree of Snopesism. The book invites us to identify ourselves only with those Snopeses who are sub-humanly "innocent" or violently lost. Thus, with the exception again of Eck, the only two sympathetic Snopeses are those guilty of sodomy and murder, two offenses that have not lost their significance in the popular mind.

Ike's romantic idyll with the cow has been widely appreciated. The episode is controlled by pity, yet done for the most part without overt sentimentality. In its invitation to us to see value in "one of the least of these," in the lost and rejected, the episode is consistent with a Christian interpretation of life which the narrative voice of this section explicitly rejects. Over and beyond its intrinsic beauty, the episode justifies itself in the scheme of the novel by its presentation of just those values—gentleness, love, devotion—the lack of which makes Snopesism the evil it is; and by its locating of those values precisely where a smarter Snopes would never think to look.

The richly lyrical, almost euphuistic prose of the section is in general finely controlled and expressive. Whatever the world may think of sodomy, this is not depravity but love, with love's gentle concern and self-forgetfulness. Flem Snopes, who if he does anything at all that pan-Snopesism would call wrong, is smart enough not to be caught, who is only a "shrewd operator," is seen as the quintessence of evil. In Ratliff's fantasy he is capable of routing the devil himself from his throne. But the two Snopeses, Ike and Mink, who are guilty of what even the Snopeses condemn, are seen as creatures deserving our sympathy. Ike's story is an effective part of *The Hamlet's* violent attack on success worship, on "business ethics" and popular philosophy, on all that Snopesism means to Faulkner.

In the portait of Mink there seems to me a certain sentimentality, less conspicuous in the version in *The Hamlet* than in the original story, published as "The Hound," but still evident.[5] Mink is seen as a "victim" but "indomitable," and therefore somehow attractive. He is a fierce little Ahab, rebelling against the injustice of the gods, unwilling to bend even in defeat. In the original story he is pictured more definitely as the product of his economic situation than in the revised version, but even here he is never shown as in any degree responsible for his actions. The question arises, of course, why Flem can be held responsible, if Mink cannot; for Flem rose from poverty as extreme as Mink's and had, presumably, as few satisfactions—until he began to rise in the world. The answer is not in the book.

Mink feels that everyone and everything is against him, and the way his story is told suggests that we should assent. As in the portraits of Popeye and Joe Christmas, an examination of the man's background leads to a denial of the possibility of moral judgment, even a judgment in which condemnation of the action would not preclude charity for the actor. Mink emerges as a cold-blooded murderer, a man for whom murder was not an exceptional departure from his normal behavior but quite in character, thoroughly to be expected. Yet we are, I think, invited somehow not only to sympathize with him but to admire him. There is the same sort of ambivalence or obscurity here that we found in the portrait of the aviators in *Pylon*: we are all victims, and Mink has the grace to be an indomitable victim, thinking of his situation

> not in remorse for the deed he had done, because he neither required nor desired absolution for that [Perhaps he didn't "desire" it, but what would it mean to say that he didn't "require" it either?] . . . and not snarling, because he never snarled; but just cold, indomitable, and intractable.

Attractive, in short, as Ahab was attractive to Melville and Manfred to Byron, a sort of Yoknapatawpha Prometheus in his rebellion against the gods, unpromethean only in his contempt for mankind:

> Perhaps he was seeking [as he went toward the sea] only the proffer of this illimitable space and irremediable forgetting along the edge of which the contemptible teeming of his own earth-kind timidly seethed and recoiled . . .

Faulkner's special power and his occasional special weakness spring in part from his ability—sometimes his compulsion—wholly to adopt the point of view, even to the errors and confusions, of his characters, rationalizing their behavior with their own rationalizations, swamping judgment in a flood of sympathy. Mink and Houston, his victim, are presented in similar terms and with apparently equal degrees of sympathy. There is an Emersonian streak in Faulkner which makes the difference between the "red slayer" and the slain seem unimportant. Brahma, or something, wipes out such petty finite distinctions, so that at times everything seems equal to everything else. If this can be called mysticism, it is a type of mysticism in which a writer of fiction cannot afford to indulge too often.

The presentation of Mink's marriage adds to the sentimentality of the whole episode. His wife is a harder and tougher Ruby Lamar of *Sanctuary*. She brags of the variety of her sexual experience, which fits her to judge Mink's virility. "I've had a hundred men, but I never had a wasp before. That stuff comes out of you is rank poison. It's too hot." Mink beats her unmercifully without provocation and she loves him all the more for it. Against every obstacle she is true to her wasp with the deadly sting, even to the extent of sleeping with one of the Varners to earn ten dollars—an act oddly presented as self-sacrificial despite her happy memories of the hundred men she once summoned repeatedly even in midafternoon to her room. It sometimes appears that when Faulkner is writing in this vein only prostitutes or the pathological are capable of making loving and faithful wives. One of the curious links between

Mink and Houston is that Houston too had for ten years or so lived with a prostitute: naturally, she made him an ideal commonlaw wife. The girl in *Pylon* was created out of the same set of attitudes, and Charlotte in *The Wild Palms* and the wife in *Idyll in the Desert*. The implication here, like that sometimes apparent in Hemingway's treatment of his heroines, is sentimental. (Not that a prostitute could not, might not, make a loving and faithful wife, but that in fact prostitutes usually don't, and to imply that they always do, just *because* of their "training," is to be sentimental in the Bret Harte manner, positing the invariable heart of gold beneath the rough surface.) From one point of view, the portrait of Mink's wife is another instance of Faulkner's sympathy for the lost and outcast, but to suggest that only the qualities of personality or experience that make for prostitution fit one for monogamy is not really compassionate but only unreasonable.

The scene in which Mink rejects as tainted money the ten dollars his wife tries to give him, preferring to face the consequences of his murder rather than accept it, is done entirely in terms of the sentimental clichés of tough modernism; and it is incredible, or credible only in other terms than those in which it is presented. Here we have the fine proud gesture of the indomitable little man striking the woman he loves *because* he loves her, rejecting the proffered help because he has that *pride* that Faulkner has so often listed as one of the indispensable virtues. If we are not prepared to recognize the anti-rational quality of the scene as presented, it is because Faulkner has bewitched us by the imagistic brilliance and emotional power of his writing in the whole Mink Snopes episode, effectively cutting off both critical judgment and the irrelevant response.

6

HOUSTON IS a larger, nobler, still more sympathetic Ahab, in rebellion against "the prime maniacal Risibility" who killed his wife after only three months of marriage. The God who would permit such things to be has earned his contempt and awakened a savage pride and fury, a violent despair almost indistinguishable from Mink's. This is what sets both of them apart from lesser men contentedly and timidly breeding along the shore: great souls seek "illimitable space" in which to exercise their fury and their grief. The portrait here is purely Melvillean, and not because of any accidental similarity of land-sea imagery, with the contemptible safety-mongers hugging the teeming land while great-souled Ahabs plunge into the depths. What theologians have distinguished as "the problem of pain"—or the problem created by the existence of natural evil in a world made by a good God—dominates the writing as much here as in *Moby Dick*.

It is not surprising that Faulkner wholly identifies himself with Houston. We have seen him identify before with less attractive and less Faulknerian characters. But it is revealing that the attitudes expressed and implied in the treatment of Houston, which are at once Houston's own and the narrator's, since there is no distinction here, are the same as those expressed by the narrator of the Ike Snopes episode. Though it might be said that the attitudes in the Houston episode, even where they are not explicitly assigned to Houston, are created by imaginative assimilation to Houston's point of view, the same cannot be said of the treatment of Ike. Ike *has* no point of view, no capacity to create a philosophy out of his despair. The voice here is not in any sense his.

Ike is another Melvillean character. He is little Pip, driven insane by his direct confrontation with the reality of the depths. The eyes are vacant, like Pip's, because of what they have seen, which is more than man can bear:

> the eyes which at some instant, some second once, had opened upon, been vouchsafed a glimpse of, the Gorgon-face of that primal injustice which man was not intended to look at face to face and had been blasted empty and clean forever of any thought . . .

This striking parallel reveals an interesting similarity between the sensibilities of Melville and Faulkner. "Melville's quarrel with God" is not more evident in *Moby Dick* than Faulkner's is in *The Hamlet*. It is in the distinct voice of the narrator that we get such a passage as this:

> Roofed by the woven canopy of blind annealing grass-roots and the roots of trees, dark in the blind dark of time's silt and rich refuse—the constant and unslumbering anonymous worm-glut and the inextricable known bones—Troy's Helen and the nymphs and the snoring mitred bishops, the saviors and the victims and the kings—it wakes, up-seeping . . .

The "it" is dawn, the first light. The light comes from below, from the earth, as in the fantasy of Hightower, who had lost the Church and the Faith. The sensibility and attitudes that shaped this image produced the explanation of Ike's idiocy. Really "authentic" Christians, the same voice tells us elsewhere in *The Hamlet*, would have to be in hell if historic Christian doctrine were true.

I have drawn attention to the parallel with Melville. There is also one, less noticeable, with Mark Twain. Several passages in *The Hamlet* as well as the quality of the sensibility in general suggest the great passage in *Huckleberry Finn* in which Huck refuses to pray a lie: better that he should be damned, if there is any damnation, than that he should betray his friend. "The weary long record of shibboleth and superstition" is a phrase Mark Twain could have written—and very nearly did, again and again—but here it is the language of the objective narrator in the Ike Snopes section. The point of view implied by this interpretation of history produces the judgment that Ike the idiot has everything, or is learning everything, as he cares for the cow, except the qualities that characterize the MacEacherns and Doc Hineses and Flems and Baptist committees: Ike,

> who has only lust and greed and bloodthirst and a moral conscience to keep him awake at night, yet to acquire.

The implied definition of conscience here is precisely that of Mark Twain. This is anti-rational primitivism: by which I do not mean to imply that certain kinds of religion have not in fact often so exacerbated the conscience as to drive men to neuroticism and violence. But if Ike is "clean" of thought, if conscience is only a goad to madness and crime, if Ike has everything except the vices, then not only faith but reason must go. The snoring bishops and the dead saviors, on the one hand, and Flem Snopes, on the other, are not "clean" of contaminations: the saviors presumably had faith, and Flem is gifted in a kind of prudential reason. Robinson Jeffers at one time pictured the world this way. Irving Babbitt would have traced some of the implications of *The Hamlet* back to "Rousseau and romanticism."

The religious ambivalence in Faulkner, which has sometimes strengthened his finest work, providing a tension which became neither confusion nor sentimentality, seems to me to have become deeper and more excruciating by the time of *The Hamlet*. The resulting conflict must qualify our admiration for this richly imaginative, at times intensely moving and at other times very funny, picaresque folk novel. The book belongs still, I think, among the great works of the American literary imagination, but it cannot carry us along with it without reservation as *The Sound and the Fury* and *As I Lay Dying* did. And some of the implications in it are ominous for Faulkner's future work. Ratliff is a sane and attractive man, one of Faulkner's finest reflectors, as has been said, but Ratliff is not always in control. Another voice, which we cannot possibly identify as his, speaks too, and speaks with "savage contempt and pity for all blind flesh capable of hope and grief." The savage pity created Ike, the savage contempt created Flem. A mind not wholly overwhelmed by either pity or contempt, a mind not yet savage with despair, produced the greater works, and the characters in them who are neither idiotic personifications of good nor intelligent personifications of evil. *The Hamlet*, despite its great virtuousity, suffers from a lack of the balance that informs the earlier greater works and keeps the agony of despair and grief from being intolerable and destructive.

CHAPTER 9

Tragic, Comic, and Threshold

THE SHORT STORIES

FROM THE BEGINNING OF his career Faulkner has been less consistently great in the short story form than in the novel. His best stories are very fine, and there are enough of them to establish him as a major short story writer; but many of the stories are merely competent, and some are weak. Faulkner's creative gifts seem not essentially those of the short story writer, just as they are not essentially those of the lyric poet—and this despite his own characterization of himself as a "failed poet"[1] and the implicit and explicit "poetry" of his fictions. His imagination is expansive, and his feeling for words is a feeling for the totality of their emotional and imaginative impact. The epigrammatist and the writer whose natural form is the short story have in common the intellectual precision and discipline necessary for the bald statement so apt in its inclusions that we do not regret the absence of what it excludes. Faulkner's typical gesture sweeps wide to try to include everything.

Yet his best short stories stand among the very greatest written in our time. Some of them, like "That Evening Sun" and "A Rose for Emily," have been adequately praised and appreciated if not always sufficiently analyzed. But others, like "Dry September" and "Was," deserve an attention they have not received. "The Bear"

seems to me justly famous—though perhaps it
a novelette rather than a long short story—
"Wash" and "Barn Burning" are also unsur
Only the stories of the First World War and th
natural seem to me to be generally no more tha

In both these last categories the imaginative
tract. In most of the war stories a feeling for the tragedy of the
doomed young men is intense but relatively meaningless. "Ad
Astra" is probably the best of the group, but even in it the profuse
echoes of Eliot's poetry and the Bible seem a little forced, as though
the fusion of meaning and feeling had not really taken place.
"Crevasse" pictures the war in terms of the circles of Dante's Hell,
but the Dantesque imagery seems more ingenious than meaningful.
The rest are straightforward enough but full of cliches. In the
stories of the supernatural in the section of *Collected Stories* called
"Beyond," the feeling for the transcendent aspects of experience,
for the mysterious and uncontrolled and uncontrollable, is strong;
but the stories usually lack the intellectual interest which, with such
subjects, could only be theological.

In both groups of stories we miss that fullness and density of
experience described by Alfred Kazin as Faulkner's special quality,
his ability to capture "so much of the simultaneous impact of human events"[2] upon the consciousness of his characters. Faulkner
has tended to write in stereotypes about the lost generation of
the First World War, from the first chapter of *Soldier's Pay* on.
His feeling for something "beyond" the limits of ordinary experience
is genuine and consistent and enriches much of his best work, but it
seems to be rather inchoate, and to remain ordinarily at the level of
minimal perception and feeling.

Yet if the stories of the explicitly supernatural are not among his
best, they keep us reminded of an interest as important in the
stories as in the novels. For when we consider all the short stories
Faulkner has published, and not only the ones included in the
misleadingly titled *Collected Stories*, we see that when they do not
develop the vein of folk humor that has been a conspicuous thread

fabric of the work from the beginning, they tend to express
of two dominant feelings. (When, as in "The Bear," they approach the novel in length, they sometimes express both.) Most of
the early stories give expression to the sense of outrage, the horror
at the unbearable quality of an experience that must yet be borne.
A good many of the later stories, in addition to those in "Beyond,"
are dominated by a feeling for what we may call, with Philip
Wheelwright,[3] the *threshold* aspects of experience. Experience for
Faulkner, more conspicuously perhaps than for most of us, is never
limited and self-contained; it is an experience of being always on
the threshold of something beyond. Past and future and the illimitable are all "beyond," but for an analysis of Faulkner's best work
the past is especially important as stimulus and vehicle of the
threshold experience.

2

"DRY SEPTEMBER" is typical in mood and theme of many of the
early stories.[4] Its account of the lynching of Will Mayes, who is
innocent of the act imputed to him by the mob, inspires in us an
almost unbearable sense of horror. Yet its violence and horror are
not the end; the story is not sensational in the ordinary sense. The
violence and horror are associated with judgment; they become
ingredients in the beauty and meaning of the story.

In the largest sense, the story may be seen as a parable of what
happens to man in the wasteland where, driven by an intolerable
sense of insecurity and isolation, faced by an overwhelming threat,
he turns to sadistic violence as a means of asserting his existence.
The story develops the insight that sadism and a sense of insecurity
are closely linked. Will Mayes is not the only victim in "Dry
September," though he is the only one who has our sympathy.
Minnie Cooper, who started the story that he had raped her, is a
victim of her sexual frustration, and the mob is a victim of the heat,
the social climate, and its own need to assert itself.

Death is everywhere present in the story, from the title and the opening sentence—and not the death of Will Mayes only. "Through the bloody September twilight, aftermath of sixty-two rainless days, it had gone like a fire in dry grass—the rumor, the story, whatever it was." All the images here, the blood, the dryness, the fall, the fire, are suggestive of death. The very air is said to be "dead," "vitiated," motionless. The background of the violent action is an utter stillness: "The screen door crashed behind them reverberant in the dead air." The death and the violence are linked by more than simple contrast: the connection is causal.

Minnie Cooper is threatened by advancing age, trapped by biology in a situation from which fantasy offers the only escape. She is "losing ground"; she wishes the rape, or the rumor of the rape, as proof that she is still sexually desirable, if only to a Negro. At thirty-eight or thirty-nine she no longer attracts the eyes of the men sitting along the sidewalk. Her fantasy is doubly pleasurable, first in itself and then as the cause of the notoriety that brought a resurgence of inspection as she walked before the men. It is Minnie's fate to be raped only in wishful fantasy, to be beyond hope of inspiring even the desire to rape.

McLendon, the active leader of the lynching party, is a victim too. When we first see him, "poised on the balls of his feet, roving his gaze," he is the very epitome of violent self-assertion. He has a "furious, rigid face," in which the apparent contradiction of "furious" and "rigid" repeats the life-death, stillness-violence contrast of the larger image pattern. He does not move in a normal tempo; he whirls, slams, flings, strikes, tears, rips. But his violence, we come to see, is a measure of the depth of his insecurity. When he returns home after the lynching he strikes his wife, then rips off his shirt and flings it away, furiously seeking relief from the intolerable heat; then hunts furiously for it again to wipe the sweat from his body and stand panting against the dusty screen.

> There was no movement, no sound, not even an insect. The dark world seemed to lie stricken beneath the cold moon and the lidless stars.

Like the river in the "Old Man" part of *The Wild Palms,* which expands in connotations until we see it as a symbol of the whole natural world in which man is precariously placed, the environment in "Dry September" is symbolic. McLendon is, though he does not know it, in flight. The only way he knows of awakening a sense that he is really alive in the midst of an almost overwhelming threat of death is to impose death. He is one with the insects attracted by the streetlights: the very heat and stillness of the air inspire him to more violent motion. "The barber went swiftly up the street where the sparse lights, insect-swirled, glared in rigid and violent suspension in the lifeless air." McLendon is fighting death in the only way he knows.

"Rigid and violent": the image is familiar. Yet there is no mere idiosyncrasy of style here. One way of asserting the story's greatness is to say that everything in it combines to justify such phrases. The rigidity, we see by the story's end, both creates and expresses the violence, and the violence creates and expresses the rigidity. So far from being a mere "stylistic device," the juxtaposition of utter death and violent action which distinguishes the imagery of the story is the chief means by which the inner meaning is expressed. McLendon is tense with destructive violence just because he is so near to nothing at all; he is hardly able to breathe in the lifeless air. Minnie feels herself too gravely threatened to be concerned with the possible repercussions of her fantasy on Will Mayes. Only the mild and timid barber seems not to need to destroy someone to assert himself, and his kindness, like Horace Benbow's, is ineffectual. The others need proof of the reality of their existence.

> They went on; the dust swallowed them; the glare and the sound died away. The dust of them hung for a while, but soon the eternal dust absorbed it again.

"Dry September" is a uniquely valuable comment on a local social condition, a compressed exploration of the psychology of the lynch mob and of the racial situation in the South. But the comment it makes on the general situation of modern man is even more memorable. An age which has needed to invent the word *genocide* has reason to be interested in the implications of "Dry September." Since the meaning is wholly implicit in a texture that conveys the most vivid sense of concrete reality, it is not easily exhausted. The story seems to me one of Faulkner's finest.

3

"WAS" EXPLORES in comic mood something of the heritage "out of the old time, the old days." The only humorous story in *Go Down, Moses,* it is nevertheless representative of a type that includes such notable stories as "Mule in the Yard" and "Shingles for the Lord" and that is also seen in many of the yarns that are woven together to make *The Hamlet.*

The fact that this humor is not "pure," not free of relevance to Faulkner's serious themes, despite its air of the uproarious tall tale, is first suggested by the rhetoric and punctuation of the opening section. The "sentences" that neither begin nor end suggest the presentness of the past, the on-going quality of time. As Faulkner has recently said,[5] he believes that "time is a fluid condition which has no existence except in the momentary avatars of individual people. There is no such thing as *was*—only is." This tale out of the remote past is not going to be remote. The humor here will not be an end but a means, a part of a total strategy aimed at domesticating the exotic. As in *Absalom,* the fact that the tale is doubly filtered, that it is Ike McCaslin's memory of his cousin McCaslin Edmonds's memory, docs not result in an increased aesthetic distance but in a controlled closeness. What "was" becomes what "is."

But to plunge in this way into one of the thematic meanings of the story, though it may be necessary for an understanding of the implications of the title and the opening section, is to get far away from the actual story we encounter on first reading. Beginning with the second section the story becomes apparently a traditional tall tale. Its description of the dogs chasing the fox through the house and Uncle Buddy chasing both the fox and the dogs, with fox, dogs, Uncle Buddy, and the flying sticks of stovewood all caught in arrested motion, might almost have been written by Mark Twain. "Baker's Bluejay Yarn" has the same exaggeration, the same treatment of the absurd as though it were normal, with the consequent rearrangement of our perspective on normality. And the paragraph describing the chase ends with another device of traditional folk humor that Mark Twain developed to perfection, extreme understatement following immediately after grotesque exaggeration: "It was a good race."

Much of the rest of the tale may be appreciated on this level. The consistent use of hunting terms to describe human actions that we should expect to find either tragic or romantic is one of the most conspicuous humorous devices in the story. From the beginning, when the captive fox "treed behind the clock on the mantel," to the end, when the runaway slave has been captured and brought home and the fox trees once again from the dogs, this time on the roof, the casual and anti-romantic diction keeps us aware of the presence of the absurd. The disparity here between the manner and the matter, between the diction and the story it conveys of slavery and courtship in the Old South, is one of the staples of traditional humor.

The situation itself, as it develops, is farcical. The moral problem of slavery is not so much ignored as denied by the perspective in which we see it here. This runaway slave must be captured as soon as possible because otherwise he will be returned by a neighbor who will bring with him a marriageable sister for a visit. He must be hunted with hounds to prevent not his escape but his return. And in the poker game, low hand wins: the loser "wins" Miss Sophonsiba. Winning and losing, slavery and freedom, are almost indistinguishable, and not simply because a conventionally "romantic" subject is treated anti-romantically.

All the clichés of romantic fiction of the ante-bellum South are present, but turned upside down. The plantation named "Warwick," the dinner horn being blown by the slave boy, the planter drinking a toddy, the runaway slave: but the slave has no desire to escape, the boy blowing the horn is merely amusing himself, the planter with the toddy sits with his shoes off and his bare feet in the cool water of the springhouse, and the guests at Warwick must step carefully over a broken board in the floor of the porch. Miss Sophonsiba's pretensions to grandeur and her ambitions for romance are seen against the reality which they distort. The broken shutter, the rotting porch, the gateless gatepost—these are symbolic items in the unromantic reality of the life portrayed. Uncle Buck, terribly aware of Miss Sophonsiba's "roan tooth," yet had the presence of mind to bow to the lady: "He and Uncle Buck dragged their foot." The courtly manners belie his feeling and the situation. The traditional gestures of hospitality, of courtship, and of slavery are as thoroughly inverted as the famous poker game.

"Was" is not Faulkner's last word on life in the Old South, but in its reduction of the stock heroic and the conventionally romantic to less not only than their traditional but even than life size it might well be kept in mind as a complement to *The Unvanquished.* It is a very funny story, and that is merit enough. But it also has some significant things to say about the human community as it is viewed in time. Time past here appears as not nearly so different from time present as we might have supposed. Uncle Buck and Uncle Buddy still live and still continue their frantic and absurd efforts to escape from women.

4

ONE OF THE meanings of "The Old People" is that if we are to be redeemed from the futility of the well-meaning Quentins and Horace Benbows and the bitter frustration of the amoral Jasons, we have to be initiated into the mysteries by the old people as Ike McCaslin is initiated. What we discover when we have been initiated is not so easily stated, but what we become is made clear both abstractly and concretely in Faulkner—abstractly in his frequent catalogues of the old virtues he celebrates, concretely in redemptive characters like Ike.

Whether Ike McCaslin, childless, propertyless by choice, a carpenter, is convincing as a Christ symbol or even as a redemptive character is a question on which Faulkner's readers have differed and are likely, I think, to go on differing. It is perhaps significant that we do not see him between his boyhood and his old age. Much in Faulkner's work besides this suggests that he finds it easier to entertain the possibility of redemption from the horror than to imagine concretely what such redemption might be like. More to the point at the moment is the fact that he has written some of his very greatest stories about the need for and the experience of a kind of redemption conceived as dependent upon mingled lore and rite.

"The Bear" has been much discussed as an initiation story, but "The Old People," which is simpler in structure and meaning, develops a part of the same theme. Its relation to "The Bear" is that of introduction to development: it defines the conditions in which the redemptive rite can take place and suggests some of the central aspects of a redemptive experience, but it does not, like the longer story, show us even the initial stages of redeemed action. It shows us, rather, what made it possible and necessary for Ike later in "The Bear," after his ritual baptism, to "renounce the devil and all his works."

The opening of the story takes us onto the thematic level immediately. "At first there was nothing. There was the faint, cold, steady rain, the gray and constant light of the late November dawn. . . ." Whatever revelation is to come to us will come in the cold rain of late November. The light, later concentrated, "condensed," will be gray and faint. The symbolic implication of the light in which Ike waits should be familiar to us from a good deal of modern literature. E. A. Robinson pictured himself waiting in the same half-light for a greater light, and Robert Frost's poetry has in effect defined our age in autumnal images. It is in the late November that the disturbance of the spring comes to Ike. "The

Old People" suggests, from this point of view, not Frost's *Masque of Reason* but his *Masque of Mercy*.

At first there was nothing: "Then Sam Fathers standing just behind the boy . . ." The old people are just behind us, preparing us, waiting to initiate us if we are ready, as Ike was. Ike comes to terms with the past as Quentin never was able to for all his probing and his imagination. It is not simply that Ike listens to the voice of Sam Fathers recreating the past. It is not even that he listens so sympathetically that he comes to identify himself with the old people, though this is necessary as a preliminary to his initiation. He is first prepared by the voice and then initiated by the action of Sam Fathers, who is figuratively always just behind him, as he is literally behind him now.

Yet the voice is necessary, if only preliminary. The story starts just before the climax of the action; later it takes us back to Ike's preparation, the talk.

> And as he talked about those old times and those dead and vanished men of another race from either that the boy knew, gradually to the boy those old times would cease to be old times and would become a part of the boy's present, not only as if they had happened yesterday but as if they were still happening, the men who walked through them actually walking in breath and air and casting an actual shadow on the earth they had not quitted.

Ike's coming to recognize, through the words of Sam Fathers, the continuity of time and of the human community in time, his awareness of the old events as "still happening," is what has prepared him to see the deer. The idea here is similar to the Christian doctrine of the "communion of saints." "Time is a fluid condition. . . ."

The buck appears suddenly, without warning or preparation except the preparation of Sam Fathers' tutelage. "Then the buck was there. He did not come into sight; he was just there. . . ." The coming of the buck has the character of an epiphany. Though he comes in the gray November light, he seems himself to shed light, "looking not like a ghost but as if all of light were condensed in him and he were the source of it, not moving in it but disseminating it. . . ." This is what all Sam Fathers' talk has been for, what it has prepared the boy for.

" 'Now,' Sam Fathers said, 'shoot quick, and slow.' " What the old people have to tell us, when we are in the presence of the deer, is a paradox, or even a mystery. "Shoot quick, and slow." Only the prepared can follow both parts of the advice. The old man speaks in mysterious paradoxes; like Nancy with her reiterated "Believe" at the end of *Requiem for a Nun,* he cannot explain. The boy shoots without being able later to remember the shot. "He would live to be eighty . . . but he would never hear that shot nor remember even the shock of the gun-butt." The killing of the deer is for Ike an experience transcendent, elusive, ineffable, a religious experience. Unlike the stories of Sam Fathers that have prepared him for it, this experience is indescribable. "He didn't even remember what he did with the gun afterward. He was running." Yet it is an experience, like the later hunting of the bear, that determines the direction of his whole life.

The symbolic parallel of the hunting experience with religious rite and mystery comes to its climax when Sam "stooped and dipped his hands in the hot smoking blood and wiped them back and forth across the boy's face." Ike has been "washed in the blood of the lamb," to use the old Christian imagery, as well as in the blood of the deer. For the story contains enough parallels of Christian rite and doctrine to make perfectly clear the role of the deer as a substitute lamb even if we disregard what we learn later in "The Bear." Which does not mean that the story is an allegory of Christian baptism or conversion. By itself, in isolation from "The Bear," it can be read in several ways, perhaps most convincingly in terms of a kind of primitivism or nature mysticism. Ike is initiated into the mysteries of the wilderness, the mysteries known to the old people before the wilderness was tamed and its knowledge lost. When Sam Fathers was born

all his blood on both sides, except the little white part, knew things that had been tamed out of our blood so long ago that we have not only forgotten them, we have to live together in herds to protect ourselves from our own sources.

The question that, as far as I can tell, cannot be answered with any certainty from a consideration of this story alone is whether the primitivism is being "used" or "expressed." If it is a vehicle for an essentially Christian meaning, Sam Fathers is priest, the only kind of priest whose counsel could be effective for Ike in the gray November light. If it is the meaning, Sam Fathers, though he has priestly functions still, is ultimately Rousseau's noble savage, knowing with his blood what we cannot know with our minds. Perhaps he is a little of both, a priest, but a priest of "Nature, and Nature's God." If we take him this way, it would not be the first suggestion in Faulkner's work that his religious feeling is, paradoxically, at once Deistic and orthodox.

What cannot be questioned is that Ike's hunting experience is essentially religious. Like Hemingway's old fisherman, he loves "the life he spills." Like the recipient of Christian baptism, he is initiated into the deer's death as well as into his life. He learns to see nature sacramentally. The enormous buck he sees at the end of the story, the buck saluted by Sam Fathers as "Chief," may not even exist so far as the public, incontrovertible evidence is concerned. Walter Ewell saw his tracks but did not credit them, did not know they were his. Walter is almost willing to believe "there was another buck here that I never even saw," but he does not in fact believe it. Only Sam Fathers and Ike saw the grandfather of all deer.

Talking to his cousin McCaslin after the hunt Ike tries to describe his experience of the great buck. "You don't believe it," he says, "I know you don't . . ." "Why not?" his cousin replies; "think of all that has happened here, on this earth." He "believes" but his belief is involved and figurative, not Ike's simple literal acceptance. He seems to feel that some kind of survival is possible— ". . . you always wear out life long before you have exhausted the possibilities of living . . . all that must be somewhere. . . ." But he has not actually seen the deer that Ike has seen; and to Ike he seems, even in his sympathetic agreement, to be explaining away the experience. "Suppose they don't have substance, can't cast a shadow," he says.

To which there is only one reply that Ike can make. " 'But I saw it!' the boy cried. 'I saw him!' "

5

THE REVELATION gained by Isaac from the wilderness in "The Old People" under the tutelage of Sam Fathers is reaffirmed, completed, and set in a historical and social context in "The Bear."[6] In view of the profusion of religious symbols in both stories, it is probably not misleading to think of the two as a sort of Baptism and Confirmation: "The Bear" confirms Isaac's membership in the "church" of nature and society.

Part IV of "The Bear" gives us Isaac's discovery of the evil that made the purification rite necessary, makes explicit the content of the wisdom learned from the wilderness, and shows us something of the result of the boy's attempting to live what he has learned. We become aware of a paradox: the ancient evil is the reason why there had to be a purification rite, but the rite itself was a precondition of the discovery of the evil. Isaac is ready now to discover that the land cannot be owned, that man's proper role is defined in the concept of what the church calls "stewardship." The terrible injustice of slavery was merely an extension of the self-assertiveness that resulted in the idea of absolute ownership of the land: from "owning" Nature to "owning" other people. Natural piety, a sense of the numinous, reverence are needed if the evils dramatized in the old ledgers are not to be perpetuated in new forms forever. Isaac learns that the earth is man's not to exploit "But to hold . . . mutual and intact in the communal anonymity of brotherhood." Man was "dispossessed of Eden" when he first asserted his right to unconditional ownership. The land is now "cursed and tainted" by the compounded results of this original sin of self-assertion. Isaac must give up his patrimony.

He learns that man is permitted to "own" anything only "on condition of pity and humility and sufferance and endurance." He must cultivate the old virtues, "honor and pride and pity and justice and courage and love," learning through suffering—"Apparently they can learn nothing save through suffering. . . ." He must learn to live in full and unrestricted community. What Ishmael discovered on a whaling ship in *Moby Dick* and Melville dramatized in the "monkey rope" scene, Isaac discovers in the wilderness and in the old ledgers: "no man is ever free." His grandfather had been like Sutpen of *Absalom, Absalom!* unable to say "My son to a nigger," but Isaac will do what he can to break the pattern of inherited injustice: he will at least refuse to profit by it. He becomes a childless, propertyless carpenter, "not in mere static and hopeful emulation of the Nazarene . . . but . . . because if the Nazarene had found carpentering good for the life and ends He had assumed and elected to serve, it would be all right too for Isaac McCaslin. . . ." Though he does not accept the "fairy tale" with which "the Jew who came without protection" has "conquered" the earth, his is, in the full sense of the word, a religious renunciation. He is attempting in his way to fulfill both the Great Commandments, to love God and to love his neighbor, but the God he loves is purely immanent, not the God both immanent and transcendent of Christian orthodoxy. The theology of "The Bear" is a kind of "demythologized" and somewhat romantic Christianity. Whether its "heretical" or its "orthodox" aspects are the more important is a question on which its readers are likely to go on differing.

For the story does not seem to me to yield a completely consistent allegory. Its symbols are suggestive but not always clear in their implications when they are examined logically. It may well be that the imaginative and emotional richness of the story is gained at the expense of clarity. William Van O'Connor in his clear-headed and illuminating discussion of the story[7] has pin-pointed some of the difficulties of an allegorical interpretation. Why, for instance, does Isaac not hate Lion, the instrument of the bear's destruction? Going at the problem genetically, Mr. O'Connor finds that Faulkner had trouble unifying the material in the original, shorter version of "The Bear," and "Lion," the two stories he put together to make the final version of "The Bear." Insofar as there is a difficulty of interpretation in connection with Lion, I suspect that Mr. O'Connor's explanation is correct.

But there is another way of looking at the matter which I should like to suggest as at least possible. It involves cutting the lines of implication somewhere short of allegory. Isaac needn't hate Lion, despite the fact that the dog foreshadows the railroad which later destroys the wilderness of which the bear is a kind of apotheosis, because the bear is not God. He is a natural symbol of the old wild times from which so much can be learned, but he is still a bear. Faulkner would have us read the story, I think, both—and at once— as "myth" and as "realism." Isaac has learned what the old people have to teach, and the Way he learns is the only Way; but there are other methods of learning it. Though he is more at home in the wilderness than in the town, he need not hate what destroys the wilderness, neither Lion nor the railroad; what he must hate is evil. Lion is morally neutral, but Boon at the end of the story hammering on his gun and claiming the squirrels as his own is repeating the primal sin.

Whatever destroys community and stewardship over nature, in other words, is evil; but the use of nature in itself is not evil. The story leaves us not with an injunction to become propertyless carpenters but with a reminder that, while no course of human action is ideal, nevertheless every man aware of his heritage, as Isaac has become aware, must seek to realize his obligations as he can. Isaac's Uncle McCaslin is quite persuasive in his argument that for Isaac to give up his patrimony is in effect to try to escape the burden of responsibility. Only the Tenderfoot Scout, as Faulkner has Gavin Stevens remind us in *Intruder*, sees simple solutions to complex moral problems. Old Ben may rightly be hunted, the wilderness *will* shrink, but man must maintain his rightful relationship to nature and other men. Lion may be, symbolically, modern civilization, for which Isaac has little taste, but he is not Evil, as the bear is not Good or God. If there is something snake-like about the logging railroad, it is because the logging operations partake of the character of exploitation. The story is not so much an allegory of Good and Evil as it is an exercise in double vision. The good and the evil are seen finally as inextricably mixed, just as the heroic and the anti-heroic merge in the incident of Boon and the squirrels at the end. The heroism of the hunting epic and the sordid injustice of the old ledgers qualify each other: Isaac must know both if he is to come to terms with the past.

If we do not insist too much on a strictly allegorical reading, the story will seem to have sufficient unity and coherence. Symbolic "loose ends" in it there may well be, but the view of life that emerges from it seems to me neither incoherent nor properly to be characterized as romantic primitivism. Rather, it is a view at once ironic and tragic, but not defeatist, for it calls us to responsibility and community.

A much later hunting story, "Race at Morning,"[8] suggests that some such reading as this approximates the one Faulkner intended. In the new story a boy of a later generation learns, even from a much shrunken wilderness, something of what Isaac had learned earlier. But his mentor tells him at the end that this way of learning the old virtues—which are still the necessary ones—is no longer good enough. " 'You're going to school. . . . You must make something out of yourself.' "

> "I am," I said. "I'm doing it now. I'm going to be a hunter and a farmer like you."
> "No," Mister Ernest said. "That ain't enough any more. . . . Now just to belong to the farming business and the hunting business ain't enough. You got to belong to the business of mankind."
> "Mankind?" I said.
> "Yes," Mister Ernest said. "So you're going to school. Because you got to know why. You can belong to the

farming and hunting business and you can learn the difference between what's right and what's wrong, and do right.
And that used to be enough—just to do right. But not now.
You got to know why it's right and why it's wrong and be
able to tell folks that never had no chance to learn it. . . .

The "old truths of the heart," in short, do not change, but our
approach to them may have to change. Isaac McCaslin is not
Christ, the bear not God. There are other ways of learning to "do
right" than hunting the bear or the great buck. In "The Bear" as
elsewhere in Faulkner the moral implications are clear and central,
the theology somewhat ambiguous and usually peripheral. What
some have taken to be Faulkner's religious "orthodoxy" is a by-
product chiefly of his view of man, not of God.

6

THE TRAGIC mood predominates in the short stories as it does in
the novels, finding two kinds of expression. In the earlier stories it
appears as "the outrage of a potential believer," to use a phrase
applied primarily to *Sanctuary* by Carvel Collins.[9] In the stories
written from about the end of the thirties on, it appears primarily
as the tragic burden of an obscure affirmation. The two expressions
of the tragic vision are linked in many ways. They are, as Mr.
Collins has also said, two sides of the same coin. "That Evening
Sun" may be seen, now that we have the benefit of hindsight, to
have prepared the way for "The Bear." Ike McCaslin's renunciation
of his hereditary plantation was motivated not only by his recognition of the moral evil of slavery but by his feeling for the reality of
death. He did not ponder the birth and death entries in the com-
missary ledgers without profit. What he learned from them com-
plemented what he learned from Sam Fathers of the wilderness.
Both lessons had the effect of destroying man's pretensions, reducing
him to his real size and power. From both the ledgers and the
wilderness he learned to see man in a religious perspective.

The comic stories are linked to the tragic by the same ultimate vision and sensibility. Faulkner's comedy, even with all his sharp awareness of social realities, is not in the last analysis social comedy but religious comedy. Like the comedy of Christopher Fry's dramas, the comedy of "Was" and "Spotted Horses" and "Mule in the Yard" has as one of its integral elements an awareness of man's situation as precarious. Man's pretensions and his folly are amusing not so much because he offends against manners and mores and good sense as because he ignores or misconceives his position in nature. Man's societies are always passing away, all of Faulkner's work says, but the truths of his relation to ultimate reality remain constant. When he is ignorant of, or misconceives, these truths the result is tragic or comic, depending on our mood.

The humorous short stories and the tragic ones, then, express the same vision of life. The horror and astonishment with which Cash viewed the antics of man in *As I Lay Dying* are implicit in all the stories in *Knight's Gambit* as well as in those like "The Old People" that attempt to suggest some sort of affirmation capable of preventing Darl's madness and Quentin's suicide. Perhaps the final impression we take from the short stories as a body of work is Faulkner's constant identification of ultimate reality with the unconditioned and uncontrolled. When Ike and his party came out of the wilderness after the hunt, they would come suddenly to "a house, barns, fences, where the hand of man had clawed for an instant. . . ." Faulkner's religious humanism, so often given overt expression when he editorializes, finds no frequent or powerful expression in the short stories. So far as the short stories are a valid clue, we may say that his creative imagination is energized by a tragic religious sense that sometimes issues in comic and sometimes in tragic stories but that always implies the threshold character of experience.

CHAPTER 10

The Artist as Moralist

INTRUDER IN THE DUST
REQUIEM FOR A NUN
A FABLE
THE TOWN

IN THE MIDDLE FORTIES Faulkner's work began to show a marked reversion toward one of the characteristics of his earliest novels. The voices of the characters began to have to compete with, even to give way to, the voice of the artist whose message was so important that he could no longer be wholly content with the indirection of fiction. It is not of course that the voices of the characters of the great novels were ever free of the evidences of their paternity. But as in a large family in which all the children bear a strong family resemblance but each is nevertheless unmistakably himself, with the unpredictable uniqueness of freedom and maturity and independence, the voices seemed to be the voices of people in a community. One of the most important differences between *Soldier's Pay* and *As I Lay Dying*, as we have seen in Chapter 4, is the greater dramatic independence of the characters in the later novel.

But in the forties Gavin Stevens was created, with an outlook and specific opinions ordinarily very similar to those of his creator.

When Stevens is not available, other voices take his place, do his job, which is essentially to supply a philosophic statement of the themes of the works themselves. To those who had watched this development for more than a decade, it was not very surprising that the old general in *A Fable* should not simply paraphrase but actually quote Faulkner, climaxing his temptation of his son by repeating parts of the Nobel Prize speech. It is as though Faulkner, having long wanted a platform and having got it at last, were determined to make the most of it, even if it became necessary to say the same things twice that they might not go unheeded.

Gavin Stevens is less obsessive and more philosophic than Quentin, and better educated than Ratliff, but to say that he is a less impressive fictional character is certainly to indulge in understatement. The voice of fin de siècle pessimism heard quoting the Rubaiyat and paraphrasing Swinburne in *Soldier's Pay* and *Sartoris* has become the voice of an obscure mid-century tragic affirmation; but the change of emphasis in the message has not rendered it any less recognizable, less personal. The latter part of Faulkner's career has been marked by three parallel developments: a new stress on the moral function of art, a gradual change of emphasis from despair to affirmation, and a tendency to make his themes explicit through the use of spokesman characters. All three developments point to a movement away from the influences under which he began his mature career, after his apprenticeship.

The new conception of the artist as having a duty to uplift and sustain mankind was first clearly announced in Stockholm in 1950 from the platform afforded by the reception of the Nobel Prize. Before that, in 1948, it was adumbrated by the role assigned to Gavin Stevens in *Intruder in the Dust*. The increased hopefulness found expression in the Nobel Prize speech too, and is apparent in most of the works of the last dozen years, most notably in two short stories, "Race at Morning" and "Of the People." The tendency to emphasize the message of hope by making it explicit may be seen in most of the work from *Intruder* on. Faulkner is clearly no longer content to create works marked by "form, solidity, color."

2

THE TITLE of *Intruder in the Dust* is ambiguous with the old ambiguity of *As I Lay Dying*. Both a radical naturalism and a Biblical view of man are consistent with the implications of the phrase. Robinson Jeffers, for example, in his poems of the twenties and thirties, pictured man as an "intruder" in nature in the sense of a biological accident, an "unnatural," temporary, incidental offshoot of the convolutions of the nebulae. On the other hand, the Bible and the Prayer Book caution man to remember that he is dust and will return to dust, that unless he be regenerated he lives only toward death.

Up to a point the body of the work keeps this ambiguity alive. At the beginning of Chapter X, for instance, Uncle Gavin, still talking, describes man as given definition in his eating, picturing him as eating his way into the substance, the body, of the world, so that he becomes the world and it becomes man. The parallel with the words of the Invocation in the service of Holy Communion sets up religious suggestions here that may seem to justify the neo-Christian interpretation of Faulkner's meanings. But Stevens continues, becoming more and more explicit (that his meaning may not be misunderstood, presumably); and the ambiguity evaporates, the parallel with Holy Communion becoming more of an adornment than a part of the meaning, as Stevens restates an explicit, still obscure but not essentially ambiguous, theology:

> eating . . . the proud vainglorious minuscule which he called his memory and his self and his I-Am into that vast teeming anonymous solidarity of the world from beneath which the ephemeral rock would cool and spin away to dust not even remarked and remembered . . .

If Steven's version of the central Christian rite is religious enough in its tone to inspire, perhaps deliberately incite, a religious interpretation, only its obscurity makes an interpretation in terms of historic Christian doctrine continue to seem possible. By eating man is united not with God but with nature. Perhaps one reason for the increasing insistence of the voice is that passages like this have been so often misinterpreted. Faulkner's article of several years ago in *Harper's* magazine on the right to privacy and related matters[1] exhibits a tone in which anger is mingled with impatience of misunderstanding. He seems to feel an increasingly urgent need to make his meanings clear.

Even in the words of Stevens the ambiguity does not of course wholly disappear. Stevens is after all a created character, not Faulkner, and he usually speaks obscurely enough to be open to a variety of interpretations. He is both obscurely profound and profoundly obscure. But something of what he intends comes through his rhetoric clearly: his unalterable, sometimes angry, religious humanism, set sharply in contrast to the institutional forms of man's ancient "delusion," the "fairy tale that has conquered the whole Western world"; his insistence, against whom it is not clear, that man is "immortal" but that the "immortality" is racial, a survival not of the "I-Am" but of the species, or at least of life, even if on another planet; his conviction that man's only salvation lies in responsible moral action in community, action guided, his creator has recently told us in accents indistinguishable from Stevens's, by "the scientist and the humanitarian,"[2] who must take over now that church and state have failed.

Enlightened responsible action in community: in this conviction of Stevens we are close to the explicit theme of *Intruder*, which poses the problem of the conditions under which morally significant and effective action can take place. Because this is so, Stevens's lengthy discussions of the South's case against the "outlanders" are not aesthetically irrelevant or unfunctional. Whatever its flaws may be, *Intruder* is not simply a tract against the Fair Employment Practices Commission. For the South is seen as an example of community—perhaps the only true one left in America—as contrasted with a mere aggregation of people. The South must solve its race problem by itself, "without help or interference or even (thank you) advice" from outlanders because only thus can the problem be solved in such a way as to benefit both parties to the guilt. Stevens tells his nephew that only the Tenderfoot Scout refuses to accept the full horror of the guilt; the Eagle Scout accepts the burden of his corporate sinfulness and goes on from there. The motto of the Tenderfoot is "Dont accept," of the Eagle Scout, "Dont stop."

According to Stevens such acceptance of mutual responsibility for moral action is likely to take place, or *can* take place, only in a homogeneous community, not among "a mass of people who no longer have anything in common save a frantic greed for money." It follows that the extended attempt to define the South as community, as contrasted with North, East, and West as mass, is essential to the development of the theme. The view that finally emerges from Stevens's monologues seems not very different from that expressed half a century before by Stephen Crane in "The Open Boat" and by Conrad in "The Secret Sharer" and elsewhere: a naturalistic moralism in which a sense of community is stimulated by a perception of the precariousness of man's situation. Men, in this nineteenth century answer to naturalistic reductionism, are driven into community by the threat of the alien universe, the failure of the conventional life-saving stations, the emptiness or indifference of the tower like a giant. As they emerge dripping from the sea, they find that there is a halo around the heads of those on the beach who come with blankets and sympathy. The direction of Faulkner's development is nowhere more clearly exhibited than in the contrast between this point of view and that of such an early story as "Dry September."

A merely legislated, forced achievement of justice, then, would short-circuit the possibility of moral action by destroying the South's existing homogeneity as a community. Regeneration cannot be legislated against the will of the unregenerate. Stevens is therefore justified, from the point of view of the novel's theme, in concluding that Lucas needs defense from the regions that would "free" him as much as he does from the South itself:

> I'm defending Sambo from the North and East and West—
> the outlanders who will fling him decades back not merely

into injustice but into grief and agony and violence too by forcing on us laws based on the idea that man's injustice to man can be abolished overnight by police . . . I only say that the injustice is ours, the South's. We must expiate and abolish it ourselves, alone and without help nor even (with thanks) advice.

There is nothing obscure about this central contention of Stevens's, whatever we may think of its tact. But in a good deal of the talk that leads up to this there is an obscurity that cannot be explained as intentional ambiguity: a kind of obfuscation, whether intentional or not, a fuzziness in the use of words, sometimes what seems a deliberate attempt to exploit irrelevant and unearned connotations. There is an obscurity in *Intruder* that is different in kind from the ambiguity of *The Sound and the Fury.* One example will suffice.

Stevens is talking, at the moment, of man's aspiration toward justice and other ideals. He finds man's "pity and justice and conscience too" evidence for his "belief in more than the divinity of individual man," or rather (after a long parenthesis) not this "but in the divinity of his continuity as Man . . . ," etc. Now I submit that in the first phrase defining Stevens's affirmation, the word "divinity" has been robbed of most of its semantic content, since clearly in the context of this book and in the larger context of Faulkner's work, we cannot take seriously an Emersonian view of man and his "divinity"; and that is the only option open to us, since traditional Christianity, the "fairy-tale" of man's "delusion," has never asserted man's divinity but on the contrary has repeatedly condemned any such notion as heresy.

It is possible of course that Stevens is equating Christianity with just this notion, despite the gap in his Oxford and Heidelberg education which such an equation would suggest. If so, this would not be the first indication in Faulkner's works that he himself in some moods equates the Christian doctrine of man with a tender-minded optimistic "idealism" capable of denying the presence in the world and in man of that evil which his own tragic vision finds there. See for example the story "Leg," in which a priest's faith is destroyed when he has to face the fact that evil exists.

A "belief in more than the divinity of individual man" is obscure because, not knowing what a belief in the "divinity" of individual man could be (every man his own god?), we cannot very well imagine what a belief in more than this would be. But the stated "more," when it comes, is even more obscure: "the divinity of his continuity as man." We may guess, of course, that this points toward some such meaning as this: man's very survival ("I decline to accept the end of man") renders him, however obscurely, divine. Why it would not equally prove the divinity of atoms or molecules or whatever else may survive is not clear. But this interpretation, though tempting, would be wrong. The belief is not in the divinity of man at all but in "the divinity of his *continuity*": continuity itself is said to be divine. If this has any meaning at all, it is certainly difficult to find out what it is. Both the point of view and the obscure way it is expressed remind us of the Nobel Prize speech of two years later.

Intruder in the Dust represents a falling-off in Faulkner's power as a novelist, though I have argued that the long-winded religio-political speeches of Gavin Stevens are not intrusive or functionless but codify the theme that without them would be implicit anyway. It is a falling-off first of all because of the very need so to insist upon the theme: it becomes the Novel of Ideas, the Novel with a Message, too easily and quickly. The timeliness of the message does not help. It appeared in the context of election time, Harry Truman and the FEPC, revolt in the South and the threat of political secession or, worse, of moral outrage: "... *you will force us ... into alliance with them with whom we have no kinship whatever in defense of a principle which we ourselves begrieve and abhor ...*" (That is, we will push the Negro down still lower in the scale of human dignity and value, make him suffer still more, much as we hate to and much as we will thereby increase our own guilt, if you don't stop urging us toward justice.) The political message of the book was so timely that it is not surprising that to many the novel seemed essentially a pamphlet announcing the candidacy of Strom Thurmond.

Without meaning to suggest an ideal of absolute "purity" for the arts, and certainly without meaning to imply that Faulkner would be a better writer if he were not so solidly a part of his native community, I should think it obvious that the kind of precise social relevance *Intruder* has weakens the book. Its temporal context makes its importance seem in some degree a matter of the correctness of its opinions. Yoknapatawpha's anger over FEPC is an interesting fact in American social history. I think a rather strong case for Yoknapatawpha's stand could be made, stronger indeed than the one Stevens makes, since his obscurantism makes even his clear ideas suspect. But it is clear enough that this sort of thing, this passionate abstract defense of a section's political anger, is not the stuff of Faulkner's greater works. Much of the writing is brilliant, especially in those numerous passages where consciousness is doubled and tripled in intensity and fullness as an event is experienced over and over ("He could see himself reaching the church . . .") first in anticipation, then in deed, then in memory, then sometimes in all three in one multiple remembering of anticipating and doing and remembering. But all the brilliance of passage after passage in the book, or the beautiful solidity of Lucas as a character, cannot finally make it seem proper to put *Intruder* in the same category with Faulkner's greatest novels, or even with *Pylon* or *The Wild Palms* or *The Hamlet*.

3

REQUIEM FOR A NUN was written apparently as a kind of relaxation from the major work in progress, *A Fable*, with which Faulkner was chiefly occupied from 1944 to 1953. *Requiem* is the sort of thing an artist of Faulkner's kind does for the fun of it, and because it's easy. A by-product of a rich imagination, it is casual, almost playful in its recapitulation of the major themes of the earlier works.

Formally, it is a daring experiment. (*A Fable*, in contrast, is safe— for Faulkner, and for our time, almost conventional.) One can

imagine Faulkner saying to himself that he would try uniting in
this work both of the two great styles of our time, his own and
Hemingway's; that he would really give the critics something to
puzzle over and misunderstand this time, writing like himself and
like the artistic opposite of himself, alternating a sensuous, lyric,
evocative style in which character and plot disappear in an
excruciating awareness of time and place, with a bare, direct,
behavioristic style in which facts—words and actions—make their
own poetry.

I said "One can imagine." I do not pretend to have any "inside"
knowledge of what was in Faulkner's mind when he conceived
Requiem for a Nun. But judging from the results, as well as from
the several explicit references to Hemingway scattered through the
work, we may at least say it is *as though* Faulkner had decided to
show that he could outdo both himself and Hemingway in a little
coda to Temple Drake's story. The hallmark of Faulkner's most
characteristic style has always been his brooding lyrical intensity.
In several of his greatest works the crucial problem for the critic
is to decide how much of the stuff of traditional fiction is left after
plot and character as we are accustomed to think of them have
seemingly evaporated in the fluid nuances of a technique which
attempts to capture the simultaneity of all experience. A lesser
problem in *The Sound and the Fury,* this is a major problem in
Absalom, Absalom! The remarkably dramatic vividness and concreteness of many characters and scenes in his best work, and the
rich vein of folk humor, do not invalidate but only qualify the idea
that Faulkner's most typical and natural vein is lyric. From the
closing scene of *Soldier's Pay* to the opening scene of *Absalom* to
the wonderful courthouse and state capitol and jail sections of
Requiem, his imagination is most fully expressed in the passages of
lyric evocation.

Hemingway, on the other hand, is of course famous for his "anti-
poetic," his bare, hard, muscular, deliberately insensitive, dramatic
style. The technique of expression he has created depends upon
using the most (one would have said) inexpressive words, evoking

emotion by controlling, repressing, or denying the emotion and concentrating on the "fact." Until a very few years ago at least one would have had no hesitation about saying that Hemingway's style had had a greater influence than Faulkner's, that it was in fact *the* typical style of our time. Certainly it has affected a whole generation of young writers, so that imitations or adaptations of it have long since sifted down from the little magazines and the first novels to the rich slicks and drug store fiction.

Faulkner has often shown himself concerned with the reputation and achievement of his great contemporary. If he has seen himself as closer to Thomas Wolfe, whose sensitivity and daring he has publicly praised, he has never been grudging in his praise of Hemingway's accomplishment. The extended definition of woman's nature in *Requiem* not by reference to "life" but explicitly in terms of Hemingway's Maria in *For Whom the Bell Tolls* is symptomatic, an overt expression of a preoccupation that must have contributed earlier to the conception of *Pylon* and *The Wild Palms*.

The dramatic sections of *Requiem* are almost a parody, by intention perhaps a distillation, of the dramatic style of modern fiction popularized and given quintessential expression in the work of Hemingway. Fiction stripped of everything except the words and actions of the characters, Faulkner seems to be saying, is this: the bare, inexpressive words, the fumbling with the cigarettes, the drinks poured and not drunk. Each act of the drama, on the other hand, begins with an expository evocation of time and place, an essay on the history of the setting—the courthouse, the statehouse, the jail. The two aspects of fiction, fiction as dramatic report and fiction as lyric poetry, both present in Faulkner's own work of course but perhaps more clearly to be distinguished in modern fiction in the great contrast between Hemingway and Faulkner, have been split apart, distilled, then juxtaposed. This is something Faulkner had not tried before, an experiment that must have intrigued him by the very outrageousness of its daring.

The result is certainly interesting but not I should think for most readers wholly successful. If it demonstrates once again that

Faulkner possesses in full measure that indispensable virtue of the great artist, courage, it does not prove that he can outdo Hemingway in Hemingway's own province. The dramatic parts are bare without being especially suggestive in their concreteness. The lighting of the cigarettes, for example, is a piece of business that suggests Henry James's attempt in his plays to control his imagination, force it to be content to find expression in the revealing word or gesture: an attempt which succeeded chiefly in eliminating most of what is most valuable in his fiction. When we think of the wonderful revelations achieved by the notations of behavior in Faulkner's earlier works—by Flem's chewing in *The Hamlet* for example or Jason's putting his hands in his pockets in *The Sound and the Fury* —we may wonder what has happened here to make these gestures so inexpressive, so banal even, or at least, when they convey what they are supposed (presumably) to convey, so uneconomical. There is a good deal of what James called "weak specification" here. One or two cigarettes offered and refused or smoked furiously or simply handled would surely have suggested Temple's nervousness and Gavin's solicitude as well as several dozen; and similarly I should think with the drinks and the handkerchiefs.

The dramatic sections show us Faulkner writing at a level considerably lower than his best, exhibiting his ideas and themes (as when Stevens says "The past is never dead. It's not even past.") standing alone, isolated from the transforming power of his unique imagination. But the lyric sections exhibit him at very nearly his best. The prose poems devoted to the courthouse, the statehouse, and the jail are recapitulations of Yoknapatawpha history, much of it familiar from earlier works, which make that history explicitly microcosmic. Yoknapatawpha is not only a part of the world, with no discernible boundaries in time or space; in some sense it *is* the world. Geologic time and astronomic space are as tangibly present to the fully conscious mind as the logs within the walls of the Holston House, which some do not know are there, or the scratched name and date on the window of the jail. The communities of Jefferson and Jackson are at once exceedingly real spots on the earth and "events" hardly discernible in time. In this vision reality is seen as process—a process moving very fast or very slowly, depending on what aspect of it our imaginations seize. This is the ultimate setting against which Temple's drama of good and evil is enacted.

The drama itself concentrates on the crisis of belief. Many readers for whom Faulkner's religious preoccupation did not emerge clearly in the earlier works were surprised by what seemed to them a change of direction in *Requiem*. With the problem of belief now explicit, they felt they had discovered a new Faulkner, concerned with a Miltonic attempt to justify the ways of God to man. But the differences between this and the earlier works are chiefly formal. The splitting apart of behavior and imagination, which is the central fact about the technical experiment, forces the old themes into explicit statement.

At the center of Temple's anguish there lies a belief not unlike Horace Benbow's discovery of the "pattern" made by evil:

> Which is another touché for somebody: God, maybe—if there is one. You see? That's what's so terrible. We don't even need him. Simple evil is enough.

Temple is more fortunate than Sutpen, for she has Stevens as mentor. He brings her to a realization that she must accept her full guilt and not only forgive but, what is harder, ask to be forgiven.

> And now I've got to say "I forgive you, sister" to the nigger who murdered my baby. No: it's worse: I've even got to transpose it, turn it around. I've got to start off my new life being forgiven again. How can I say that? Tell me. How can I?

Stevens and Nancy together bring her to a point where she is willing to consider the idea discovered by Isaac a decade before in "The Bear," that man's redemption depends in some way upon suffering accepted freely to prevent suffering. ("Stevens: 'The salvation of the world is in man's suffering. Is that it?' Nancy: 'Yes, sir.'") Nancy, if she could, would take Temple still further, to an acceptance of Christ as Lord and Savior, to justification by faith through grace—"All you need, all you have to do, is just believe."

Nancy goes straight to the heart of Apostolic preaching when she distinguishes between the *didache* and the *kerygma* and makes the *didache* dependent upon the *kerygma:* precisely the Pauline order, of course:

> Menfolks listens to somebody because of what he says. [The ethical maxims; Protestant modernism; ethical human-ism] Women don't. They don't care what he said. They listens because of what he is. [That is, the unique Son of God, whose words therefore have the character of Revela-tion.]

But at the end Temple is still not sure that she has a soul, or that, if she has one, it is worth saving, or that God, if there is one, would trouble Himself to save it. "What kind of God is it that has to blackmail His customers with the whole world's grief and ruin?" Nancy's answer, though it exhibits the firmness of her simple faith, presumably is not such as could possibly convince Temple: "He dont want you to suffer. He dont like suffering neither. But he can't help Himself. . . . He dont tell you not to sin, he just asks you not to. And he dont tell you to suffer. But he gives you the chance." Though she compresses and foreshortens the theological explanation of historic doctrine, Nancy is actually surprisingly articulate in her outline of orthodox belief. Her statement of it connects her with Dilsey, who acted as a Christian but did not talk about the belief that made her so different from the Compsons.

The comparison of Nancy with Dilsey reminds us, though, of the degree to which *Requiem* is a lesser achievement than *The Sound and the Fury*. Like Dilsey, Nancy is a sympathetic character. Her words have power and authority because she is a redeemed char-acter who has much to teach Temple, whether or not there is a part of her belief which cannot be accepted by more sophisticated minds. Yet we see very little of her before the climactic scene in the jail; we do not learn to trust her as we do Dilsey. We hear about her hymn-singing, and about Stevens's willingness to join her in the singing; but she is more nearly a composite of all that we have learned to expect a Faulkner redemptive character to be than a convincing human being. We know the implications of *nigger, whore, dopefiend, murderer*: transposition of the world's values, redemption through suffering for the lost and rejected. But we do not see her in action enough to understand why she felt driven to murder the child to prevent suffering. We suspect her of being a little mad.

What comes through with power in *Requiem for a Nun* is not a world created and sustained in all its immanent meaningfulness but a theme. It is a significant theme, significantly felt and expressed, but still a theme rather than a world. And this despite the "realism" of the dramatic sections. We remember Temple saying, as she leaves the jail, "Anyone to save it. Anyone who wants it. If there is none, I'm sunk. We all are. Doomed. Damned." And Stevens replying, "Of course we are. Hasn't He been telling us that for going on two thousand years?" And the question remains: Are we in fact then "Doomed. Damned"? Whether Christianity is more than a moral paradigm, an instructive myth which teaches that the only redemption comes through guilt acknowledged and suffering accepted, *Requiem* does not attempt to tell us. Nancy says yes, Temple recognizes her need to believe, Stevens is uncommitted but not unsympathetic. The long conflict between heart and head in Faulkner is left unresolved. Still, this is the book, instead of *A Fable,* on which Faulkner's publishers should have lavished the decorative crosses.

4

IN A FABLE the preoccupation with religious issues which has been apparent in Faulkner's work from the beginning breaks into systematic allegory. The novel was intended, it seems apparent, as Faulkner's *magnum opus,* a definitive statement of the themes of a lifetime. Its meaning is so elaborately schematic, and its structure and texture so completely dominated by its abstract meaning, that it should perhaps not be thought of as a "novel": the very word carries with it traditional expectations that *A Fable* does not, perhaps is not intended to, fulfill. The book is an intricate, multi-leveled, massively documented and sustained imaginative statement of Faulkner's opinions on the possibility of salvation for man. It attempts to explain what Gavin Stevens has been saying obscurely for so long. To those who have followed Faulkner's great career with sympathetic interest and admiration and concern, it is very unpalatable to admit that the widespread disappointment which the book aroused was justified.

The disappointment did not spring from any sense that the book failed to respond to the mood of the times. With isolated exceptions there was a general readiness to welcome it as a great work by a great writer. In the twenty-five year interval between *The Sound and the Fury* and *A Fable*, particularly in the last several years before *A Fable*, an immense public had discovered Faulkner. Reviewers were prepared to be overwhelmed, mystified, even shocked. What they were not prepared to be was bored. I doubt that any other Faulkner work has been put aside unfinished by so many readers of taste and adequate preparation—some of whom at least were Faulkner enthusiasts of long or recent standing.

Neither untimeliness nor insistence once more on themes long familiar can account for this reaction. Readers were prepared to be impressed by any Faulkner novel but especially by a work of this sort, exploiting myth and elaborating symbols, religious in tone without being committed to any religious orthodoxy, compounding Dostoyevsky, Eliot, Freud, and the Bollingen Series. *A Fable* is as timely as the issue of *The Partisan Review* that came out a few months after the novel with a "Self Portrait in Questions and Answers" of Ignazio Silone.[3] To the question "What do you consider the most important date in world history?" Silone is said to have replied, "December 25 of the year 0"; and to a later question, "Have you confidence in man?" his answer is given as

I have confidence in the man who accepts suffering and transforms it into truth and moral courage. And so now I think that out of the terrible polar night of the Siberian slave labor camps, Someone may come who will restore sight to the blind.

The interview ends with the question, "Someone? Who?" and the reply "His name does not matter." The very different backgrounds of Silone and Faulkner, the one a repentant Communist and the other a Southern conservative, have led them at last to remarkably parallel developments of opinion and attitude. The interview, like the book, is an indication of the climate of opinion in the mid-fifties. If *A Fable* disappoints us, then, it is not by a failure to express the mood and attitude and preoccupation of the present.

Nor does it represent any sharp change of direction in Faulkner's own thinking. As long ago as the writing of the stories in *Dr. Martino* he had opened the story "Black Music" with a passage that foreshadowed *A Fable* more clearly than the image of the falling spire in *Soldier's Pay*:

> This is about Wilfred Midgleston, fortune's favorite, chosen of the gods. For fifty-six years, a clotting of the old gutful compulsions and circumscriptions of clocks and bells, he met walking the walking image of a small, snuffy, nondescript man whom neither man nor woman had ever turned to look at twice, in the monotonous shopwindows of monotonous hard streets. Then his apotheosis soared glaring, and to him at least not brief, across the unfathomed sky above his lost earth like that of Elijah of old.

The old gutful compulsions, the lost earth, and Elijah: this is a vision compounded of the naturalistic discovery of the mechanisms of man and of his dreams, revealing both a sense of man's utter loneliness in the "alien universe" and a sense of the degree to which he finds definition and hope only in religious myth. The tensions that characterize much of the best of Faulkner's work spring from the outlook expressed in this description of an ordinary man; and the meaning of the allegory in *A Fable*, so far as I can make it out, springs from it too. The opinion that *A Fable* shows us a Faulkner who has decisively changed his mind seems to me not merely wrong in emphasis but quite mistaken. *A Fable* makes one doubt whether there has been any essential change in outlook from the earliest work to the latest.

"Out of Nazareth," one of the first things Faulkner ever published, takes a direction that nothing in *A Fable* contradicts or even sharply qualifies. The sketch portrays a modern Jesus who is a fine young dreamer and idealist, sympathetically drawn, but doomed to failure. The old general in *A Fable,* an older Gavin Stevens, could be describing this poor idealistic young man when he addresses the Christ-figure of the novel: "You champion of an esoteric realm of man's baseless hopes and his infinite capacity—no: passion—for unfact." The sympathetic Christ-figure in "Out of Nazareth" carries around with him a copy of *A Shropshire Lad.* Another sketch of life in Chartres Street pictures the kingdom of God as revealed in the splinting of the stem of a broken flower loved by an idiot, thus foreshadowing not only one of the most moving scenes in *The Sound and the Fury* but the final impotence of the Christlike corporal in *A Fable.* Early and late, Faulkner's Christ is like Melville's: a deaf-mute in cream-colored clothes, a beautiful good young man with a stutter, a corporal going voluntarily to his death knowing himself forsaken and his mission a failure, going only because not to go would mean betrayal of the hopes of man.

In one significant sense *A Fable* is obscure without being ambiguous. Its title suggests not only its form—that of a fable, or morality, or allegory—but something of its underlying theme. The "fable" that is the subject here is identical with the "fairy-tale" that some thirty years earlier Faulkner had referred to, in "Mirrors of Chartres Street," as having conquered the whole western world. The allegory of Holy Week is detailed and systematic. Beginning with an ironic Triumphal Entry, it proceeds through the major events of Holy Week with parallels too close to seem mere allusions. From the profuse trinitarian imagery of the opening scene, through the Last Supper to the death and "resurrection" of the Christlike corporal as the Unknown Soldier, the writing is overtly allegorical. The major figures of the Gospel story are here, recognizable by name or symbolic action if not by their characteristics—John the Baptist, Martha, Mary, Peter, Judas, St. Paul, Christ. Everything in the story is Biblical except the meaning. For the correspondences are at once close and twisted, obvious on the surface and obscure at a deeper level. The meanings that emerge from the Biblical framework would make the identifications seem ludicrous if it were not clear that this, like Robert Graves's *Nazarene Gospel Restored,* is an interpretation of Scripture based on the supposition that historic Christianity was founded upon a hoax. It is as though Faulkner had set out to found, by rewriting the Gospel story, a sect humanistic in its ultimate theology but traditional, even orthodox, in its moral and psychological understanding of man. The process is almost the opposite of symbolic, as though Dilsey had been given Jason's character and outlook and then labeled Mary and called a virgin. Not the real nature of the people and events here, but their arbitrary designations remind us of the people and events of the Gospel.

This seems an unprofitable matter to dwell upon: I shall give only one illustration. The supposedly Christlike corporal does not suggest the historic Jesus to me in the least. Not only is he a dim and shadowy figure about whom we know too little as a person and about whose expressly symbolic activities we know too much, he appears to be a young man without radiance or magnetism or eloquence or even, so far as we can really know, vision. Granted that in reading the Bible every man has a right to be his own interpreter, surely we may agree that the weight of history throws the burden of proof on anyone who would envision Jesus in so negative and colorless a way. Such an interpretation would not have seemed valid even to the spiritualizing "ethical Christianity" of the past. The corporal not only would not have been recognized as a type of Christ by Dante or Milton or Donne; he would not have been recognized by Matthew Arnold or Renan. Even Faulkner's St. Paul figure, the runner, though quite un-Pauline in his naivete, is more satisfactory as a character. The runner's last words on the corporal seem appropriate in a way we are not sure was intended. The sisters offer to show him the grave. " 'What for?' he said. 'He's finished.' " In view of the way the Christ figure has been presented, one's response to this is likely to be that he was "finished" before he ever began. Not his nature as we come to know it in the book but only his allegorical function makes the corporal seem in any way Christlike.

But even that is open to question. Jesus after all is recorded as having said that the peace he brought was not peace as the world knows it, and there has always been an important segment of Christian opinion which has held that wars and rumors of wars will continue until the end. At the very least we may say that there is no Biblical evidence that Jesus conceived his mission exclusively, or even primarily, in terms of stopping war. Faulkner's Christ is likely to strike almost everyone as impoverished rather than ambiguous or luminant.

So far as I can understand them, I find the theological ideas in the book banal when they are not muddled or obscure. R. W. Flint has put the matter temperately. The book, he has said, "is everywhere vitiated by rampaging ideas, ideas divorced and disembodied, muddled and self-defeating."[4] Yet the effect of the realistic texture in which the Biblical allegory is embedded is to destroy the allegory. Reading the book, we have constantly to readjust our understanding as passages of vivid, but not meaningful, realism give way to Biblical echoes. A character is about to come alive for us, is almost created; but suddenly we are reminded that he is Peter or Judas or the Devil tempting Christ, and the likelikeness fades, the allegory seems questionable, and we find ourselves objecting that Peter or whoever was almost certainly not like this, would not have done or said this, looked like this. There are some scenes of heightened and powerful writing in the book, and a few more or less lifelike characters, but insofar as the events and people become lifelike, fictionally real, they cease to be credible allegorical types. What moves these people is never in the last analysis anything but the author's opinions. The incarnation never takes place here, aesthetically or theologically. Fact and meaning do not blend and illuminate but destroy each other.

A *Fable* was presumably intended to leave open the possibility of some sort of hopeless hope—or at least to say that some such hope would in fact endure.[5] Not, certainly, the Christian hope of Heaven suggested by the crosses so lavishly used in the book's design: the final meaning here is clearly humanistic, obscurely naturalistic. When the shattered Runner at the end spits out blood and broken teeth to proclaim his confidence that he is never going to die, his meaning is a hidden one. But we may guess that the "immortality" he proclaims, like the survival in which Gavin Stevens affirms his, and Faulkner's, faith in *Intruder,* is such as will be brought about by "the scientist and the humanitarian," or perhaps even, as one of the mammoth slick magazines has recently opined, by the scientist alone.[6]

It is, perhaps, possible to argue that, since Faulkner has made it impossible to be certain that the body of the corporal was the one exhumed and placed in the tomb of the Unknown Soldier, there is still a minimal ambiguity attaching to the central meaning. Perhaps there was a resurrection, not just an exhumation, even though probability seems to suggest otherwise. Perhaps so. At any rate, there still remains the belief in hope, the almost hopeless hope of "prevailing" through endurance, or because of endurance. But it seems to me that "prevailing" and "endurance" so conceived have very little meaning. This is pagan stoicism without spiritual or ethical content. It may be argued that the structure of the book does not finally and irrevocably deny the possibility of some sort of Christian faith.[7] But I think we must insist, first, that if anything is clear about the book it is that the supernatural is in effect, though probably not in intention, ruled out. Finally, we should have to answer that it does not seem to matter very much: the meaning of whatever religious faith we can conceive to be asserted here is so impoverished that it does not appear an attractive, even if we can imagine it as a possible, option.

"I decline to accept the end of man," Faulkner has said; and also, in a similar context, that he believes that

> man is tough, that nothing, nothing—war, grief, hopeless-
> ness, despair—can last as long as man himself can last; that
> man himself will prevail over all his anguishes, provided he
> will make the effort to; make the effort to believe in man
> and in hope—to seek not for a mere crutch to lean on, but
> to stand erect on his own feet by believing in hope and in
> his own toughness and endurance.[8]

This was Faulkner speaking to the Japanese people not long after *A Fable* appeared. If the book's achieved theme is not so much a firm belief in hope as an infirm hope that hope may, somehow, endure, I think the reason is that *A Fable*, despite its "rampaging ideas," is also, partially and intermittently, a product of Faulkner's deeper imagination. And his imagination has always been characterized by grief narrowly escaping despair. Despite its too conscious, its elaborately contrived, conception, *A Fable* is of the heart as well as of the head. The only parts of it that really live are of the heart.

5

IN THE HAMLET Snopes took over Frenchman's Bend, in *The Town* he took over Jefferson, in the forthcoming *The Mansion* we are promised the spectacle of Snopesism triumphant in the state. By calling his latest book both *The Town* and "Volume Two" of *Snopes*, Faulkner has invited comparison of this work with *The Hamlet* and at the same time suggested that we should reserve judgment of this second part of the three-part novel until the whole thing is before us. But *The Town* suffers greatly in any comparison with *The Hamlet,* and any attempt to think of it as the second part of a unified work of which *The Hamlet* is the first part presents considerable difficulties.

The difficulties center in the conception of Snopesism, of the old order, and of the conflict between them. As far as Snopesism is concerned, we learn nothing essentially new about it in the new work, except Flem's impotence, which is symbolically so appropriate that we ought to have guessed it from *The Hamlet*. But this is not the whole difficulty. In a sense we do learn something more about Snopesism—but what we learn does not so much develop as weaken and confuse the indictment of modernism made by *The Hamlet*. The real stumbling block to our reading this book as a continuation of *The Hamlet* is that, in terms of achieved content rather than repeated asseveration, Snopes has now become passive.

When Eula reveals Flem's impotence to Gavin Stevens, she says

> He's—what's the word?—impotent. He's always been. Maybe that's why, one of the reasons. You see? You've got to be careful or you'll have to pity him.

This sudden revelation of Flem as victim more than evil-doer is the old Faulknerian change of perspective, from judgment of the deed to compassion for the doer.

In earlier works this reversal only (at most) threatened to destroy the work by deepening ambiguity to ambivalence, and at the same time strengthened the work, in another sense, by reminding us that the character in question was not just a symbol. But here it reinforces the abstractly symbolic interpretation of Snopes, encouraging us to do what we are already too strongly tempted to do. In *Sanctuary* we were reminded that Popeye, with his black rubber knobs for eyes and his stiff mechanical gestures, was not simply a symbol of evil modernism: he was an unhappy child. But in *The Town* we are invited to see the symbol of soulless modernism as properly to be pitied, not hated; invited easily, quickly, abruptly, with no dramatic embodiment of the new perspective. The result is that instead of coming suddenly to see Flem as a human being we begin to wonder what judgment of modernism is required of us.

Flem approached being an incarnation of pure evil in *The Hamlet*, and we may have speculated about why he was uniquely exempt from the otherwise universal Faulknerian rule of compassion. But the structure of that book did nothing to encourage any such speculation. Flem was something of an anomaly, to be sure, but there was a symbolic consistency in all that we saw and thought of him. We saw him act in "soulless" ways, doing things that were vividly credible; and we equated him, when we came to think about him and the book abstractly, with soulless modernism. But now we scarcely ever see him at all, and when we do he is not especially either hateful or vivid; yet we are asked to see him as victim. The familiar shift of perspective becomes ineffective here. There is no adequate fictional embodiment of the evil to make the pity difficult; nor is there any convincing presentation of the conditions that should inspire pity, there is only the surprise of the withheld information. The pity we are invited to feel looks more like sentimentality than like compassion set in a framework of clear moral judgment.

Paralleling the change of emphasis in the conception of Snopes is a change in the conception of the old order from which Snopes inherits. It is almost as though in *The Town* Faulkner were saying to his critics, particularly to the traditionalist critics, No, no! I was never so naive as to romanticize the old times, *I* never thought they were glamorous. *The Town* strikes one as protectively anti-romantic, acknowledging the romanticizing tendency only to repudiate it: "Because we all in our country, even half a century after, sentimentalize the heroes of our gallant lost irrevocable unreconstructible debacle," and

> Bayard Sartoris drove too fast for our country roads (the Jefferson ladies said because he was grieving so over the death in battle of his twin brother . . .).

But of course, as we have seen, it was not just the Jefferson ladies who "romanticized" Bayard Sartoris, it was the total design of the book of which he was the center.

The faults of *Sartoris* are glaringly obvious today—to us and, it would seem, to Faulkner. One of them is a too immediate, and uncontrolled, identification with the old order, as in the final apostrophe to the Sartoris name. The fault in *The Town,* so far as the presentation of the old order is concerned, is just the opposite: not too much passionate identification but too little. Or rather, the tendency to identification is controlled by a protective irony which serves no aesthetic purpose—though it may serve a personal one—and actually undercuts the apparently intended theme. For if the old order does not somehow, after whatever necessary qualifications, stand for a superior way of life, then Snopes has no opponent and there is no conflict.

And that is very nearly the case. We hardly ever witness Snopes doing anything particularly outrageous. In fact, until very near the end we never even *hear* of his doing anything very shocking; rather, we hear of his receiving, passively, the favors showered on him by the representatives of the old order itself. Stevens and Ratliff debate endlessly what he will do next, but as far as we can tell for sure he seldom does anything at all. Mayor de Spain gives him the super-intendency of the power plant, the vice-presidency of the bank, and finally the bank itself and his home. Gavin Stevens designs and executes the monument to Eula; and we are not convinced when Ratliff assures us that nevertheless "it was Flem's monument."

At one point Ratliff, speculating as usual on the triumph of Snopes, remarks on the lack of conflict: "No, not a contest. Not a contest with Flem Snopes anyway because it takes two to make a contest and Flem Snopes wasn't the other one." Rather, he thinks, it is as though Flem were playing a game of solitaire—against Jefferson. But Ratliff's shrewdness is for once inadequate: for if it is true that Flem is passive, as Ratliff notes, it is equally true that "Jefferson" is compliant, even, at crucial moments, active against its own presumed interest. Whereas in earlier books representatives of the old order were often pictured as Prufrock characters, helpless to preserve values which they adequately appreciated and at least passively embodied, here there is no conflict at all. What, then, is the book about, what does it say?

Perhaps when we have the third part of *Snopes* the answers to these questions will be clearer. At the moment it seems truer to say not that *The Town* adds nothing to *The Hamlet's* portrayal of the crisis of modernism but that it subtracts something. And its subtraction is not only abstract, from our sense of the issues involved—because the nature of the conflict has become unclear—but emotional and imaginative. *The Town* is a lesser work than *The Hamlet* in every way. Its humor is tamer, almost tired at times, especially when the material has been used before. Its compassion is less pure and less revealing—compassion for Eula, for whom one might quite easily feel sorry, rather than for Ike or Mink, for whom one's natural feeling is disgust or contemptuous rejection. Its grief is less intense—not dramatically localized in a Houston, but spread over the broad view of things as seen from the hill above Jefferson.

In a key passage toward the end of the work Faulkner pictures Gavin Stevens looking down on Jefferson from this hill and seeing "all Yoknapatawpha in the dying last of day beneath" him. Stevens is more than ever a mask for Faulkner at this point. What he sees is, quite clearly, what Faulkner sees:

> And you stand suzerain and solitary above the whole sum of your life beneath that incessant ephemeral spangling . . . yourself detached as God Himself at this moment above the cradle of your nativity and of the men and women who made you, the record and chronicle of your native land proffered for your perusal . . . you to preside unanguished and immune above this miniature of man's passions and hopes and disasters . . .

There is no distinction here between the voice of Stevens and the voice of Faulkner. In effect Faulkner is telling us what he feels as man and artist, and the final emphasis is on the achievement of a difficult detachment: "unanguished and immune." But Faulkner in earlier and better works was not detached, not immune. The greatness of the best early works is certainly inseparable from the intensity of their passion, their grief, their attachment, an intensity always threatening to become excessive and unbearable but always just being controlled by technique. The immunity, the distance from the subject, the detachment so evident in *The Town* whether we look at the old order or at Flem, was bought at a high price.

Flashes of the old Faulkner are here, but only intermittently. The unresolved conflicts that we have noted over and over again in the earlier works have not been resolved, they have been put aside. *The Town* must have been easy to write, and it is easy to read. But it is not great Faulkner.

CHAPTER 11

"A Passion Week of the Heart"

WHEN FAULKNER REVIEWED HEMINGWAY'S *The Old Man and the Sea* several years ago he was very brief and pointed: the novel showed Hemingway at a new peak of achievement because he had at last brought God into the picture.[1] The pronouncement was consistent with the religious tone of the Nobel Prize acceptance speech, with the more recent address to the Japanese people in which they were urged not to despair, to have faith, and with one of the most recent observations of Gavin Stevens, who seems clearly to speak with an authority not solely his own. Stevens says in a recent short story, with Ratliff agreeing, that what we need to make America survive is "to trust in God without depending on Him. We need to fix things so He can depend on us."[2]

Together with the profuse religious imagery and symbolism in his fictions, and with the fact that (if religion be defined, with Tillich, simply as "ultimate concern") all of Faulkner's works are religious, such pronouncements as these have led to a widespread agreement that Faulkner should be aligned with the movement of neo-Christianity among artists and intellectuals of our time, or even with orthodoxy.[3] There is undoubtedly considerable justification for seeing him in such terms. But I submit that the problem of attempting to determine what, in general and in the last analysis, Faulkner means, what he has to say to us, is partially clarified but not really solved by this alignment.

There is, in the first place, the difficulty that emerges when we examine all the pronouncements of Faulkner the man, outside his works of fiction, and try to find out precisely what *they* mean. In the Nobel Prize speech, for instance, despite the clearly religious tone of the whole, despite too the use of terms like *prevail* that are susceptible of interpretation in Biblical terms, there seems to me to be a crucial ambiguity about the central affirmation. One wonders if the rhetoric is tortured because the conviction is not clear. What will man prevail over, and how? Over the world, himself, his machines, his folly, death? By virtue of the Atonement or by education, science, his own ingenuity? By the efforts of what Faulkner has called elsewhere "the humanitarian in science and the scientist in the humanity of man?"[4]

When the Bible uses *prevail,* as it often does, it is clear in general how the word should be interpreted: always the frame of reference is theistic in a fully supernaturalist sense. Man's hope rests in a transcendent God. In the Old Testament man will prevail because God keeps his promises despite the faithlessness of man; in the New, man will prevail by virtue of Christ's victory over death on the cross, which is interpreted as precisely God's way of keeping his promise. But when Faulkner says man will "prevail," it is not easy to find out exactly what he means.

Or again, when we study the message of faith to the Japanese and look for indications of the object of faith, we find a similar difficulty. In effect the speech says that we are to have faith in hope and in man's ability to continue to hope. The message is clearly "affirmative," but what it affirms, apart from the old need for endurance, seems to be the process of affirmation itself: "believing in hope and in . . . [man's] own toughness and endurance."[5] If we are tempted to interpret this in a clearly and exclusively humanistic sense ("man's *own* toughness"), we are given pause by putting it in context, and the context includes the affirmation by Stevens and Ratliff just noted, the terms in which *The Old Man and the Sea* was praised, and the answer Faulkner gave to a Japanese audience when asked if he believed in Christianity: "Well, I believe in God."[6]

There is a problem of interpretation here not easily to be solved in any terms, and not solvable at all I think if we consider only the evidence of Faulkner's public pronouncements in recent years. We may of course prefer to put the problem aside by saying that he is in a muddle. Or we may more charitably stop short of the desired clarity by reminding ourselves that he is a man of our time, with all the tensions and ambiguities bequeathed us by the rediscovery in a positivistic age of the fundamental truth of the Biblical view of man and his situation. No wonder, we may say, Faulkner's mind dwells habitually in paradox. In an age at least partially character-ized by its interest in Kierkegaard and Kafka, by existentialism and Barthian theology, what else would satisfy a sensitive mind?

Considerations such as these may "explain" the ambiguities in Faulkner's stated opinions on religious matters, but they do not clarify them. The one thing that seems clear at this point is that Faulkner is torn between attachment and rejection, between what in his frame of reference appears as the conflict of tradition and reason, between heart and head. If this is so, we are unlikely to make much progress in attempting to find out what his works mean by trying to untangle the threads of his personal theology.

2

BUT WHEN we turn back to the works themselves with the public pronouncements in mind, we are immediately confronted by a further difficulty. Not only are Faulkner's stated opinions them-selves ambiguous and conflicting, but the chief implications of the whole body of his fiction are partially inconsistent with the general drift of implication in the statements. If we may disregard for the moment a whole host of problems of interpretation, we may put the difficulty in this way: the main drift of Faulkner's statements has been essentially humanistic, and in his fictions and elsewhere he has repeatedly warned us against accepting the "fairytale" as a "crutch"; but the finest works of his imagination have presented the issues of life in traditional religious terms. It would seem that his fiction is more susceptible of traditionally religious interpretation than Faulkner the man, as distinct from the artist, intends it to be. The man who urges us to have faith in hope and in man creates a Dilsey who has faith in neither but in God and then forces us, aesthetically, to identify with her.

The problem we face here, of the partial discontinuity between Faulkner's art and his opinions, is completely insoluble only if we hold to the romantic notion of art as distinctively and primarily confession. That Faulkner's fiction is a kind of personal testament springing from his identification with Yoknapatawpha is certainly true in a number of senses, most importantly perhaps in the sense that where we find the greatest evidence of passionate identification with the material, there, in general, the fiction is greatest. But if this were the whole truth we should be brought to a halt in any attempt to understand the problem.

A more fruitful approach is to recall the climate of opinion about the nature of art and the role of the artist when Faulkner first achieved his artistic maturity. Despite his increasing tendency to write and speak as moralist, Faulkner has never abandoned the idea of the artist expressed in *Mosquitoes*. He may be driven by a sense of the urgency of our problems to speak out and save the Republic, but he still holds to an "impersonal" theory of art. As he has said of his use of Christian allegory in *A Fable*, "The Christian allegory was the right allegory to use in that particular story."[7] And he added on the same occasion a statement that leaves no doubt at all about what he thinks on this subject, though it raises a number of interesting questions when we think of it in connection with some of his other statements and with some of his later practice: "The writer's only responsibility is to his art."

In short, Faulkner says that he makes use of Christian myth in his stories to deepen and enrich them. He uses it, he insists, because it is at hand, available, as something with which he can work, without any implication of personal commitment to it. But I think we may doubt that this is the whole truth, despite Faulkner's insistence upon it to the interviewer. The very insistence seems defensive; we wonder about the conditions of the interview, the opinions of the interviewer. Faulkner is not simply being true in these statements to his old conception of the impersonality of art; he is also, by implication, picturing himself as "unanguished and immune." But the finest works of his whole career are sufficient evidence that any such characterization of himself is at least partially false. When he works at his best, he works from the depths of his mind and his experience and creates *novels* that "believe," whatever their creator may say, much later, to interviewers. When Faulkner talks off the top of his mind, as he frequently does in public situations, he seems to me often to misrepresent both himself and his work. Nevertheless, the fact that he talks as he does in such situations is in itself revealing. Defensiveness springs from a sense that one is vulnerable.

To this extent a study of Faulkner's opinions expressed outside his fiction is helpful—though the reminder it offers us, that we must move warily in any identification of the man with his works, hardly comes as a total surprise. But it seems unprofitable to go beyond this in surveying the opinions of the man as a basis for understanding his works. The dangers of the genetic or intentional fallacy in criticism have undoubtedly been exaggerated in some quarters in the recent past, but the element of truth in the notion was never more apparent than when one is dealing with the work of Faulkner. With the notable exception of his comments on his conscious intention in *The Wild Palms,* his opinions on his work are seldom helpful. Indeed, the matter should be put more strongly than this: a great many of Faulkner's public statements of meaning and intention lead us not toward but away from an understanding of the achieved meanings of the works themselves.

A single illustration should suffice. In the same *Paris Review* interview Faulkner has said that "No one is without Christianity, if we agree on what we mean by the word." Whatever we mean by the word, are we to interpret Jason as not without Christianity? What are we to make of Nancy's plea in *Requiem for a Nun*— "Believe. Just believe"—if everyone already is Christian? Is Flem Snopes in *The Hamlet* also in some sense Christian? Would it help, in deciding these matters, to find out what Faulkner himself says he means by the word? Christianity, he goes on to say in the same place,

> is every individual's individual code of behavior by means of which he makes himself a better human being than his nature wants to be, if he followed his nature only. What-ever its symbol—cross or crescent or whatever—that symbol is man's reminder of his duty inside the human race.[7]

If we assume that Faulkner was not deliberately pulling the interviewer's leg with this definition, we shall have to decide that he was talking through his hat. Even if Christianity were to be defined as simply a moral code—a definition both historically and philosophically irresponsible—it would obviously not be *any* moral code ("every individual's individual code"). If we were to take such foolishness seriously and use it as a basis for interpreting *The Sound and the Fury*, we should find it impossible to make any sense at all of that work. What Faulkner has to say, he says well only through the symbolic language of his art. When he uses the abstract language of philosophy and theology, his meanings are usually vague and often apparently confused.

About all we may conclude with any degree of certainty from the statements Faulkner has made in recent years is that he considers himself a theist and an anti-naturalist. The stance is clearly religious, but the meaningful core of religion for Faulkner seems to be morality. Glands and conscience are always in conflict, and our only hope is that conscience may win. Religion, for Faulkner, is summed up in the call to self-transcendence. There is an important strand in Faulkner's thought that looks at times remarkably like old-fashioned eighteenth century deism. Neo-naturalists might reasonably charge that his attacks on naturalism in the name of religion are "dated": they have force only if we define naturalism in the reductive and essentially materialistic terms very common a generation ago but much less common now. A good many people, perhaps most, who think of themselves as naturalists today hope for the same kind of self-transcendence Faulkner calls for, though they would insist that this hope does not make them "religious." But their categories of thought and Faulkner's do not overlap enough to make a real argument possible.

When we turn our attention back to the fiction, we are likely to realize with renewed force the difficulty of relating art and philosophy in any direct and simple way. For however deistic and humanistic Faulkner's religious convictions may be, it is abundantly clear that his imagination works effectively only when it works in Biblical terms. In *Requiem for a Nun,* for instance, it would hardly be possible to argue convincingly that Nancy is not presented as a sympathetic character, perhaps *the* sympathetic character. She is one of the redeemed, precisely because as "negro, dopefiend, whore" she has suffered and learned her need for someone to save her. So far as Nancy expresses the theme of the work, the meaning of *Requiem for a Nun* is subsumed under classic Christianity.

But Nancy with her formula of simple faith in Him is not the only clue to the effective, achieved, theme of *Requiem for a Nun.* When in the end Temple acknowledges that she cannot save herself and Stevens agrees, though he does not share Nancy's simple faith, we see the coming together of all the lines of implication and are close to the meaning of the work. And when we arrive at this point we find that we have been here before, many times. The conflict of heart and head, of desire and scruple, has not been resolved but only restated.

Requiem for a Nun is a late novel and has sometimes been taken as evidence for the spiritual journey toward orthodoxy that has been posited for Faulkner. But if we turn back to the beginning, we find an anguished response to the falling spire. The religious meaning of *Requiem* is not essentially different from the meaning of the closing scene of *Soldier's Pay.* Again, *The Sound and the Fury* is finally, in *achieved* content, Dilsey's book, not, despite Faulkner's stated intention, Caddy's or her daughter's; and Dilsey knows a time not our time. But Dilsey is one of the ignorant and simple. Between Dilsey's redemptive but inaccessible faith and Quentin's intelligent despair the early fiction offers no middle ground except endurance.

The later fiction sometimes offers us the way of Isaac McCaslin, Ratliff, and Gavin Stevens. All three seem to have found some viable faith permitting an escape from the alternatives of credulity or despair. Viewing man in traditional terms, they see his situation as desperate but not hopeless; and the hope, as they see it, lies in his assumption of moral responsibility in community. McCaslin and Stevens are, apparently, theists; all three seem to have taken the categories in which they think from Biblical Christianity.

Beyond this it would seem that the theology they imply cannot be clarified by considering them alone. Any further definition of the meaning they hold for us must come, if at all, from considering their place in the whole body of fiction of which they are a part.

3

THE THEOLOGY implied in the fiction strikes us as orthodox or heterodox not only according to the novels we have in mind but according to the position from which we view it. If we are thinking primarily of the main currents of thought expressed in American literature in the last hundred and fifty years or so, we shall be likely to see Faulkner as continuing the tradition of Hawthorne, Melville, James: the ironists with a tragic vision, an unwillingness or inability to deny the clear fact of the presence of evil in the world, yet with hope too. In the illuminating categories of R. W. B. Lewis in *The American Adam,* this is the tradition of the center. Faulkner clearly belongs to this tradition more than to that of Emerson and Whitman or of Horace Bushnell.

But to place Faulkner in this tradition is to begin an inquiry, not to end it. For one thing, Mr. Lewis's categories fit the nineteenth century better than the twentieth: from a purely contemporary point of view, it would seem that Faulkner does not really belong in the "middle," despite his kinship with Hawthorne. His sensibility is in many ways closer to Eliot's than to Hawthorne's, and Eliot is not a "middle" figure if we derive our categories from American literature. Eliot is certainly an ironist, and orthodox, and he has a very firm hope—but not at all Whitman's or Emerson's kind of hope. Or again, in significant respects Faulkner's point of view is more like that of his contemporary Reinhold Niebuhr, with his combination of neo-orthodoxy and social gospel, than it is like that of any nineteenth century figure; but Niebuhr does not fit neatly into any of Mr. Lewis's categories.

In similar fashion the revealing concepts of the true Prometheus and the false Prometheus applied by Richard Chase to Melville light up an area of Faulkner's work, without achieving the kind of definition in which it is possible finally to rest. We have seen Faulkner's sympathy with the Promethean archetype again and again, and noted too his warning against the false Prometheus's tendency to rely on machinery, gadgets, anything that will ease the burden of being human and having to face responsibility for our choices. But the Promethean theme appears more often in the early part of Faulkner's career than in the later. Though the sensibility that created Houston was close to that which created Ahab, the settled convictions expressed in the creation of Ike McCaslin as a redemptive character are not notably Promethean. The archetype behind Ike is not Prometheus but Christ; and though the concept of the suffering servant draws the two together, there are also, clearly, significant differences. Ike is not in rebellion.

Beginning with "The Bear" Faulkner's work is characterized by its repeated attempts to restate for modern man what Faulkner takes to be the essential meaning of Christian myth. This is just as surely the intention of *Intruder in the Dust* as it is of *A Fable*. The fundamental assumption that shapes many of Faulkner's works of the forties and fifties is that the dogmas of the Christian creeds are at once figurative and profoundly true. This, ultimately, is at the root of that remarkable kinship between Faulkner and Hawthorne that Randall Stewart and William Van O'Connor have correctly emphasized.

In short, if we think of "orthodoxy" in American literature in a sense as extended as the "neo-orthodox" definitions often are, we find that Faulkner belongs in the orthodox camp. However often and heatedly he may condemn the churches, he is closer in his view of man and the nature of the moral life to Jonathan Edwards than to Franklin, to Hawthorne than to Emerson. He belongs with those who, whatever their heterodoxies, have felt and expressed a kinship with the historic Christian view of man and his situation.

4

FROM SUCH a point of view, the meanings of Faulkner's fiction are for the most part basically consistent with the broad outlines of the classic Christian view of man and the world as expressed by American writers. Yet, when viewed in relation to a tradition older than American literature, when viewed as a part of the Christian literature of two thousand years, the meanings of Faulkner's works may come to seem Christian only in a sense. It is not simply that Faulkner is not Dante or Milton or Bunyan: neither is Eliot. It is rather that in Faulkner's works the crucifixion is central and paradigmatic, but the resurrection might never have occurred. Grant all objections that may reasonably be made at this point, grant the difficulty of defining not only "orthodoxy" but "belief" of any sort, grant all this and more, and it still remains true that the common core of belief that has united Christians of all persuasions in all ages is acceptance of the miracle of the first Easter. Without it the early church would have had no gospel, no "good news"; without it, there would be no essential distinction between Christianity and other theistic religions.

But within a Christian frame of reference the crucifixion without the resurrection is pure tragedy. Unlike Emersonian optimism, Christianity does not by-pass or deny tragedy, but neither does it rest in the final tragic dilemma: it holds that "in the end," when all things are made manifest, it will become apparent that perfect power and perfect love are one. Tragedy has been once and will be again transcended. Tragedy is, as it were, an *interim* condition; perhaps better, the purely *human* condition.

In Faulkner's greatest works the tragedy seems final, unrelieved, inescapable in any dimension. This is very nearly the same as saying that when he writes at his best we find all the categories of Christian thought and feeling except faith and hope in the classic, and Pauline, sense. The body of his fiction is built of Christian thought and feeling, shaped by Christian images and symbols, and deepened and enriched by constant Christian and Biblical allusions; but within all this is a core of what we may call religious humanism, or old-fashioned Protestant modernism—or simply deism tinctured with romantic nature mysticism.

The religion implicit in Faulkner's works is, then, as what seems to be becoming the prevailing opinion would have it, very "orthodox"—but only insofar as that is possible with a "demythologized" Christianity. Bultmann in theology and Faulkner in fiction belong to the same intellectual generation. Clearly, Faulkner's definition of Christianity as simply a moral code is not an adequate statement of his position. He takes credal Christianity, apparently, as unhistorical myth containing profound and redemptive moral and psychological truth which he has undertaken to reinterpret in modern terms. If this is so, it is really no wonder that his best imaginative works and the statement of his personal credo that he makes on public occasions seem often discrepant.

In a time when the reaction against secular optimism has made it fashionable to rediscover original sin, it is easy to conclude, as a good many today seem to be doing, that Faulkner's tragic vision is sufficient to make his works Christian. But as Hawthorne told us long ago in "Young Goodman Brown," it is not enough for a Christian to discover the universality of guilt. If to deny the radical nature of evil is to make Christianity seem irrelevant, as it came to seem to the believers in the "religion of humanity" and the followers of the gospel of Progress in the nineteenth and early twentieth centuries, to affirm evil without also affirming the effectiveness of the Atonement is to stop in the position that St. Paul characterized as pre-Christian and conducive to despair.

Hope can only subsist where faith is, faith in God or in man or in both. Some of Faulkner's works, like *Sanctuary* and *Pylon*, remain close to despair at all times; others, like *The Sound and the Fury* and "The Bear" and *Intruder in the Dust,* include a movement toward faith, and consequently a note of hope. But the object of the faith—man or God—is often left unstated, and when God is its object the faith is embodied in simple believers like Dilsey and Lena and Nancy. In the former case we have Christian terms without necessarily Christian meanings; in the latter, Quentin's problem is still with us, for however strong our sympathy for the Dilseys of the world may be, we cannot by wishing attain to their simple faith. It may be said of many of the earlier works that they hover between present despair and the memory of a lost faith, and of the later ones that they seem to be bidding us to repent and believe in God and man, as we wish, or can, or must.

In short, the view of God and Revelation implicit in the fiction is open to question; the view of man's nature and his human situation is not, or not in the same way. There is no doubt about what Ike McCaslin thinks about man; what he thinks about God and ultimate reality is not so clear. We know where Stevens's heart lies, but his opinions seem inchoate when they approach ultimate questions. Ratliff's shrewdness is insufficient to define the way of redemption. I think we must say of the redemptive characters in the later works that they end by leaving the themes they are intended to carry not very far from where they picked them up.

Faulkner's fiction is best understood in Biblical categories. It proceeds from piety and is conducive to piety. If we would go beyond some such statements as these, we must be content to leave clarity behind.[8]

5

WE ARE FORCED, even in conclusion, to fall back upon paradox: when Faulkner's work seems most obviously Christian, it is often least so, and when it does not seem Christian at all, or seems even explicitly non-Christian or anti-Christian, as in the excoriation of

Baptist and Presbyterian "orthodoxy" in *Light in August,* then Christian meanings often emerge most powerfully. If that seems too positive a way of putting it, let us say that the terms in which experience is analyzed are such as to make the historic Christian answers to the questions implicitly raised seem pertinent and natural.

I take it, for example, that in *As I Lay Dying* Addie is the "saved" and saving character, not Cora Tull with her conventional piety. Though the book is replete with Biblical echoes and Christian symbols, an important meaning in it would seem to be that deeds and not words (or doctrines, or faith) save us. It is, of course, possible to point out that this emphasis too is within the Christian tradition, is even Biblical. We need only recall the Epistle of St. James with its warnings against the dangers of a "dead" faith: "Be ye doers of the word, and not hearers only. . . . Pure religion and undefiled . . . is this, to visit the fatherless and widows in their affliction." But Addie seems to want us to be doers *instead of* hearers. She is not so much reminding believers to practice what they believe as rejecting their belief. Addie is certainly in rebellion against the "prime maniacal risibility": which is to say that *Moby Dick* is at least as relevant to her story as the Jamesian Epistle. But if we continue very far in this direction we reach an interpretation like the readings of *Moby Dick* that resulted from identifying with Ahab and forgetting Ishmael. *Absalom, Absalom!,* on the other hand, which does not have the problem of belief at its center in the way that *As I Lay Dying* does, contains nothing that would contradict a Christian interpretation and much that would support it.

Light in August is probably the most striking example of this dualism in Faulkner's work. With professed Christians in the roles of antagonists and with its reflective character expressing opinions about the failure of the churches that Faulkner has often expressed himself, it yet implies at its deepest level a meaning which is Christian not merely in some broad or figurative sense but precisely and Biblically Christian. "Inasmuch as ye have done it unto the least of these, ye have done it unto me." The characters are finally judged in terms of their response to Joe Christmas, and the professed

Christians are convicted of having a faith that is dead because it never issues in works of love. However Faulkner may have "intended" the novel, however he would now interpret it himself, Christians are certainly justified in seeing in it a powerfully expressed Christian theme.

Faulkner's fiction is existentialist, and to say this is not really to change the subject. It is existentialist as much of modern painting is existentialist, and the fiction of Kafka, and the earlier poetry of Eliot, and the theology of Paul Tillich. And as Tillich himself has recently said, existentialist art rediscovers in a manner appropriate to our time "the basic questions to which the Christian symbols are the answers."[9] Faulkner's fiction breaks up and reconstitutes the conventional and expected elements and patterns and feelings of experience, imposing on us the burden of painfully fresh perception. From its sometimes violent dislocations of the familiar, the old questions of man's nature and destiny emerge with fresh relevance and unexpected urgency. The culture of the recent past tended to forget not just the answers but the questions that must be put before the answers can seem meaningful. Faulkner's Passion Week, in short, may only be "of the heart," obscurely and ambiguously related to history, but a wholly pragmatic and positivistic frame of reference would produce no Passion Week at all.

CHAPTER 12

"From Jefferson to the World"

FAULKNER'S USE OF THE SOUTHERN PAST, his conception of time, and his search for a living image of man are all connected. Toward the end of *The Town* there is a passage that will open up the subject. It seems to say "This is what it has been like to be William Faulkner," though the experience is attributed to Gavin Stevens. A life and a career are epitomized in a single view of Jefferson, embodied in an image and held off at a distance for inspection and appraisal. The first two paragraphs of the passage give us what amounts to Faulkner's own summary of his career:

> There is a ridge; you drive on beyond Seminary Hill and in time you come upon it: a mild unhurried farm road presently mounting to cross the ridge and on to join the main highway leading from Jefferson to the world. And now, looking back and down, you see all Yoknapatawpha in the dying last of day beneath you. There are stars now, just pricking out as you watch them among the others already coldly and softly burning; the end of day is one vast green soundless murmur up the northwest toward the zenith. Yet it is as though light were not being subtracted from earth, drained from earth backward and upward into that cooling green, but rather had gathered, pooling for an unmoving moment yet, among the low places of the ground so that ground, earth itself is luminous and only the dense clumps of trees are dark, standing darkly and immobile out of it.
>
> Then as though at signal, the fireflies—lightning-bugs of

the Mississippi child's vernacular—myriad and frenetic, random and frantic, pulsing; not questing, not quiring, but choiring as if they were tiny incessant appeaseless voices, cries, words. And you stand suzerain and solitary above the whole sum of your life beneath that incessant ephemeral spangling. First is Jefferson, the center, radiating weakly its puny glow into space; beyond it, enclosing it, spreads the County, tied by the diverging roads to that center as is the rim to the hub by its spokes, yourself detached as God Himself for this moment above the cradle of your nativity and of the men and women who made you, the record and chronicle of your native land proffered for your perusal in ring by concentric ring like the ripples on living water above the dreamless slumber of your past; you to preside unanguished and immune above this miniature of man's passions and hopes and disasters—ambition and fear and lust and courage and abnegation and pity and honor and sin and pride—all bound, precarious and ramshackle, held together by the web, the iron-thin warp and woof of his rapacity but withal yet dedicated to his dreams.

"First is Jefferson": here the passion week of the heart was discovered and, because it was discovered in depth, was found to be universal. Any claim of greatness for Faulkner must rest primarily on the way he has rendered the local, the particular, and the concrete with amazing vividness while evoking the most far-reaching symbolic implications. The "historian of Yoknapatawpha" has both recorded and created a world; and he could have done neither so well if he had not done the other too. Though several of the works laid outside Yoknapatawpha are very fine, it remains as true for Faulkner as it was for Hawthorne that the past of his region is his best subject, the one in which he is surest of himself and least likely to falter in thought or feeling. And the spokes of the wheel whose hub is Jefferson radiate farthest in those works in which the past is treated with the most passionate attachment and surveyed with the most intense grief. The most significant meanings in Faulkner all start in Jefferson and radiate outward to meanings as various and as inexhaustible as myth.

Beginning with *Sartoris*, in which both a subject and a way of treating it were effectively discovered, his stories chart and plumb, isolate and define, Faulkner's situation and our own. Exploiting to the limit the fracturing of the image of man, the destruction of any given, assumed meaning, they carry on a continuous conversation on the possibility of finding or creating another image, new or old, which will affirm and foster life, not deny and defeat it. *Absalom, Absalom!* may be taken as the key to Faulkner's career, both formally and thematically. Before it had become commonplace to speak of modern man as "in search of a soul," *Absalom* defined not only the necessity but the method and controlling conditions of the search. A commentator on Freud's letters has said recently, in connection with the shifting problems of psychotherapy, that the task of the contemporary analyst is not so much helping his patient to adjust his personality to a given reality as helping him to discover or create a personality. The problem becomes one of the ego's survival. "What was once the province of religion now becomes the substance of a personal therapy. . . ."[1]

The chief value attached to the past in Faulkner's works is the value of a clear, and clearly human, image of man. In a way very much like that of Hawthorne a century before, Faulkner has searched the past of his family and his region in an effort to understand where it went wrong and where it was right. The Civil War and Reconstruction have been for him what the witch trials were for Hawthorne, not simply available as subjects but demanding to be treated, ghosts to be exorcized, personal wrongs to be expiated. *The Sound and the Fury* and *The Scarlet Letter* were both "wrung from the heart," compulsively, by writers who went on later to create lesser works with more premeditation and detachment.

As Faulkner has Gavin Stevens say in *Intruder,* the past is not dead, it is not even past. It not only makes us what we are; it *is* what we have to work with. No opinion about Faulkner's treatment of the past seems to me more mistaken than the idea that he has sentimentalized or idealized it, holding up for our adoption its specific beliefs, attitudes, or mores. If this opinion were right, then *The Unvanquished* should document it; but if there is any validity at all in the foregoing analysis of that work, that is precisely what it does not do: father was not large, the heroism not untinctured with heroics, the ethical code of Granny not wholly in keeping with her actions. If there is nostalgia in Faulkner's treatment of the past, it is nostalgia—though that is perhaps hardly the word—for a definition of man that will not deny or obscure his humanity.

In the works of his deeper imagination, Faulkner's search for a living image of man has been conditioned always by a feeling for the past and for true community—two things not entirely distinct. Faulkner has always written as though the doctrine of the communion of saints were a part of his operating creed. "The old people," at their best, had a sense of community, and were a community; and we, Faulkner's works imply, if we are to find an acceptable definition of ourselves, must come to a sense of community with them as well as with each other.

Much has been written in Faulkner criticism of the nature and function of the code by which the society of the Sartorises and the Compsons once lived. Faulkner himself has not been reticent on the subject, listing for us again and again, in and out of his fiction, the features of the old code that he admires. But more significant than any reiterated catalogue of virtues is the fact that in the past man could conceive of virtue and could therefore create, or hold, a code which he took to be binding no matter how often it was violated. In the world of Faulkner's fiction men are human because they can sin. What the old people have to teach us, *can* teach us once we have entered imaginatively into communion with them, is not simply the value of courage, honor, pride, humility, and the rest, but the difficult belief that man is called to self-transcendence. Animals cannot sin, and Faulkner's thorough naturalists, his Jasons and Sutpens, calculate the probabilities of effectiveness on the assumption that man can't either. But the old people knew otherwise: they had at once a higher opinion of man's potential and a lower opinion of his unredeemed nature. This seems to me the chief effective, aesthetically valid, affirmation that Faulkner's fiction up to now has made.

A feeling for the human community conceived as extended in time as well as in space—a view with a vertical as well as a horizontal dimension—has this gift in its power. It can make us human again, arrest the dispersion, halt the evaporation, and start a process of creative condensation. The affirmation that man will not simply endure but prevail, left obscure in the Stockholm speech, can be interpreted in the light of the fiction: man will prevail, if he continues to believe in man, over all that defeats and dooms him. If he continues to believe in man: full, integral man, man with a conscience as well as glands, a soul as well as "gutful compulsions." The disappearance of vision and its replacement by fact and technique (the fact "neutral," "value-free," and the technique designed for manipulation, for "human engineering,") must first be halted before hope for man can be affirmed. Both the behaviorist conception of man, as an animal whose behavior can be fully understood without reference to such concepts as mind, soul, or purpose, and man's own tendency to ease the burden of his existence by relying on anything that will render decision and commitment unnecessary, must be denied and fought, as they have been all through Faulkner's works, before the hope can have any meaning. Quentin's father's definition of man as "the sum of what have you" must be replaced by the view held by "the old people." *Pylon* suggests that even in the conditions of a machine-dominated culture, man can retain his essential humanity. A recent letter of Faulkner's to a newspaper makes the same point, more obscurely. The letter comments on an airplane accident apparently caused by the pilot's depending solely on his instruments in attempting to land:

> [The pilot of the plane that crashed with great loss of life] dared not flout and affront, even with his own life too at stake, our cultural postulate of the infallibility of machines, instruments, gadgets. I grieve for him, for that moment's victims. We all had better grieve for all people beneath a culture which holds any mechanical gadget superior to any man because the one, being mechanical, is infallible, while the other, being nothing but man, is not just subject to failure but doomed to it.[2]

The point had been made years before in *Pylon*: our image of reality, and the object of our trust, is the machine—to our ultimate grief.

Nowhere is Faulkner's kinship with Melville more apparent than in this aspect of his thought. Though he has used different imagery to express it, his meaning I take it is very close to that of Melville in "The Bell Tower," or in "The Lightning Rod Man," in which the protagonist refuses to be frightened into relying on gadgets, either theological or technological. He takes his stand on the hearth, precisely the most dangerous spot according to the purveyor of lightning rods. Man is doomed to "failure," and gadgetry will hasten, not avert, the doom; nevertheless he will "prevail," if he dares to be man. It is the distinctive gift to us of "the old people" that at their best they dared.

But it is not simply a sense of the presentness of the past that is created, and drawn upon for guidance, in Faulkner's works. It is also the complementary sense of the pastness of the present. It is not uninstructive that *doom* is one of the recurrent words in all the works, as it is in the letter to the editor I have just quoted. If it is the function equally of art and of code and ritual and myth to arrest, if only momentarily, the rush to doom, it is the prerogative of man, if he would take up his burden, to endure it. In a sense all of Faulkner's works not only end but begin and continue with death, even though, in many of them, there is a strong hint of the possibility of new birth. The stories are written out of, and help to define for us, the inescapable anxiety of modern man.

Faulkner's themes and situations could very appropriately be studied in Kierkegaardian terms: paradox, the absurd, the concept of dread and the dialectic of despair, man's contradictory nature and precarious situation—these and other Kierkegaardian themes are central in the fiction and an existential analysis of them would illuminate without distortion if it were never forgotten that Kierkegaard's central category, faith, is present in Faulkner only in some very un-Kierkegaardian form. For in the end, despite his traditionalism, the *existential* quality of Faulkner's work is probably closer to Heidegger than to Kierkegaard. A feeling that life is a one-way street leading to death is the burden felt not only by the young Bayard Sartorises and the Quentins but by the Sutpens and the Joe Christmases.

In Faulkner's work present experience is seldom realized until it is already past. Life is interpreted in terms of death: as Kierkegaard would have put it, the finite in terms of its relation to the infinite. It is no simple technical device that supplies the basic organizing principle common to *The Sound and the Fury, Absalom, Absalom!*, and *The Unvanquished*, or that shapes the rhetoric and syntax of the opening of "Was." Memory here and elsewhere in Faulkner's fiction is not adjunctive but central and enabling. It gives the fiction much of its special quality and value, and a significant part of its meaning. By creative remembering man may rise to the level of humanity and community. The remembering will not be easy or always pleasant, no mere escape into sentimental recollection. It will involve embracing all that we have known and suffered and endured, all that we are, all that it means to be alive and conscious in a *now* that is past before we can identify it. As Faulkner put it to the interviewer for the *Paris Review*, "There is no such thing as was, only is."

2

AS FAULKNER'S meanings have offered a prescription for keeping man alive, so the forms of his work have helped to keep the possibility of serious fiction alive. The elaboration of myth and symbol that led finally to *A Fable*, which is located somewhere off the main road of fiction as we conceive it today, should not blind us to the formal accomplishment of the great works of the late twenties and thirties. We are far enough from the intellectual climate of that time, to be sure, to be nostalgic for simplicities. We appreciate the virtues of a story straightforwardly told. Having learned fully to appreciate the complexities of the James of "the major phase" and of

Conrad, equipped with our guides to *Ulysses* and a mounting ac-
cumulation of close readings which concentrate on fiction's symbolic
effects and ignore its verisimilitude, its "rendering," we are ready to
listen to arguments intended to show that even Howells's kind of
realism was not naive. We think we have had enough, for a while,
of fiction which has been assimilated to poetry.

Nevertheless there is a sense, and I think an important one, in
which Faulkner's practice in his greatest novels *did* keep fiction
alive. It may well be that we are now at the end of an era. If so,
literary history of the first half of our century will have to be
rewritten in the light of the newly discovered possibilities for
fiction. But in the second quarter of the century it seemed as
though there were only two important alternatives to Faulkner's
way for the writer of serious fiction.

One we may call the way of Hemingway, the way of the arti-
ficially limited perspective imposing its vision on us as "fact"; or,
superficially different but finally much the same, the way of
doctrinaire fiction, the way of the "proletarian" novel. The framework of simple, clear conviction behind both makes for an appearance of clarity and factual objectivity which is at the farthest
remove from the contextualism or perspectivism of *Absalom* or the
symbolic density of *As I Lay Dying*. Yet it would be naive to suppose that these "objective" modes of fiction are less "symbolic" or
"subjective" in a philosophic sense than Faulkner's: they simply
do not acknowledge their interpretations to be interpretations, they
present their symbols as facts.

Only if we grant the ultimate truth of the presuppositions on
which they rest will they seem to us to be presenting reality "as it
is in itself," without exclusion or symbolic distortion. In the very
best of Hemingway's work the enormous exclusions seem not to
matter, the creative distortions seem not distortions at all but "the
way it was." Hemingway at his best is a great enough artist to
make his experience our experience. But the doctrines are there,
and are in control, just as thoroughly as they are in the more
obviously doctrinaire proletarian novel.

Faulkner's way was superfically more personal and subjective, but in a deeper sense it was objective: springing from a hunger for truth and reality, it explored and exploited the baffles and barriers between us and Truth. The forms of Faulkner's fiction grew out of a creative response to the situation of man revealed by modern knowledge. In an important sense Faulkner's fiction is characterized by its openness to experience, to all experience, even that which resists interpretation.

The other major alternative to Faulkner's way was that of Virginia Woolf, in whose work the "public" world becomes completely fluid and subjective and eventually disappears. The stream of consciousness comes finally to have as its object only itself, and fiction becomes lyrical evocation of states of mind and feeling. Though Woolf's fiction is closer to *Absalom*, for instance, than Hemingway's work ever is, there is a crucial difference: even in *Absalom*, probably the most extreme example of the subjective method in Faulkner, the object of the search that creates the form of the novel is an assumed objective reality. We are searching for *something*; and what we discover is not just a state of feeling but a meaningful action, an objective fact that can be imaginatively appropriated just because it does have meaning.

Faulkner's way is a strategy for writing fiction about truth in an age when no one knows any more what truth is. The dissipation of a "known" world of absolute truth signalized by Einstein and, ultimately, though not in his own conception of the matter, by Freud, lies behind the novels. When *everything* becomes problematical, a matter of perspective or of the health of the unperceived unconscious, when one may choose one's assumptions for the construction of a geometry or an ego, when even the homeliest matters of status lose their translucence, it becomes impossible for the fully conscious man to write traditional fiction. Manners, character, plot —everything evaporates or loses significance. The novelist begins to write for a limited audience with whom he can share certain enabling assumptions; or he extends his idea of creation to include creation of belief. The drama, which depends even more directly than the novel on shared conventions of attitude and belief, comes to seem hardly possible.

These are critical commonplaces and perhaps only partly true. But their relevance to Faulkner's achievement seems so direct that they can hardly be avoided. Structure in Faulkner's works is the product of a created, not an assumed, truth. But the creation is undertaken for the purpose of discovery, and the building blocks used in the created structure are given. That is the chief reason why his relation to a small Southern community has been on the whole advantageous to him. If he had had to create not only his forms and his meanings but his plots and characters and culture too, I cannot imagine that he would have been able to succeed. He has not in fact succeeded when he has tried to do something like this in his stories of Europe, from the early stories of World War I aviators to *A Fable*. Some things a gifted artist can, perhaps must, create as it were *ex nihilo*, but not everything he has to work with. Yoknapatawpha has served him well, permitting him to record and create at once.

Faulkner was once commonly claimed for the naturalists, who thought of themselves as "objective recorders." More recently he has been claimed exclusively for the Gothic writers and the symbolists, the "creators." His importance is closely connected with the fact that both claims are in some sense true, though the later one, typical of the best writing on Faulkner for the last decade, represents a more sensitive response to his work than the earlier one.

Passages and stories may be cited to illustrate Faulkner's kinship in aim and method with his naturalistic predecessors. We are perhaps in danger today of forgetting that the stream of consciousness method itself may in one sense be thought of as a late development of the fundamental naturalistic ideal of achieving truth beyond illusion and totally independent of belief. When it became clear, finally, that the artist could not achieve aesthetically valid "truth" by substituting scientific abstractions for felt or intuited reality, that no reliance on even the most up-to-date scientific doctrines would solve his problems as artist, later "naturalists" turned to experience itself as immediately known in their search for "objectivity." The "poetry" of the new naturalism was intended not as a way of escaping from or denying objective truth but as a means of entry into it, into the only reality the artist could grasp. Faulkner was not being irresponsible, despite his clear kinship with writers of a different tradition, when he told the interviewer for the *Paris Review* that Sherwood Anderson "was the father of my generation of American writers and the tradition of American writing which our successors will carry on."[3]

But as he has also said, on the same occasion, "The two great men in my time were Mann and Joyce."[4] That both Mann and Joyce, in their different ways, transcend the conflict of naturalism and symbolism is the important point here. The relation between philosophic theory and aesthetic development is nowhere clearer than in the parallel between modern philosophy's refusal to accept either of the alternatives offered in the realist-idealist battle carried on in traditional metaphysics from the time of the Greeks, and modern art's reluctance to accept, in the form in which they were offered, the inherited alternatives of naturalistic realism and idealistic symbolism.

Randall Stewart has put the case for the interpretation of Faulkner as an anti-naturalist most strongly: "Paradoxically, although Faulkner's works could hardly be what they are had they not been preceded by the great works of Dreiser and the other naturalists, Faulkner, in a deeper sense, represents a break with naturalism and a return to the older tradition of Hawthorne."[5] It is impossible to quarrel with this if we are thinking of the *aesthetic* credo of the early naturalists, with its demand that the artist abdicate to make way for the scientist, that he renounce responsibility for his creation and offer a "slice of life." But if we are thinking of naturalism in more philosophic terms, we may decide that Stewart's words *break* and *return* are a little too strong, that we should speak instead of a something like a synthesis or a transendence.

A more genuine and relevant problem than the question of whether Faulkner is a "naturalist" or a "symbolist" arises when we try to apply the twin terms *symbolism* and *allegory* to Faulkner's

work. It would seem true in general to say that Faulkner's development has been in the direction of a more allegorical method. Despite
the broken clock, Benjy's age, Quentin's death by water, and the
narcissus, *The Sound and the Fury* is surely less allegorical, more
symbolic, than *A Fable*. Or we may arrive at the same conclusion
as to the direction of development if we compare *The Hamlet* and
The Town. Though much of the material in the latter is presumably
closer to Faulkner's personal experience than that in *The Hamlet*,
surely *The Town* is more allegorical.

Yet it will not do to say that Faulkner started writing realistically
and is now writing allegorically. It would be nearer the truth to
say that Faulkner wrote his greatest early works compulsively and
now writes with more conscious premeditation. What he has told
us of the way he composed *The Sound and the Fury* and what we
know of how he worked on *A Fable* will illustrate. Of *The Sound
and the Fury* Faulkner has said to the *Paris Review* interviewer that
he

> wrote it five separate times trying to tell the story, to rid
> myself of the dream which would continue to anguish me
> until I did. . . . It began with a mental picture, I didn't
> realize at the time it was symbolical.[6]

With this we may compare the *Life* magazine illustrated story of
Faulkner at work composing *A Fable*: elaborate diagrams, schemes
of cross reference, outlines. The earlier book began with a picture
and ended in realistic symbolism; the latter began with a design
and a message and ended as a kind of realistic allegory. Both works
are "symbolic" and both are "realistic," but they are very different
in their effect. *The Sound and the Fury* is of course incomparably
more "realistic" in the sense of creating for us an illusion of reality,
even while it flouts the older realists' insistence on accurate notation
of surface fact. *A Fable* records more facts and records them more
straightforwardly, within any given segment of its complicated time
scheme. It is generally closer in texture, despite its allegorical intention, to history conceived as chronicle than *The Sound and the
Fury* ever is. "Realism" in the historic sense of the word and a successfully created "illusion of reality" are not synonymous.

In *Sartoris* Faulkner found a way of fusing "fact" and "idea." We may call it the symbolist way, the way of attending to what Joyce called epiphanies, of treating facts as translucent. In *A Fable* and in parts of *The Town* facts are not so much translucent as illustrative. *Requiem For A Nun* was Faulkner's deliberate experiment in taking fact and meaning apart and treating them separately. *A Fable* tries to put them together again, starting with the meaning. The result is a paradox: the book is at once much more "realistic," as realism has traditionally been defined, than *Absalom*, and much more allegorical. To compare Faulkner with Hawthorne once again, *Absalom* is to *A Fable* as *The Scarlet Letter* is to *The Marble Faun*.

When he was teaching at the University of Virginia recently Faulkner was asked "whether man's best hope to prevail and endure lay with the mind or the heart." Accepting the Hawthornesque terminology, Faulkner is reported to have given a Hawthornesque answer: "I don't have much confidence in the mind. . . . It lets you down sooner or later. You have to feel." But despite this declared lack of confidence, the direction of Faulkner's development in recent years would seem to be toward writing more and more from the mind.

3

A STUDY OF a living author cannot hope for completeness, still less for definitiveness. Faulkner has said that he will complete his Doomsday book, the Snopes saga, and then break his pencil. The ultimate shape and significance of his career remains not only to be defined but to be achieved.

But some conclusions are already inescapable. That Faulkner's achievement can be fairly judged only if we think of him as continuing the traditions of the greatest American writers is already clear. His roots are in the past, in more than one sense, and the values of the past that he has kept alive are richly inclusive. The line Eliot once traced "from Poe to Valery" could be extended: from Poe to the French Symbolists to the expatriates of the twenties to Faulkner. Like Hawthorne, Faulkner has dedicated his art to probing deep into "the truths of the human heart." The phrase is Hawthorne's, but the idea of the role of the artist it implies is equally Faulkner's. The symbolic implications of Melville's images of land and sea are continued in Faulkner's of town and wilderness. No wonder the Rockwell Kent portrait of Ahab is said to have been at one time the only picture hanging in Faulkner's study in Oxford. The white whale and the great bear are first cousins.

Had he lacked the courage to experiment, Faulkner could not have renewed and refreshed his heritage. When he broke with the conventions that were dominant at the beginning of his career, he did not break with tradition. Between Hawthorne's Coverdale and Faulkner's Horace Benbow there are only two intermediate stages, James's John Marcher and Eliot's Prufrock. Ahab and Houston, Pierre and the woman in "Idyll in the Desert": their common gestures reveal a sensibility and a world. Mark Twain's Huck Finn and the narrative voice of Anderson as it is heard in "Death in the Woods" establish a precedent for Addie's determination to penetrate beyond words to the reality of deeds. Faulkner approaches "the real thing" with no less confidence in "the alchemy of art" than James had. The burden of the ironic and tragic vision that Faulkner's characters must learn to endure is not new in American literature, or in any great literature. When the young poet from Oxford raided "Sweeney Among the Nightingales" to express his sense of the irony of life, he was beginning to discover a relationship between tradition and his talent that would soon help to shape his finest works:

> The raven beak and Philomel
> Amid the bleeding trees were fixed.
> His hoarse cry and hers were mixed
> And through the dark their droppings fell.

The bleeding trees, the fact and the dream: only art as fine as Faulkner's at its best could hold them in perfect tension. Tension, not stasis. There may be more to be endured than to be enjoyed in Faulkner's world, but there is still another sense in which he joins his voice with the voices of the great writers of the past and present with whom he must be compared: starting from a perception of man's absurdity, he recalls us to a knowledge of our condition and our hope. With Hawthorne, he warns us against expecting redemption by a celestial railroad. His tragic vision, again like Hawthorne's, and like Melville's, does not deny democracy but sustains it. Nor does it suggest that we try to escape the world: rather, that we do what we can to transform it, and be prepared to endure it. His tragic vision does not deny or restrict freedom, it demands and magnifies it, but recognizes the forces that limit it. With the Mark Twain of *Huckleberry Finn,* he affirms the underlying worth of the common life, even in a situation replete with tragedy and absurdity. With James, Faulkner says in his work that only moral choices freely made are ultimately significant. With Eliot, Faulkner tells us that if we hold to a purely positivistic definition of man we shall misconceive his nature and his situation.

This much is already clear. Faulkner is the inheritor of a great tradition and he has augmented his inheritance to the enrichment of us all.

Notes

CHAPTER 1

1. Interview in *The Paris Review*, Spring, 1956, reprinted in Malcolm Cowley, ed., *Writers at Work: The Paris Review Interviews*, Viking Press, 1958, pp. 122-141; p. 141.

2. Carvel Collins, ed., *William Faulkner: New Orleans Sketches*, Rutgers University Press, 1958, p. 54.

3. I am not suggesting that *Portrait of the Artist* was an *influence* on Faulkner when he was writing *Mosquitoes*, only that the two books are comparable in their relation to the developing careers of the two writers. I know of no evidence that Faulkner had read Joyce's *Portrait* by 1925. That he read *Ulysses* about this time seems to me very likely from internal evidence. Faulkner himself has dated his reading of the novel only roughly—as the middle of the twenties (Robert A. Jelliffe, ed., *Faulkner at Nagano*, Tokyo, Kenkyusha, Ltd., 1956, p. 203). He once denied having read it before writing *The Sound and the Fury*, while admitting that he might have been influenced by what he had heard about it. See William Van O'Connor, *The Tangled Fire of William Faulkner*, University of Minnesota Press, 1954, pp. 42-43, n.

4. Both Hemingway and Faulkner were personally indebted to Anderson for his efforts to help them in their careers, both paid him the compliment of imitating him, Hemingway in "My Old Man" and Faulkner in his newspaper sketch "Cheest," and both parodied him. Hemingway's *The Torrents of Spring* concentrates on the absurdities of Anderson's less successful works, particularly *Marching Men* and *Dark Laughter*, absurdities that generally fall under the heading of romantic primitivism. Faulkner's parody in *Mosquitoes*, as in the work which he did with his friend Spratling, *Sherwood Anderson and Other Famous Creoles*, concentrates on the qualities of the man who produced the works. But the two young writers came to essentially similar conclusions: Anderson was to be respected, but by no means to be followed.

   Faulkner's several recent comments on Anderson do not suggest that he has basically changed his mind about the older writer. Depending on the situation, and presumably also on Faulkner's mood, the recent comments either alternate between or mingle praise for the man, vague statements about his importance as a writer, and specific praise for one book and several short stories. A feeling of guilt for having parodied a benefactor may be what complicates the statements and makes them at times seem self-contradictory, but behind them I think we may discern an essentially unvarying estimate. To the interviewer for *The Paris Review* Faulkner speaks of Anderson as "the father of my generation of American writers and the tradition of American writing which our successors will carry on." (*Writers at Work*, p. 135.) And he adds, apparently in the interest of justice to one who has been injured, "He has never received his proper evaluation." But to his questioners in Japan, with what would seem to be less thought of making a statement for the record, he said:

> Why, [Anderson] was one of the finest, sweetest people I ever knew. He was much better than anything he ever wrote. I mean by that he was one of those tragic figures that had just one book, which was *Winesburg, Ohio*. . . . [Several of the short stories are also] very fine, but after that it got worse and worse and he tried and he tried and he tried—that was the tragedy. And I think that's what he died of. (*Faulkner at Nagano*, pp. 54-56.)

The son who achieves independence of the father without incurring guilt is rare indeed. Faulkner's repeated judgments of Anderson achieve rough justice. In general, Faulkner's early judgments anticipated what has come to be widespread critical agreement. See, for example, Faulkner's 1925 *Dallas Morning News* article containing specific comments on Anderson's works; the article is reprinted in the William Faulkner Number of *The Princeton University Library Chronicle*, 18 (Spring, 1957), 89-94.

5. It would seem from internal evidence that Faulkner was first strongly impressed by Eliot about 1925. Any attempt to date the reading from Faulkner's poems is complicated by the fact that the publication dates of Faulkner's poems are misleading if taken as evidence of date of composition. *The Marble Faun*, published in 1924, was written in 1919. It shows no influence of Eliot or the "new" poetry; its influences are from the nineteenth century. The poems in *Salmagundi*, published in 1932, were written, apparently, in the early and middle twenties and show some new influences. "Portrait," dated June, 1922, suggests, though faintly, that Faulkner may have read "Prufrock" as early as this. "Lilacs," dated June, 1925, is the earliest poem clearly showing the influence of the new poetry. Most of the Eliot echoes in Faulkner's poetry are to be found in *A Green Bough*, published in 1933 but made up of poems written in the twenties. They are undated, but I suspect that they were written, most of them at least, in the middle years of the decade. For the clearest Eliot echoes see the following (the poems are numbered, not titled): II (cf. "La Figlia che Piange"); XIX (cf. the ending of "Prufrock"); XXVII (cf. "Sweeney Among the Nightingales").

   For dates of first publication of Faulkner's poems, see James B. Meriwether, "William Faulkner: A Check List," the William Faulkner Number of *The Princeton University Library Chronicle*, 18 (Spring, 1957), 136-158. See also George P. Garrett, Jr., "An Examination of the Poetry of William Faulkner" in the same issue. Mr. Garrett discusses the apparent influences on the poems ("Among the principals were Eliot, Housman, Cummings, Hart Crane, Rossetti, and Swinburne."), the evidence of Faulkner's frequent revisions, and the conjectural dates of composition of some of them.

6. *Writers at Work*, p. 135. Carvel Collins has commented on Faulkner's debt to Joyce in "The Pairing of *The Sound and the Fury* and *As I Lay Dying*," *The Princeton University Library Chronicle*, 18 (Spring, 1957), 114-123.

7. *Writers at Work*, p. 132.

8. See Karl E. Zink, "Flux and the Frozen Moment: The Imagery of Stasis in Faulkner's Prose," *PMLA*, 71 (June, 1956), 285-301; and Walter J. Slatoff, "The Edge of Order: The Pattern of Faulkner's Rhetoric," *Twentieth Century Literature*, 3 (October, 1957), 107-127.

CHAPTER 2

1. *The Explicator*, 14 (April, 1956), 7.

2. Faulkner has Horace Benbow in *Sanctuary* say of Dreiser, expressing what one suspects was Faulkner's own opinion at the time, "Nobody ever had more to say and more trouble saying it than old Dreiser."

3. O'Connor, *The Tangled Fire*, p. 36.

4. The Eliot allusions that run through *Soldier's Pay* and *Mosquitoes* continue in *Sartoris*, though less frequently and less obviously. One of them, on page 55 of the 1951 edition, is to a poem also alluded to in *The Sound and the Fury*, "Mr. Eliot's Sunday Morning Service." On the same page of *Sartoris* there is an image that I suspect was derived from "La Figlia che Piange."

CHAPTER 3

1. Robert Coughlan, *The Private World of William Faulkner*, Harper, 1954, p. 89.

2. Harry Modean Campbell and Ruel E. Foster, *William Faulkner*, The University of Oklahoma Press, 1951, pp. 51-52.

3. *Writers at Work*, p. 130.

4. George R. Stewart and Joseph M. Backus, in " 'Each in Its Ordered Place': Structure and Narrative in 'Benjy's Section' of *The Sound and the Fury*," *American Literature*, 29 (January, 1958), 440-456, have analyzed the "clues" to the order of events in Benjy's section. They present a table by which the various events may be dated in the story, if one wishes to date them precisely. One of their conclusions is that "The evidence seems to show that the section was consciously constructed as a puzzle or a mystery story, or both combined." I doubt it; but whatever may have been in Faulkner's mind when he wrote the section, I can see no reason for reading it as either a puzzle or a mystery story. The kind of order Mr. Stewart and Mr. Backus try to clarify is not the kind of order that is aesthetically important in the section.

5. An interesting discussion of Benjy's redemptive role is to be found in Lawrence E. Bowling, "Faulkner and the Theme of Innocence," *Kenyon Review*, 20 (Summer, 1958), 466-487.

6. For a discussion of Christian parallels in *The Sound and the Fury*, see Sumner C. Powell, "William Faulkner Celebrates Easter, 1928" *Perspective*, 2 (Summer, 1949), 195-218.

7. *Writers at Work,* pp. 123-124, 132.

8. An excellent analysis leading to the conclusion that it is Dilsey who supplies order and moral perspective in the novel is to be found in Olga W. Vickery, "*The Sound and the Fury:* A Study in Perspective," *PMLA,* 69 (December, 1954), 1017-1037. See also Peter Swiggart, "Moral and Temporal Order in *The Sound and the Fury,*" *Sewanee Review,* 61 (Spring, 1953), 221-237.

9. Irving Howe, *William Faulkner: A Critical Study,* Random House, 1951, p. 119.

10. T. S. Eliot, *Selected Essays,* Harcourt, Brace, 1950 ed., p. 380.

11. Quentin even uses a word in his revery that one suspects Faulkner of having picked up from "Mr. Eliot's Sunday Morning Service"—"philoprogenitive," with the "poly" which prefixes the word in the poem lopped off because it does not apply to one who has loved only Caddy. There are other Eliot echoes in the section in addition to this, including of course Quentin's choice of death by water.

   I suspect that Faulkner's conception of Benjy also owes something to Eliot. In "Rhapsody on a Windy Night" Eliot had written: "Midnight shakes the memory/ As a madman shakes a dead geranium." It would seem to be not too far from this to Benjy cherishing his memories and bawling as he shakes his narcissus or jimson weed. Compare Faulkner's early picture of an idiot clutching a broken flower in "The Kingdom of God" in *New Orleans Sketches,* Carvel Collins, ed., Rutgers University Press, 1958.

12. As do the Snopeses of Faulkner's world. If it seems an exaggeration to suggest that Jason has become a Snopes (since he is the only "sane" Compson) we may compare his statement on Negroes and Jews with the following by Flem Snopes in *Sanctuary:* " 'I'm an American,' he said. 'I don't brag about it, because I was born one. And I been a decent Baptist all my life, too. Oh, I aint no preacher and I aint no worse than lots of folks that pretends to sing loud in church. But the lowest, cheapest thing on this earth aint a nigger: it's a jew.' " The best discussion of Faulkner's attitude toward the Jasons and Snopeses of the modern world is still George Marion O'Donnell's 1939 essay, "Faulkner's Mythology," reprinted in Hoffman and Vickery, ed., *William Faulkner: Two Decades of Criticism,* Michigan State College Press, 1951, pp. 49-62.

CHAPTER 4

1. *Writers at Work,* p. 139.

2. Roma A. King, Jr., in "The Janus Symbol in *As I Lay Dying,*" *The University of Kansas City Review,* 21 (Summer, 1955), 287-290, interprets Addie's role in part in terms of horse symbolism in classic myth. The result reinforces the redemptive aspect of Addie and the humanistic aspect of the theme of the novel.

3. William Van O'Connor in his balanced and perceptive discussion of the novel seems to me to have offered the strongest case for finding a clearer meaning than I am here suggesting. He concludes that "The theme . . . would seem to invite the dividing of people into those who accept the bitterness and violence of living and those who do not." See *The Tangled Fire,* p. 53.

CHAPTER 5

1. Introduction to the Modern Library Edition, and *Faulkner at Nagano*, pp. 62-65.
2. *The Tangled Fire*, p. 57.
3. An interesting discussion of the moral theme of *Sanctuary* in terms of the idea of initiation is to be found in George Monteiro, "Initiation and Moral Sense in Faulkner's *Sanctuary*," *Modern Language Notes*, 73 (November, 1958), 500-504.
4. Lena's last name, one recalls, is *Grove*. For comments on her relation to nature, see, for instance, Cleanth Brooks, "Notes on Faulkner's *Light in August*," *The Harvard Advocate*, 135 (November, 1951), 10-11, 27 (special Faulkner Issue); and Karl E. Zink, "Faulkner's Garden: Woman and the Immemorial Earth," *Modern Fiction Studies*, 2 (Autumn, 1956), 139-149 (special Faulkner Issue).
5. For a perceptive comment on Byron as the "engaged" man, committed to life in all its impurity, see Richard Chase, "The Stone and the Crucifixion," in *William Faulkner: Two Decades of Criticism*.
6. Faulkner uses this image of light coming, or seeming to come, from the earth itself at least twice again, in later works, once in *The Hamlet*, on page 207 of the original edition, and once, in a key passage, in *The Town*, on page 315.
7. I am not unaware that the passage can be defended on the allegorical level as appropriate to the symbolic meaning of the character of Christmas. Allegorically, it is shocking to Christmas to discover that there are people for whom the difference between black and white is not important, who do not share his demand for purity. But when Faulkner is writing at his best we do not need to try to defend in allegorical terms what offends our sense of character.

CHAPTER 6

1. *The Portable Faulkner*, Viking Press, 1946, p. 540.
2. Quoted in O'Connor, *The Tangled Fire*, p. 92.
3. Many of the features of modern life described in such a way in *Pylon* as to imply rejection are discussed from a neutral point of view as a "democratization of culture" by the late Karl Mannheim in his posthumous *Essays on the Sociology of Culture*, London, Routledge and Kegan Paul, 1956. See also Robert A. Nisbet, *The Quest for Community*, Oxford University Press, 1953.
4. For a reading of the novel stressing Faulkner's sympathy with the fliers, see George Monteiro, "Bankruptcy in Time: a Reading of Faulkner's *Pylon*," *Twentieth Century Literature*, 4 (April-July, 1958), 9-20.
5. *Writers at Work*, p. 133. See also W. R. Moses, "The Unity of *The Wild Palms*," *Modern Fiction Studies*, 2 (Autumn, 1956), 125-131.
6. *The Tangled Fire*, p. 105.
7. *Writers at Work*, p. 133.

CHAPTER 7

1. Kathleen Nott, *The Emperor's Clothes*, Indiana University Press, 1955, p. 5.

2. For a discussion of the way in which the style (i.e., grammar and rhetoric) is functional, see Robert H. Zoellner, "Faulkner's Prose Style in *Absalom, Absalom!*," *American Literature*, 30 (January, 1959), 486-502.

CHAPTER 8

1. *William Faulkner*, pp. 27, 34-35.

2. The only exception to this that I am aware of is Andrew Lytle's brief excursion on *The Unvanquished* in the course of his review of *A Fable*, in the *Sewanee Review*, 63 (Winter, 1955), 114-137.

3. *The Tangled Fire*, pp. 100-102.

4. For the best discussions of the moral and social meanings implicit in the structure of Yoknapatawpha, see the essays by George Marion O'Donnell, Robert Penn Warren, and Malcolm Cowley in Hoffman and Vickery, *William Faulkner: Two Decades of Criticism*.

5. The first version of the story appeared in *Harper's*, 163 (August, 1931), 266-274. Reprinted in *Doctor Martino*, it was revised before being used in *The Hamlet*. In the original version there was a stronger suggestion that the murderer's situation as a sharecropper was sufficient to account for his rage and his deed. But not all sharecroppers, however "underprivileged," become murderers. In revising the story, Faulkner lessened, but did not entirely eliminate, his reliance on this cliché of the early Depression; traces of it remain as one of the elements of simplistic thinking in the episode.

CHAPTER 9

1. *Writers at Work*, p. 123.

2. "Faulkner's Vision of Human Integrity," *The Harvard Advocate*, 135 (November, 1951), 8-9, 28-33 (special Faulkner Issue). "Faulkner burdens his characters with the integral human state; he will not let them off. . . . [his] imagination seems to be characterized by a velocity of memory that one finds only in writers of genius. . . . what I see and hear in the soar and thud of these details is an effort to present—not merely *to* the consciousness of a single mind but *along* the whole circuit of time and thought through which we move—that which *is* our life in all its presentness. . . . Faulkner's insistence on embracing all actuality in the moment is . . . an attempt to realize continuity with all our genesis, our "progenitors" . . . with all we have touched, known, loved." Mr. Kazin's article is one of the most perceptive, and most important, comments ever made on Faulkner's fundamental strategy, and on an important aspect of his achievement.

3. *The Burning Fountain*, Indiana University Press, 1954.

4. Except as noted later, all the stories discussed in this chapter are to be found in *Collected Stories* and *Go Down, Moses,* and it is these versions of the stories that I have in mind.

5. *Writers at Work,* p. 141.

6. Once again, the reference is to the version in *Go Down, Moses,* which incorporates an earlier, shorter story, "The Bear," published in *The Saturday Evening Post,* May 9, 1942, and "Lion," *Harper's Magazine,* December, 1935. A later version of the story, without the fourth section, is reprinted in *The Big Woods.*

7. *The Tangled Fire,* pp. 129-133.

8. *The Saturday Evening Post,* 227 (March 5, 1955), 26ff.

9. "A Note on *Sanctuary,*" *The Harvard Advocate,* Faulkner Issue, p. 16.

CHAPTER 10

1. "On Privacy . . . The American Dream: What Happened to It?" *Harper's Magazine,* 211 (July, 1955), 33-38.

2. *Ibid.* By "humanitarian" Faulkner seems to mean, judging from the context, a practitioner in what are called, in academic circles, "the humanities," as contrasted with the natural and social sciences.

3. The issue of November-December, 1954.

4. "What Price Glory?" *The Hudson Review,* 7 (Winter, 1955), 602-606. Mr. Flint goes on, in his valuable review, to make a more general point that bears on the failure of *A Fable:* "Faulkner's good instincts are profoundly temperate as well as orderly, but they deal profoundly only with experienced realities, not, as in *A Fable,* with received ideas. He is wisely critical of modern life, but to a degree unusual even among novelists, can criticize convincingly only in terms of tone, character, temperament, and conduct." (p. 603.)

5. In "Race at Morning," published shortly after *A Fable* came out, Faulkner has his wise character say: "'Maybe . . . The best word in our language, the best of all. That's what mankind keeps going on: Maybe.'"

6. "Is death from 'natural causes' inevitable? No one can say categorically that it is. . . . The attainment of human immortality must be the goal of medical research." *Life,* 38 (April 25, 1955), 55.

7. As Roma A. King, Jr., has argued in "Everyman's Warfare: A Study of Faulkner's *Fable,*" *Modern Fiction Studies,* 2 (Autumn, 1956), 132-138.

8. *Faulkner at Nagano,* p. 186.

CHAPTER 11

1. *Shenandoah,* 3 (Autumn, 1952), 55.

2. "By the People," *Mademoiselle* (October, 1955), 86-89, 130-139.

3. For example, Randall Stewart, *American Literature and Christian Doctrine*, Louisiana State University Press, 1958, pp. 136-142.

4. "On Privacy . . ."

5. *Faulkner at Nagano*, p. 186.

6. *Ibid.*, p. 23.

7. *Writers at Work*, p. 132.

8. Edwin A. Penick, Jr., arrives at a similar conclusion in his discussion of Faulkner's theology in "The Testimony of William Faulkner," *The Christian Scholar*, 38 (June, 1955), 121-133.

9. "Existentialist Aspects of Modern Art," in Carl Michalson, ed., *Christianity and the Existentialists*, Scribner's, 1956, p. 147.

CHAPTER 12

1. Sonya Rudikoff, "Freud's Letters," *Hudson Review*, 7 (Winter, 1955), 630.

2. From a letter to *The New York Times*, reprinted in *Time*, January 3, 1955, p. 19.

3. *Writers at Work*, p. 135.

4. *Ibid.*

5. "Hawthorne and Faulkner," *College English*, 1 (February, 1956), 258-262.

6. *Writers at Work*, p. 130.

Index